Great Careers

IN

2 Years

The Associate Degree Option

**HIGH-SKILL AND HIGH-WAGE JOBS
AVAILABLE THROUGH
TWO-YEAR PROGRAMS**

SECOND EDITION

PAUL PHIFER

D1113477

Ferguson
An imprint of  Facts On File

Great Careers in Two Years, Second Edition

Ferguson
An imprint of Facts On File, Inc.
132 West 31st Street
New York NY 10001

Library of Congress Cataloging-in-Publication Data

Phifer, Paul.
    Great careers in 2 years : the associate degree option by Paul Phifer.-- 2nd ed.
      p. cm.
Includes index.
Summary: Presents an overview of careers that can be obtained by earning an associate degree, different types of institutions that offer that degree, and how to determine if this is the right option for oneself.
    ISBN 0-89434-415-3 (pbk. : alk. paper)
  1. Vocational guidance--United States. 2. High school students--Vocational guidance--United States. 3. Associate in arts degree. 4. College majors--United States. [1. Vocational guidance. 2. Associate in arts degree.] I. Title: Great careers in two years. II. Title.

HF5382.5.U5 P447 2003
331.7'0235--dc21   2002151307

Ferguson books are available at special discounts when purchased in bulk quantities for businesses, associations, institutions, or sales promotions. Please call our Special Sales Department in New York at (212) 967-8800 or (800) 322-8755.

You can find Ferguson Publishing on the World Wide Web at
http://www.fergpubco.com

Project Editor: Nora Walsh
Managing Editor: Andrew Morkes
Senior Editor: Carol Yehling
Editorial Assistant: Laura Walsh
Proofreader: Jon Bieniek
Indexer: Sandi Schroeder

Cover design by Cathy Rincon

Printed in the United States of America

EB 10 9 8 7 6 5 4 3 2

This book is printed on acid-free paper.

TABLE OF CONTENTS

Foreword vii

Introduction 1

Chapter One: Associate Degrees and More 7

Chapter Two:
Should I Attend an Associate Degree Program? 13

Chapter Three:
Accreditation: Not All Schools are Created Equal 35

Chapter Four: Transfer Options 41

Chapter Five: Career Profiles
    Adult Day Care Coordinators 47
    Aeronautical and Aerospace Technicians 50
    Agribusiness Technicians 53
    Agricultural Equipment Technicians 56
    Aircraft Mechanics 59
    Alcohol and Drug Abuse Counselors 62
    Automobile Collision Repairers 65
    Automobile Service Technicians 68
    Biomedical Equipment Technicians 71
    Broadcast Engineers 74
    Cardiovascular Technologists 77
    Carpenters 80
    Cartoonists and Animators 83
    Caterers 86
    Chemical Technicians 89
    Civil Engineering Technicians 92
    Computer and Office Machine Service Technicians 95
    Computer Programmers 98
    Computer Support Service Owners 101
    Computer-Aided Design Drafters and Technicians . . . 104
    Cooks and Chefs 107
    Corrections Officers 110
    Court Reporters 113

Dental Assistants 116

Dental Hygienists 119

Desktop Publishing Specialists 122

Diagnostic Medical Sonographers 125

Dialysis Technicians 128

Dietetic Technicians 131

Dispensing Opticians 134

Drafters 137

Electricians 140

Electroneurodiagnostic Technologists 143

Electronics Engineering Technicians 146

Emergency Medical Technicians 149

Environmental Technicians 152

Fashion Designers 155

Fiber Optics Technicians 158

Fire Safety Technicians 161

Firefighters 164

Fluid Power Technicians 167

Funeral Home Workers 170

Graphic Designers 173

Heating and Cooling Technicians 176

Horticultural Technicians 179

Hotel and Motel Managers 182

Human Services Workers 185

Industrial Engineering Technicians 188

Laboratory Testing Technicians 191

Landscapers and Grounds Managers 194

Laser Technicians 197

Legal Secretaries 200

Library Technicians 203

Licensed Practical Nurses 206

Marine Services Technicians 209

Massage Therapists 212

Mechanical Engineering Technicians 215

Medical Assistants 218

Medical Laboratory Technicians 221

Medical Record Technicians 224

Medical Secretaries. 227

Medical Transcriptionists. 230

Microelectronics Technicians. 233

Musicians 236

Nuclear Medicine Technologists. 239

Occupational Therapist Assistants and Aides 242

Office Administrators 245

Orthotic and Prosthetic Technicians 248

Packaging Machinery Technicians 251

Painters and Sculptors. 254

Paralegals 257

Pedorthists 260

Pharmacy Technicians 263

Phlebotomy Technicians 266

Photographers 269

Physical Therapy Assistants 272

Plastics Technicians 275

Plumbers and Pipefitters. 278

Police Officers. 281

Preschool Teachers 284

Quality Control Technicians 287

Radiologic Technologists. 290

Real Estate Agents and Brokers 293

Recreation Workers 296

Registered Nurses 299

Respiratory Therapists. 302

Restaurant and Food Service Managers. 305

Retail Managers 308

Robotics Technicians 311

Security Guards 314

Semiconductor Technicians. 317

Surgical Technologists 320

Surveying and Mapping Technicians 323

Systems Set Up Specialists 326

Teacher Aides 329

Technical Support Specialists 332

Veterinary Technicians 335

Wastewater Treatment Plant Technicians 338

Webmasters 341

Wireless Service Technicians 344

Chapter Six: Related Resources 347

Index 349

FOREWORD

by George R. Boggs
President and CEO
American Association of Community Colleges

Each fall, over 5.4 million students attend classes for credit in our nation's nearly 1,200 regionally accredited community colleges. (I am using the term community college to include those two-year institutions that call themselves technical or junior colleges as well as those that are called community colleges.) A nearly equal number of students are enrolled in non-credit classes in these colleges. In fact, 45 percent of all first-time college freshmen in the United States attend community colleges. Community colleges have changed the paradigm for higher education from having to "go away to college" to having access to quality higher education in local communities. Community college campuses are within commuting distance of over 90 percent of the population of the United States, and a growing number of these schools are making education even more accessible through distance learning opportunities.

Community colleges provide access to higher education to all who can benefit, and they attract the most diverse student body in history. Students of all ages, ethnicities, degrees of preparedness, socioeconomic statuses, and degrees of disability are welcomed. The colleges generally offer all of the general education courses found in the first two years at any university, but they also respond to the educational needs of their communities by offering important vocational, contract education, and community service educational programs.

The diversity of American higher education presents students with many options. For some students, such as those who are independent learners, those who can afford to attend a residential four-year college or university, or those who could benefit by getting away from home for four years, a university may be the best choice. However, community colleges have significant advantages for many students. Community colleges are clearly focused on the success of their students. Class sizes are much smaller than those found in major universities. Classes are taught by fully qualified professors rather than teaching assistants. A variety of student services, including financial aid, counseling, and tutoring, are offered to help students to be successful. In addition, community colleges are generally far less expensive to attend than are other institutions of higher education.

Twenty-eight percent of non-credit community college students already have a bachelor's degree or higher, reflecting the fact that many university graduates are attracted to community colleges to obtain the practical skills they will need for employment. Many people are also attending community colleges to keep their skills updated.

The U.S. Bureau of Labor Statistics projects a continuing increase in the number of jobs requiring professional skills that are obtained by education beyond high school and a decreasing number of unskilled jobs that do not require some higher education. The world is changing, and education beyond high school is ever more important to achieving the American dream. Occupations requiring an associate degree are projected to increase more rapidly in the next 10 years than those requiring any other level of education. Initial salaries for holders of technical associate degrees are often higher than those of the holders of bachelor's degrees.

Great Careers in 2 Years is a great resource. It gives students an opportunity to assess their own temperaments, skills, values, and interests. It points out the disadvantages of attending an unaccredited college, and it provides information on how to find programs at accredited community colleges. And most importantly, this helpful book provides information about careers obtainable with an associate degree, including information on their personal and professional requirements, earnings potential, and employment outlook. Programs for all these careers are available at community colleges in the United States. If a local community college does not offer a specific program of interest, there are others that do. The Web site of the American Association of Community Colleges (http://www.aacc.nche.edu) has links to all its member community colleges throughout the United States, where potential students can find further information about the programs offered by specific community colleges.

I wish the reader all the best in finding a career option that will provide satisfaction and security. Education is the key to success in today's society, and community colleges are there to help.

INTRODUCTION

A COLLEGE STUDENT HAS PULLED AN ALL-NIGHTER to finish an English paper. From her window, she can see the horizon gradually growing lighter as the sun begins to rise. Her class begins in less than an hour, and she is nearly finished. As she types the last paragraph, her computer suddenly "freezes." She pounds on the keyboard unmercifully, but to no avail. She calls her college's computer hotline, and 15 minutes later, a **computer service technician** arrives, "unfreezes" the computer, and helps the student retrieve her paper. The student is elated and, with relief, completes her project.

∎

EVER SINCE SHE COULD REMEMBER, Jessica has loved being outdoors, particularly out in the woods. She believes her fondness for exploring forests was cultivated by her late father, who had been a forester for many years. He had shared with her numerous adventure stories, and he took her on camping trips, hikes, and a number of exciting expeditions to Yellowstone National Park. On occasion, Jessica was even allowed to observe her father at work. Over the years, she developed a strong passion for protecting America's forest areas from damage and disease. This strong interest motivated Jessica to enroll in a forestry technology curriculum at a nearby community college. After successfully completing the two-year program, she will receive an associate's degree and qualify to work as a **forestry technician.** It seems in Jessica's case, the apple has not fallen far from the tree.

∎

IT'S THE HEIGHT OF SUMMER in the Texas Panhandle. Temperatures are in the 90s and rising. The city has issued a severe heat warning. A woman with a chronic respiratory ailment, who can get around the house only with a walker, is faced with a problem: her air conditioner has broken down. She can already feel her house heating up. Fortunately, she has the telephone

number of a qualified **heating and cooling technician.** Within a half hour, the technician has the air
back on, thus helping her to avoid a health emergency.

■

THEY SAY A DOG IS MAN'S BEST FRIEND. But who is
Fido's best friend when he's sick or injured? One good
friend is the **veterinary technician.** Pete recently had
to take his yellow labrador Charley in to the vet's
office after the dog stopped eating for several days
and appeared lethargic and sluggish. The veterinarian
and a veterinary technician examined Charley and
diagnosed him with a mild stomach ailment, treatable
with medication. On Pete's way out, the technician
shared a valuable hint as to how to get his dog to take
the prescription without having to force it on him:
hide the pill in some cottage cheese. Sure enough,
Charley ate it up. After only a few days, he's his old
self again, getting into everything—including the
garbage can. Though happy with his chosen vet, Pete
hopes he won't have to take Charley back there again
so soon.

■

EVER SINCE HIS UNCLE lost his left leg in a motorcycle
accident 10 years ago, Jerry has been intensely interested in orthotic and prosthetic devices. After
researching the field, Jerry is amazed to find out how
the results of work done by **orthotic and prosthetic
technicians** have helped improve the lives of many.
Jerry is pleased at the way his uncle's disposition
improved from bitter resignation, feeling that he'd
never walk again, to triumph over his ability to use his
artificial leg almost as well as his original. The prosthetic device was constructed and fitted by a prosthetic technician. Jerry can't believe how similar his
uncle's artificial limb is to a natural human leg. It is
this experience, along with an awareness of how this
type of work can positively impact people's lives, that
has helped Jerry decide to pursue a career in orthotics
and prosthetics.

■

ON A RECENT FIELD TRIP to the county courthouse, Miss Stahler's fourth-grade classroom sat in on a legal proceeding. One student was particularly curious about a man sitting in the front of the room, typing furiously at an odd-looking typewriter while the case was presented to the judge. She asked her teacher, "Why is that man typing a paper while everyone is talking?" Miss Stahler thought it a good question, and instead of simply giving her an explanation, she arranged to have all the students meet the **court reporter** at the end of the day to ask him to explain his record-keeping duties to the class. The students were even able to try out his typing equipment, called a stenotype machine. Upon meeting the reporter, the same student told Miss Stahler, "I couldn't decide between becoming a lawyer and becoming a writer— now I know what I want to be when I grow up!"

■

These examples represent just a small number of situations that we encounter in our daily lives. We rely on trained workers of all backgrounds to keep us safe, healthy, and productive at home, school, and work. You might think that such important jobs require individuals with a bachelor's degree or higher. However, the workers in these previous scenarios became qualified to do their jobs by completing educational programs shorter than the traditional four-year bachelor's degree. Most of these workers received all or a significant portion of their preparation through an associate degree program. Such programs have become crucial to the preparation of workers in high-demand occupations, many of which are experiencing severe labor shortages. With these areas begging for workers, the associate degree has become the preferred postsecondary choice for millions of Americans. This belief, in part, is supported by a growing number of scholars and business leaders. Many express the concern that too many of America's colleges and universities have for too long concentrated primarily on pushing students into bachelor's-degree programs. These institutions have failed to keep pace with a society that increasingly needs workers with technical skills. Such skills not only require a different curriculum, but also usually require less time to prepare.

Many experts are also concerned that high schools and colleges neglect the fact that the majority of their graduates will never earn a bachelor's degree. According to the report "Counseling For High Skills," compiled by researchers at Kansas State University, 83 percent of parents hope their children will graduate with a bachelor's degree. In reality, only approximately 30 percent of high school graduates go on to obtain a bachelor's degree. While it appears that some parents realize that their sons and daughters do not need to pursue a bachelor's degree to be successful, there is still a long way to go before the associate degree option is more widely accepted.

According to the National Center for Education Statistics, there were 1,732 two-year colleges in the United States in 2000-01.

Many communities and educational institutions have realized the need for more practical connections between school and work. The proliferation of School-To-Work, Tech Prep, applied education, and other similar educational programs clearly attest to this fact. Community colleges tend to offer a comprehensive array of courses and programs beyond what School-To-Work and Tech Prep programs can provide. The community colleges' curriculum allows students to take a wide variety of courses, granting students an associate degree or certificate upon completion. Other students use community colleges as a springboard, transferring to a bachelor-degree program. Along with many other factors, the steady increase in tuition at the average college or university is expected to make community colleges more attractive to a growing number of individuals.

Not many will argue that education is one of the most important keys to personal success in life. National, state, and local government officials regularly allocate millions of dollars for education at all levels. In addition, businesses are spending larger sums on training and corporate education for both current and incoming employees. Community organizations and religious institutions have traditionally been committed to providing strong educational initiatives for the people they serve.

Our nation continues to experience increasing global competition, economic fluctuation, rapid technological changes, an overwhelming explosion of knowledge, and, in the opinion of many, a growing scarcity of effective leadership. Never before in America's history has the need for adequate, quality education appeared to be as acute as it seems today. This need is not expected to diminish, particularly in light of our most recent president's emphasis on education as one of his top priorities. Many states are earmarking millions of dollars for the preparation of educators and students in all grade levels to prepare students for in-demand, high-wage jobs. Many of these occupations require two years or less of full-time education and training. Change is now occurring at such a rapid pace that many career counselors are advising clients to prepare and brace themselves for increasing ambiguity and uncertainty in the job market.

Therefore, in light of these changing realities, there is an urgent need for practical answers to the following questions:

• What type of education does the future workforce need in a society such as ours? What institutions can best deliver these services?

• How, and in what form, should education be provided?

• What types of workers will help employers to effectively compete and meet their needs for today and tomorrow?

I firmly believe this nation's two-year colleges can address the questions above. Evidence supports the belief that community colleges will become crucial in America's economic future. The community college, which has traditionally placed emphasis on flexibility and outreach, is particularly suited to a society in need of rapid, customized responses. Communities, businesses, and industries all across the country are relying on cooperative efforts with nearby community colleges to educate and train the future workers.

> *Over 564,933 students earned associate degrees in 1999-2000, according to the National Center for Education Statistics.*

It is important for current and future college students, parents, and educators to take a closer look at how the two-year institution and its associate degree and programs can provide for millions a viable and fulfilling educational option. Therefore, in order to continue to heighten awareness for both current and potential students, we have written this second edition of *Great Careers in 2 Years: The Associate Degree Option*. This revised edition highlights the question of whether an associate degree is the right option for you, and it offers suggestions for preparation. In addition, we have added a chapter on transfer options, as some students of two-year colleges may later decide to finish a four-year degree. The remainder of the book identifies and describes 100 high-demand jobs. Each career article provides a description of job duties; certification, licensing, and personal requirements; ways to enter the field; salary statistics; employment outlook; and sources of additional information to contact to learn more about the career.

We hope this second edition of *Great Careers in 2 Years* will prove to be even more valuable than the original, expanding your knowledge of the associate degree option and helping you to make informed career decisions.

Chapter One

ASSOCIATE DEGREES
AND MORE

Two-year educational institutions have unique goals that are geared to meet the labor needs of their local communities. Included among these institutions are community and junior colleges as well as technical colleges and technical institutes. After these brief definitions below, I will refer to all of these institutions as two-year colleges.

Junior colleges have traditionally focused on providing students with the first two years of a bachelor's degree program. However, many junior colleges have expanded their focus and changed their name to community college. Now, few junior colleges restrict their programs to students planning to transfer to a four-year institution.

Technical colleges or *technical institutes* are primarily aimed at job training. However, many of these institutions are essentially community colleges with an emphasis on technical employment areas that are high in demand. These schools tend to provide specialized and intense training in trade or skill areas, such as electronics, computers, dental assisting, and respiratory therapy.

Students who desire a direct approach, wanting to learn only the essentials of a certain trade or skill area in the shortest period of time, may prefer a technical college experience.

Community colleges are probably the most popular choice among two-year institutions. Most of these colleges offer a wide variety of curriculum offerings. These schools present an attractive, economical, and realistic option for students who may not otherwise be able to attend college. For a significant number of students, a community college education provides the needed training to acquire a satisfying job and personal fulfillment.

Community colleges are usually well respected in their local areas. Typical curriculum offerings mirror those offered in the first two years of a variety of bachelor's degree programs. However, most community colleges offer additional courses aimed at the general community, such as continuing education classes and customized training for local businesses and industries. Minorities, veterans, immigrants, the disabled, and economically disadvantaged students may find that the community college's "open door policy" is the best avenue to higher education.

Community colleges usually grant at least two documents that officially recognize a student's successful completion of a program of study: the certificate (which we will cover a bit later) and the associate degree.

An *associate degree* is awarded when a student has successfully completed the minimum academic and related graduation requirements in a particular curriculum area. Generally, it is the equivalent of two years of study beyond the high school level. However, the actual time spent can vary greatly. Some students may finish earlier by taking summer classes or having taken previous college-level courses. Others may take longer than two years if they choose their subject concentration late, if they are slower to meet course requirements, or if they have personal interruptions. The following represent the most common associate degrees granted by most two-year colleges.

An *associate in applied science* (or *associate in applied arts and sciences*) is a degree that prepares students for immediate employment or advancement after its completion. Many or most courses may be transferable to selected four-year colleges.

An *associate in arts* requires a curriculum of study that basically mirrors the first two years of a four-year, liberal arts bachelor's degree.

An *associate in science* requires a curriculum of study that constitutes the first two years of a four-year, bachelor's of science degree.

Other popular degrees include the associate degree in nursing, associate in business, and the associate in music.

Associate degree programs have been developed for almost every interest. If you want to take an associate degree program in professional pilot technology, you might want to attend Miami-Dade Community College (http://www3.mdcc.edu). If you prefer to become proficient in the paper industry, then the pulp and paper technology curriculum at Bay de Noc Community College (http://www.baydenoc.cc.mi.us) in the Upper Pennisula of Michigan may be just the answer. Maybe you are more interested in the outdoors and backpacking; then the wilderness studies program at Colorado Mountain College (http://www.coloradomtn.edu/campus_alp) will sound attractive to you. Or you may choose to enroll in a boat maintenance and repair program at Honolulu Community College (http://www.hcc.hawaii.edu) while a friend of yours, thousands of miles away, completes her associate degree in instrumentation and controls at Northern Maine Technical College (http://www.nmtc.net). The above represent only the tip of the iceberg when it comes to the rich variety of associate degree options. The following is a sampling of other degree programs:

> Alcohol and drug abuse, accounting, aquaculture, arboriculture (urban forestry), computer programming, communication technology, civil engineering, culinary arts, chiropractic medicine, diesel equipment, equine studies (horses/harness racing), entrepreneurship, fire protection, funeral service education, food service management, fish and wildlife technology, farm and ranch management, recreational management, gerontology, graphic design, gunsmithing, horticulture technology, human services, health insurance claims management, occupational therapy, physical therapy, nursing, resort management, sports management, water technology, and welding.

Top 5 "Hot Programs" Reported by Community College Administrators

Program Name	Average Starting Salary
Registered Nursing	$32,757
General Computer Technologies	$34,242
Computer Networking	$38,768
Engineering-Electric/Electronics	$29,464
Computer Technician/Networking	$36,092

Source: American Association of Community Colleges, *"Hot Programs at Community Colleges,"* 2000

While the main focus of this book is on the associate degree, two-year colleges offer a variety of other programs. A brief description of each follows.

Certificates are awarded when students have successfully completed the minimum academic and related requirements of a particular curriculum area, usually equivalent to one year of study beyond the high school level. However, in a growing number of colleges, a variety of certificates of completion may be awarded for special or customized training that require shorter or longer periods of time.

Apprenticeships are written agreements between employers and individuals (referred to as apprentices). In this agreement, the individual agrees to be trained and supervised by a skilled craft person for roughly three to five years. Apprenticeships combine classroom instruction and on-the-job training that adds up to a minimum number of required hours. During this time, the apprentice is paid at a gradually increasing rate. After the apprenticeship is completed, the apprentice can apply for a Journey Worker's (or Journey Person's) Card, which proves his or her status as a skilled craftsperson in the particular area of training. Apprenticeship training has long been a vehicle used by thousands of manufacturing and construction firms to help meet the continuing scarcity of highly skilled, technically trained workers. Not only is the demand for such training still high, it is expected to continue to be so in the foreseeable future.

The academic courses required in apprenticeship programs are frequently taken at a local two-year college. The main advantage of apprenticeships is that students can acquire high-demand skills while earning college credit and an income. Possible careers obtainable through apprenticeship programs are too numerous to list, but here is a sampling of jobs:

> Automotive-body repairer, automotive mechanic, baker, barber/cosmetologist, boilermaker, butcher, bricklayer, carpenter, cement mason, ceramic layer, construction electrician, drywall finisher, firefighter, glazier, industrial electrician, industrial millwright, insulation worker, iron worker, machinist, operating engineer, painter, patternmaker, pipefitter, plasterer, plumber, roofer and waterproofer, sheet metal worker, sprinkler fitter, tool and die maker, and welder.

Business and industry programs are geared to meet the immediate and short-term needs of private businesses, industries and special interest groups, and nonprofit and governmental agencies. Examples of programs may range from crisis intervention strategies to professional development. Although private businesses and industries are often the designated employer for a majority of students in these programs, agreements are also made with economic development groups, high school districts, labor unions, and other colleges. Organization of these programs can vary and can be conducted on or off campus. Business and industry programs may include highly specialized seminars and workshops, professional development inservices or short-term classes, structured off-campus experiences, or one-time presentations.

Licensure is not considered a "program," but it is mentioned here because a number of two-year occupations require licensure before individuals can work. Many occupational programs prepare student graduates to not only proficiently perform in a job but also succeed in licensure exams.

Licensure is a form of legal authorization and recognition that permits an individual to perform a service within a particular area, region, or (in most instances) state.

Be sure to find out if your chosen career path requires or recommends a license or certification in order to practice or perform. The department chairperson of your school or an informed counselor should be able to provide you with this information. College catalogs and departmental publications may include general information about licensure requirements for certain career areas. When you talk to a school representative, remember to ask if there are statistics available on how well past graduates have done on licensure exams. In addition to meeting other criteria, students may be required to pass an exam, sometimes referred to as "boards," to become licensed. The following represent a sampling of the various licenses two-year occupational programs prepare their students for:

> Certified shorthand reporter (court reporter), dental assistant, dental hygienist, emergency medical technician (EMT), firefighter, insurance agent, occupational therapy assistant, optician technician, practical nurse, real estate appraiser, registered nurse, social work technician, and veterinary technician.

For more information, contact your state's department of labor, bureau of occupational licensing, or the state government headquarters, and ask for the office that can provide occupational license information.

I have only scratched the surface regarding some of the basic characteristics of two-year colleges. In light of the current and predicted workplace challenges, the future looks bright if students become actively motivated to prepare for high-demand fields. During this century, the two-year college will continue to be a driving force in vocational education and training.

Notable Community College Alumni

Gwendolyn Brooks, Pulitzer Prize-winning author and poet (City Colleges of Chicago, Illinois)

Billy Crystal, actor and comedian (Nassau Community College, New York)

Walt Disney, film producer (Metropolitan Junior College, Missouri)

Morgan Freeman, actor (Los Angeles City College, California)

Dennis Hayes, Earth Day co-founder (Clark College, Washington)

Jeanne Kirkpatrick, educator, stateswoman (Stephens College, Missouri)

Jim Lehrer, broadcast journalist (Victoria College, Texas)

John Cougar Mellencamp, singer, musician (Vincennes University Junior College, Indiana)

Natalie Merchant, singer (Jamestown Community College, New York)

Kweisi Mfume, president-NAACP, former U.S. Congressman (Baltimore City Community College, Maryland)

H. Ross Perot, corporate executive, 1992 and 1996 Presidential candidate (Texarkana Junior College, Texas)

Source: American Association of Community Colleges

Chapter Two

SHOULD I ATTEND AN ASSOCIATE DEGREE PROGRAM?

"Anybody can get into a junior college."

■

"Community college gave me a solid first two years compared to what some of my friends got out of their schools."

■

"My grades were terrible in high school, and our technical college was the only place that would accept me!"

■

"I'll go anyplace except a community college."

■

"I won't have to quit my job if I go to a community college."

■

"I really want to experience dorm life and leave home."

■

"I only want to go to school for a year or two."

■

"Community college gave me a few extra years to mature."

■

The statements above, both positive and negative, are similar to those often voiced by students when asked about technical schools, community colleges, and other associate degree institutions. You might be conflicted after reading over the statements. Which are actually true? How can you know if a two-year associate degree program is right for you? The latter question is certainly a difficult one for many people.

AN ASSOCIATE DEGREE PROGRAM
MAY BE RIGHT FOR YOU IF...

• You are interested in math and/or science but do not like the prospect of spending three or four years doing a lot of reading, writing papers, and taking courses that may not be directly related to what you want to do in a career

• You are the type of person who will work hard in school, but only want to do so for a year or two

• You want to have a more secure occupational future but do not qualify or want to apply for financial aid

• You have no scholarship possibilities and have limited financial resources

• The curriculum you are most realistically suited for is offered only at the associate degree level

• Going to a bachelor-degree granting institution would push you into a financial crisis—a situation you cannot afford to have, particularly at this time in your life

• You don't want to attend college, but your current employer requires future education courses in order to advance or keep your position

• You want the results of your efforts to be visible, practical, and more immediate than would be with a four-year program

• Either because of illness (you or a family member) or other personal problem, you need to stay close to home and work full-time while attending school

• You are seeking an attractive option to the high cost of many bachelor-degree granting institutions

• You want to acquire training that requires two years or less at a highly reputable, accredited institution

• You are applying for an apprenticeship program at a local company and will need to take classes at a local community college

• You want both an associate and bachelor's degree

• After working several years in a job that pays low wages and offers no benefits, you are strongly motivated to find something better

AN ASSOCIATE DEGREE PROGRAM
MAY NOT BE RIGHT FOR YOU IF...

- For personal reasons, you need to get away, for example, to leave a situation that is harmful to your academic, emotional, and/or physical health

- You have a strong desire to leave home, live on campus, and experience a more comprehensive college experience

- The major that you are interested in is only offered as a bachelor's degree

- Your values and personality configuration (self-assessment) are more suitable to a typical bachelor's degree program

- You have a scholarship to a four-year institution and attending would save money

- There are no two-year institutions (community colleges or technical schools) close to where you live, or they are not accredited or have a poor reputation

- Your father or mother works at a nearby college or university, which makes you eligible for reduced tuition

These are only a few of the many possible situations you will have to consider. It is more than likely that a combination of these situations, rather than just one, will eventually help you make a decision. I believe that dropping or flunking out of school is largely due to selecting the wrong curriculum or college.

Putting all these considerations together might sound like an overwhelming task, but it doesn't have to be done alone. Most community colleges will be able to help you or can refer you to a career guidance professional. Ultimately, though, the choice is up to you.

The decision to attend or not attend an associate degree program should start with a basic awareness of your life's direction. Attending a school without proper direction is not only a potential waste of money, it can also be a possible waste of your time, energy, and effort. Learning how to establish your life direction usually requires deep scrutiny and introspection. Career counselors call this process a *self-assessment*. A self-assessment, if honestly and thoroughly conducted, can help you uncover helpful personal information, which, too often, remains undiscovered. Learning such information can help you decide whether you should join the military, attend an associate degree program, apply for a job, or enroll in a four-year degree program.

Contrary to what many educators might suggest, it is my belief that students should not be encouraged to take a variety of exploratory courses as a strategy for identifying an appropriate major or career. I have personally witnessed the frustration and discouragement of too many students after they have explored a number of courses with no success.

Several years ago, I sat in on my son's freshman orientation session, and I was rather disappointed to hear the college administration recommend to the incoming freshmen that they should delay taking a career development class until at least their second semester, even suggesting they wait until their sophomore year. If students did some career planning on their own during this period, this might be good advice. However, most students fail to undertake career research on their own. The administrator went on to say that many students take five or more years to graduate, so there was plenty of time to make career decisions. With this attitude, it's no wonder there is a growing number of what many call "professional students"!

Imagine how you might feel if the results of your self-assessment and other factors strongly suggest that a two-year technical program, rather than the four-year art curriculum you are currently enrolled in, would be more appropriate for you. Imagine further that you had already taken art classes for roughly three years and had accumulated 72 credit hours during this "exploratory" time period. At this point, switching career gears would most probably be time consuming and costly.

> *The Department of Labor predicts that the number of jobs requiring an associate degree will grow 32 percent from 2000-2010.*

It is my hope that the following Self-Assessment Survey and Profile Sheet will help you to determine who you are and what you want to do with your future. This section may appear to be time consuming. But if you complete it earnestly, it could save you thousands of dollars in pursuit of inappropriate education as well as numerous hours of misdirected study time.

SELF-ASSESSMENT SURVEY AND PROFILE SHEET

Note: Feel free to duplicate any of the following self-assessment sheets for your own personal use. Responses can also be simply written on a sheet of paper.

PERSONALITY ATTRIBUTES: GENERAL

Personality attributes (sometimes referred to as *traits*) are qualities that help to distinguish one individual from another. A partial list of attributes appears on the next few pages. Carefully look over this list and identify those attributes you believe reflect yourself. Place an **S** beside those you believe are **strong** for you and a **W** beside those you are **weak** in. If some of the words are unfamiliar, you may want to have a dictionary on hand to use as a reference. Feel free to add attributes not listed that you believe may be more representative. When you are finished, list your five strongest and five weakest attributes in the space provided.

___ Able	___ Charming	___ Decisive
___ Active	___ Clever	___ Dedicated
___ Adaptable	___ Clumsy	___ Dependable
___ Admirable	___ Cocky	___ Determined
___ Adventurous	___ Commanding	___ Disciplined
___ Affectionate	___ Committed	___ Discreet
___ Aggressive	___ Compassionate	___ Dishonest
___ Alert	___ Competent	___ Disorganized
___ Aloof	___ Competitive	___ Disrespectful
___ Ambitious	___ Condescending	___ Distrustful
___ Amiable	___ Confident	___ Domineering
___ Analytical	___ Conforming	___ Earnest
___ Anxious	___ Comforting	___ Efficient
___ Apathetic	___ Convincing	___ Emotional
___ Argumentative	___ Conscientious	___ Encouraging
___ Articulate	___ Consistent	___ Energetic
___ Athletic	___ Considerate	___ Enthusiastic
___ Beautiful	___ Cooperative	___ Envious
___ Boastful	___ Courageous	___ Expressive
___ Capable	___ Creative	___ Extroverted
___ Caring	___ Critical	___ Fair-minded
___ Casual	___ Cruel	___ Faithful
___ Cautious	___ Curious	___ Fearful
___ Cheerful	___ Deceptive	___ Flexible

___ Flippant	___ Loving	___ Promiscuous
___ Forceful	___ Loyal	___ Punctual
___ Forgetful	___ Mannerly	___ Purposeful
___ Forgiving	___ Materialistic	___ Pursuing
___ Frank	___ Mature	___ Quiet
___ Friendly	___ Merciful	___ Reliable
___ Frugal	___ Methodical	___ Reserved
___ Gentle	___ Moody	___ Resourceful
___ Good listener	___ Motivated	___ Respectful
___ Graceful	___ Musical	___ Responsible
___ Grateful	___ Negative	___ Rigid
___ Gullible	___ Naive	___ Rude
___ Handsome	___ Neat	___ Sacrificing
___ Helpful	___ Nonconforming	___ Sarcastic
___ Honest	___ Obedient	___ Secretive
___ Hospitable	___ Objective	___ Self-confident
___ Humble	___ Obnoxious	___ Selfish
___ Humorous	___ Observant	___ Self-directed
___ Imaginative	___ Open-minded	___ Sensitive
___ Impatient	___ Optimistic	___ Serene
___ Impulsive	___ Orderly	___ Serious
___ Inconsistent	___ Original	___ Sharing
___ Independent	___ Organized	___ Shy
___ Industrious	___ Outgoing	___ Sickly
___ Inflexible	___ Overbearing	___ Smart
___ Initiating	___ Passive	___ Sociable
___ Inquiring	___ Panicky	___ Spontaneous
___ Insensitive	___ Patient	___ Steady
___ Insightful	___ Peaceful	___ Strong-willed
___ Intuitive	___ Perfectionist	___ Stubborn
___ Intelligent	___ Persistent	___ Sulky
___ Integrity	___ Persuasive	___ Systematic
___ Intense	___ Pessimistic	___ Tactless
___ Intolerant	___ Picky	___ Tactful
___ Irresponsible	___ Planner	___ Talented
___ Joiner	___ Pleasant	___ Thoughtful
___ Judgmental	___ Poised	___ Tolerant
___ Kind	___ Practical	___ Trustworthy
___ Lazy	___ Precise	___ Understanding
___ Liar	___ Prejudiced	___ Unselfish
___ Logical	___ Procrastinator	___ Other

Strongest Attributes   Weakest Attributes

_____   _____

_____   _____

_____   _____

_____   _____

_____   _____

TEMPERAMENTS

Temperaments are personality attributes that relate to your way of thinking, feeling, and behaving and help determine whether you are comfortable or uncomfortable in a given situation. Weigh each of the temperaments below on a comfort scale of **1-10.** (A rating of **10** would be the situation in which you feel the **most comfortable.**) Place your rating on the line beside the appropriate letter. If you feel equally comfortable about more than one, do not hesitate to use the same number twice. When you are finished, list your five most comfortable and five least comfortable situations to find your strongest and weakest temperaments.

____Situations involving a variety of duties often requiring frequent **change**

____Situations involving **repetition** according to set procedures or sequences

____Situations involving doing things only under **specific instruction,** allowing little or no room for independent action or judgment

____Situations involving **dealing with people** in job duties beyond giving and receiving instructions

____Situations involving **directing, controlling, and planning** of entire activities

____Situations involving **working alone or apart** from others

____Situations involving **influencing people** in their opinions, attitudes, or judgments about ideas or things

____Situations involving **working under pressure,** often confronting unexpected occurrences and taking risks

_____Situations involving making decisions based on **personal judgment**

_____Situations involving making decisions using **measurable or verifiable data**

_____Situations involving creatively **interpreting and expressing** feelings, ideas, or facts

_____Situations involving **precise work** in terms of set limits, tolerances, or standards

_____Other:

Strongest Temperaments   **Weakest Temperaments**

_____   _____

_____   _____

_____   _____

_____   _____

SKILLS

Skills can be divided into two major categories: abilities and aptitudes. _Abilities_ can be defined as things you can do, usually as a result of continuing rehearsal and/or practice. Abilities and skills are often thought of as having the same meaning. However, being skilled usually implies that you can do something very well and at a high degree of proficiency.

Aptitudes are those abilities that you perform well and that seem to come naturally, with little or no practice required. Some people have aptitudes they are either unaware of or have been unable to develop to their fullest. Becoming aware of your aptitudes can help you to better understand your natural strengths.

Place an **AB** to the left of the areas for which you feel you have **ability**. Place an **AP** to the left of the areas for which you believe you have an **aptitude.** Feel free to write in any ability or aptitude you may have in addition to or instead of the sampling listed. Leave blank any area of which you are unsure. After you are finished, list your five strongest and five weakest abilities and aptitudes in the spaces provided.

____Understanding facts and underlying reasoning

____Understanding the meaning of words and ideas

____Doing arithmetic quickly and correctly

____Looking at flat drawings of objects and forming three-dimensional mental images (visualizing height, width, and depth), such as in reading blueprints and patterns

____Observing details in graphic material and effectively making visual comparisons

____Observing details and recognizing errors in numbers, spelling, and punctuation

____Moving your eyes and hands together to perform a task rapidly and correctly

____Moving your fingers to work with small objects rapidly and correctly

____Moving your hands with ease and skill, as in placing and turning

____Moving your hands and feet together in response to visual signals

____Seeing likenesses and differences

____Finding errors in writing

____Asking the right questions

____Following instructions

____Improving what others have done

____Explaining things clearly

____Planning and organizing

____Operating mechanical equipment

____Exploring and doing research

____Budgeting

____Being exact and to the point

____Accepting constructive advice

____Being creative

____Getting along with others

____Counseling others

____Doing artistic things

____Keeping records

____Leading and supervising others

____Teaching others

____Gardening

____Typing

____Giving others helpful advice

____Being flexible

____Drawing or designing things

____Training others to do things

____Driving vehicles

____Performing in front of others

____Taking risks

____Solving conflicts

____Staying with a task until done

____Repairing and servicing computers

____Getting others to believe in something

____Making good decisions during emergencies

____Simplifying what appears to be complex

____Learning from mistakes and past experiences

____Working alone for long periods of time

____Listening or picking up on what others say

____Seeing the underlying reasons for behavior

____Estimating costs

____Interpreting the feelings and emotions of others

____Reading articulately

____Doing activities that require heavy physical work

____Writing

____Copying things or activities done by others

____Collecting things

____Constructing things out of wood, metal, or other materials

____Speaking in public

____Working with numbers

____Operating computers

____Motivating others to perform or do something

____Being thorough

____Expressing feelings

_____Managing time

_____Distinguishing sounds

_____Doing things for others

_____Communicating to others

_____Controlling emotions

_____Thinking before acting

_____Team sports (basketball, football, etc.)

_____Individual sports (tennis, golf, etc.)

_____Studying English or related subjects

_____Studying social studies or related subjects

_____Studying science or related subjects

_____Other:

Strongest Abilities   **Weakest Abilities**

_____   _____

_____   _____

_____   _____

_____   _____

_____   _____

Strongest Aptitudes   **Weakest Aptitudes**

_____   _____

_____   _____

_____   _____

_____   _____

_____   _____

For a more comprehensive and personalized listing of skill terms, read Richard Bolles's _What Color is Your Parachute Workbook_ (Berkeley, CA: Ten Speed Press, 2003).

LIFE VALUES

Life values are deeply cherished things, activities, or relationships that you place the most importance on and aspire to obtain or engage in. Complete the survey below to determine your own life values.

First, read through the entire list. After reading, go back and circle each value's level of importance to you. After you are finished, go back and select your five most important and five least important life values in the spaces provided.

Achievement: Being able to see or experience results that have been brought about by persistence or hard work

Not important   Important   Very important

Aesthetics: The appreciation and enjoyment of beauty, as in the arts and/or nature

Not important   Important   Very important

Altrusim: Dedication to the welfare of others

Not important   Important   Very important

Autonomy: Being able to make one's own decisions

Not important   Important   Very important

Creativity: Being able to try out new and original ideas

Not important   Important   Very important

Emotional well-being: Being able to identify and resolve inner conflict; being relatively free from anxiety

Not important   Important   Very important

Health: Being relatively free from pain, discomfort, sickness, etc.

Not important   Important   Very important

Helping mankind: Engaging in activities that will positively influence the lives of many

Not important   Important   Very important

Honesty: Being genuine, truthful, and sincere with yourself and others

Not important   Important   Very important

Justice: Treating others fairly and impartially; holding to truth and reason

Not important   Important   Very important

Knowledge: Having desire to learn or know; seeking truth

Not important   Important   Very important

Love: Warmth, caring, and unselfish devotion that freely accepts others without conditions

Not important   Important   Very important

Loyalty: Keeping allegiance to a person, group, or institution

Not important   Important   Very important

Morality: Believing and keeping ethical standards and personal honor

Not important   Important   Very important

Physical appearance: Having concern for being neat, clean, and well groomed

Not important   Important   Very important

Pleasure: Having satisfaction, fun, joy, and gratification

Not important   Important   Very important

Power: Having possession, control, authority, or influence over others

Not important   Important   Very important

Recognition: To be positively noticed and receive attention

Not important   Important   Very important

Religious faith: Having strong spiritual beliefs

Not important   Important   Very important

Security: Having visible or concrete support behind one's endeavors or involvements in life

Not important   Important   Very important

Skill: Being very good at something, regardless of whether it comes naturally or as a result of continuous practice

Not important   Important   Very important

Wealth: Having many possessions and plenty of money

Not important   Important   Very important

Wisdom: Having good sense and judgment; being able to make appropriate and effective decisions

Not important   Important   Very important

Other:

Strongest Life Values	**Weakest Life Values**
_____	_____
_____	_____
_____	_____
_____	_____
_____	_____

WORK VALUES

Just like life values, work values are things, activities, and relationships you place the most importance on and aspire to obtain or engage in, but they are relative to an occupation. Work values tend to reflect much of who you are on the inside. Complete the survey that follows to determine your own work values.

Read through the entire list. Then go back and circle the level of importance each work value suggests to you. After you are finished, determine your five most important and five least important work values, and list them in the spaces provided.

Advancement: Being able to advance into a position of higher authority, pay, and responsibility

Not important   Important   Very important

Achievement: Doing something that requires considerable effort and/or difficulty

Not important   Important   Very important

Assisting others: Being directed and supervised by others

Not important   Important   Very important

Benefits: Having adequate medical and life insurance coverage, unemployment benefits, and paid vacation time

Not important   Important   Very important

Calculating numbers: Creating charts, statistical reports, and summaries

Not important   Important   Very important

Competition: Being challenged to produce or perform; being measured against others' performance

Not important   Important   Very important

Creativity: Being able to try out new ideas; being innovative

Not important   Important   Very important

Good environment: Having physical or social surroundings that are suitable to your temperaments and values

Not important   Important   Very important

Hands-on contact: Working with things, objects, or equipment

Not important   Important   Very important

Helping others: Engaging in activities that directly aid and assist others

Not important   Important   Very important

Independence: Having little or no supervision; Being able to make own decisions

Not important   Important   Very important

Industrious: Having work that keeps one busy and active continuously; having little or no "down time"

Not important   Important   Very important

Interactive: Doing work that requires cooperation with others

Not important   Important   Very important

Interesting: Being positively excited and motivated most of the time in what you are doing

Not important   Important   Very important

Leadership management: Being in charge of others

Not important   Important   Very important

Learning: Gaining knowledge and understanding; being intellectually stimulated

Not important   Important   Very important

Money: Earning a high salary

Not important   Important   Very important

Off-work sensitivity: Doing work that is reasonably flexible; may include options such as overtime, vacation, split shifts, and an on-site day care

Not important   Important   Very important

Positive relationships: Being able to get along very well with co-workers and supervisors

Not important   Important   Very important

Prestige: Having a position that is recognized as being very important and influential and that commands great respect

Not important   Important   Very important

Religious faith: Doing work that reflects one's spiritual beliefs

Not important   Important   Very important

Security: Being relatively free from the fear of layoffs, job loss, reduced hours, etc.

Not important   Important   Very important

Self-direction: Being able to determine what you are going to do and how you are going to do tasks, procedures, pace, etc.

Not important   Important   Very important

Skill: Being able to do something that requires special effort, training, or education

Not important   Important   Very important

Support: Having a work environment that provides emotional support, praise, and backing

Not important   Important   Very important

Travel: Being able to travel within a local community as well as from city to city as a part of your job responsibilities

Not important   Important   Very important

Variety: Doing different tasks and activities; not repetitive

Not important   Important   Very important

Words, ideas, and information: Working with oral, visual, and written information, knowledge, facts, ideas, and/or symbols

Not important   Important   Very important

Other:

Strongest Work Values	**Weakest Work Values**
_____	_____
_____	_____
_____	_____
_____	_____
_____	_____

INTERESTS

Interests are things, activities, and experiences that you are attracted to, enjoy, and are excited about. Much of what we do during our leisure time tends to reflect our interests. Interests often reveal some of our most important values. A sample of interests and/or leisure-time activities has been included in the following list. Complete the survey to determine your interests.

First, go through the entire list, placing an **S** to the left of those things, activities, or experiences that represent a **strong interest** for you. Place a **W** next to those that represent a **weak interest.**

When you are done, list your five strongest and weakest interests in the spaces provided.

_____Being the leader

_____Cooking

_____Acting

_____Gardening

_____Solving math problems

_____Visiting museums

_____Organizing events

_____Water sports and games

_____Canoeing, sailing

_____Doing hard physical work

_____Working with words

_____Working with ideas

_____Drawing

_____Helping the poor

_____Hunting, trapping

_____Biology, life science

_____Working on cars

_____Team sports (baseball, football, etc.)

_____Individual sports (tennis, golf, etc.)

_____Reading

_____Writing

_____Selling things

_____Going to plays

_____Music

_____Teaching

_____Parenting

_____Earning money

_____Competing with others

_____Talk shows

_____Video/computer games

_____Listening to the radio

_____Watching TV/movies

_____Dining out

_____Bowling

_____Arts and crafts

_____Traveling

_____Antiques

_____Talking

_____Foreign languages

_____Politics

_____Collections

_____Surfing the Internet

_____Computer games

_____Computer programming

_____Interior decorating

_____Backpacking

_____Bird watching

_____Camping

_____Exploring

_____Hiking

_____Horseback riding

_____Sailing

_____Sightseeing

_____Walking

_____Big Brother/Big Sister programs

_____Counseling others

_____Peace Corps

_____Military involvement

_____Red Cross

_____Spending time with the elderly

_____Visiting the sick

____YMCA/YWCA

____Conferences/conventions

____Debating

____Editing

____Organizing activities

____Researching

____Science exhibits

____Studying

____Working in a day care center

____Writing in a diary

____Auto shows

____Religious study

____Faith-based activities

____Singing in a choir

____Playing music or singing

____Circuses

____Craftwork

____Photography

____Pottery

____Dancing

____Entertaining others

____Fairs/festivals

____Nightclubs/parties

____Poetry

____Talent/variety shows

____Visiting libraries

____Zoos/planetariums

____4-H

____Conservation

____Health/nutrition

____Investments

____Junior Achievement

____Motorcycles

____Scouting

____Sororities/fraternities

____Broadcasting

____Doing housework

____Exercising

____Learning new things

____Magazines/newspapers

____Sleeping

____Shopping

____Teaching a craft or sport

____Gymnastics

____Ice skating

____Skiing

____Weight lifting

____Cross country

____Other:

Strongest Interests

_____

_____

_____

_____

_____

Weakest Interests

_____

_____

_____

_____

_____

SELF-ASSESSMENT PROFILE SHEET

Your **Self-Assessment Profile Sheet (SAPS)** appears on the next pages. Record the summary information that you were asked to identify in each section. If you feel there are skills, interests, etc., that should be added because you believe they are of equal weight (or tied in terms of rank order), feel free to add them.

After you are finished, try to identify the occupations and/or college majors you believe most realistically reflect your results. You can generate your own list of occupations and majors or use a career interest survey such as the Kuder or COPS Survey to help you determine appropriate career direction (see end of chapter for contact information). It is my hope that after you complete the reading and exercises in this book, you will be well on your way toward a more directed and fulfilling life.

Strongest Attributes

_____

_____

_____

_____

_____

Weakest Attributes

_____

_____

_____

_____

_____

Strongest Temperaments

_____

_____

_____

_____

_____

Weakest Temperaments

_____

_____

_____

_____

_____

Strongest Abilities

_____

_____

_____

_____

_____

Weakest Abilities

_____

_____

_____

_____

_____

Strongest Aptitudes

_____

_____

_____

_____

_____

Weakest Aptitudes

_____

_____

_____

_____

_____

Strongest Life Values

_____

_____

_____

_____

_____

Weakest Life Values

_____

_____

_____

_____

_____

Strongest Work Values

_____

_____

_____

_____

_____

Weakest Work Values

_____

_____

_____

_____

_____

Strongest Interests

_____

_____

_____

_____

_____

Weakest Interests

_____

_____

_____

_____

_____

SIGNIFICANT INFLUENCING FACTORS

Remember that your profile is subject to change in time due to what are called *significant influencing factors (SIFs)*. SIFs can and often do influence your life and career direction. SIFs are situations, events, or incidents that significantly alter your thinking patterns, activities, and relationships. Consequently, these factors can motivate you to make adjustments in terms of important occupational decisions. Examples of SIFs are illness, disease, an accident, floods or other natural disasters, war, a change in religious beliefs, divorce, drug or alcohol abuse, loss of job, change of job, and new legislation. The list is almost endless. Therefore, it is suggested that you periodically review your self-assessment and adjust whenever necessary.

FOR ADDITIONAL RESEARCH

While a self-assessment should provide you with a good start in determining your interests and abilities, there is no one test or survey that can measure all the factors that must be considered when planning your future. Most career counselors rely on a variety of surveys, tests, and instruments to assist clients with life direction. Other useful assessment tests are listed below.

Career Occupational Preference System: Helps to identify interests, abilities, and values. EdITS, PO Box 7234, San Diego, CA 92167, Tel: 800-416-1666, Web: http://www.edits.net.

Kuder Career Planning System: Provides rank order of selected occupational and college major interests. National Career Assessment Services, Inc., 601 Visions Parkway, Adel, IA 50003, Tel: 800-314-8972, Web: http://www.kuder.com.

Self-Directed Search: Measures personality, environments, and interests. Psychological Assessment Resources, Inc., 16204 North Florida Avenue, Lutz, FL 33549, Tel: 800-383-6595, Web: http://www.self-directed-search.com.

Western Michigan University Career Guidance Inventory: Comprehensive test that measures skills, interests, work values, and personality traits and provides rank order list of occupations and values. Western Michigan University, Kalamazoo, MI 49008-5201, Tel: 616-387-1000, Web: http://www.wmich.edu.

Chapter Three
ACCREDITATION: NOT ALL SCHOOLS ARE CREATED EQUAL

MARY ATTENDED a small community college in Washington state, working two part-time jobs in order to pay tuition, car payments, rent, and other expenses. Although her hometown is thousands of miles away in Georgia, she decided to go away to school after reading an attractive brochure for the college. At the end of her first year, Mary developed an unexpected illness, causing her to withdraw from classes and return home to live with her parents and recover. Once she felt well enough, she decided to stay home and enroll at a nearby community college to finish her first year. However, Mary was shocked to find out that the community college she had previously attended was not accredited. As a result, none of her first-year credits would be accepted. Mary was understandably discouraged and somewhat bitter as she faced the reality of starting the year all over again.

■

RAPHAEL JUST COMPLETED an associate degree program at a local electronics institute. He was excited to begin his career because he had read that there was a shortage of workers in the electronics field. Raphael's grades had been consistently good, and he had graduated near the top of his class. He eagerly applied for a number of jobs at some of the area's most prestigious firms, only to be repeatedly rejected. Disappointed and puzzled, Raphael contacted a hiring manager at one of the firms that he had interviewed with and politely inquired as to why he had not been selected for the job. To his surprise, he discovered that the electronics institute he had attended was not accredited, and worse, it had a long-standing reputation of graduating poorly qualified students. Unfortunately, Raphael did not take the time to research or visit the school prior to enrollment.

■

The scenarios above occur far too often to unprepared students who neglect the important task of researching schools to determine, prior to enrollment, whether a college is properly accredited. After conducting a thorough and accurate self-assessment, considering all appropriate significant influencing factors that may apply, your next step is to check the credentials of your chosen institution.

WHAT IS ACCREDITATION?

Accreditation is the official stamp of approval given by a committee of evaluators to an educational or training institution that demonstrates a certain level of quality or service. For example, an accredited school might need to have an adequate number of faculty with advanced degrees and appropriate course offerings.

Lack of accreditation sometimes, although not always, can give schools a less than favorable public image and result in a possible loss of potential students and qualified teachers. In short, accreditation is a systematic way a college can assure students, employees, and the community of the quality of services being provided.

Accreditation is voluntary and usually consists of two types: institutional and specialized programs. *Institutional accreditation* is concerned with the human, financial, and physical resources; educational purposes; effectiveness; and integrity of the institution. *Specialized program accreditation* is concerned with technical or professional programs within an institution, such as nursing, automotive technology, electronics, dental hygiene, and occupational therapy programs. Accredited specialized programs need to meet the minimum quality standards of recognized agencies in the field. Examples of areas evaluated usually include course content, equipment used, and length of program.

A brief summary of the five criteria used by the Higher Learning Commission of the North Central Association to evaluate and grant accreditation to higher education institutions (including two-year colleges) appears on the next page.

1. The institution has clear and publicly stated purposes consistent with its mission and appropriate to an institution of higher education.
2. The institution has the human, financial, and physical resources necessary to accomplish its purposes.
3. The institution is accomplishing its educational goals and other purposes.
4. The institution can continue to accomplish its purposes and strengthen its educational effectiveness.
5. The institution practices integrity in all of its practices and relationships.

Advantages of attending an accredited college

- It gives you a sense of confidence that you are being trained and educated well
- Credits are more likely to transfer if you change schools
- Employers may be more likely to hire you

Disadvantages of attending an unaccredited college

- You may not be able to transfer credits if you change schools
- You may have trouble finding a desirable job and/or pay
- You may waste money and time
- You may not receive a quality education
- You may not be properly trained for your chosen career

Check to see if the two-year college of your choice is accredited by contacting the appropriate regional accreditation agency listed below. Accreditation can and does have tremendous impact on helping you acquire a desirable career and meeting life goals.

This organization accredits schools, colleges, and universities in the following states and territories: Delaware, Maryland, New Jersey, New York, Pennsylvania, District of Columbia, Puerto Rico, U.S. Virgin Islands, and selected overseas schools.

Commission on Secondary Schools/Middle States Association of Colleges and Schools
3624 Market Street
Philadelphia, PA 19104-2680
Tel: 215-662-5603
Web: http://www.css-msa.org

This association accredits schools and degree-granting colleges and universities in the following states: Connecticut, Maine, Massachusetts, New Hampshire, Rhode Island, Vermont, and approximately 86 American and international institutions around the world. It is reported to be the nation's largest accreditation association.

New England Association of Schools and Colleges
209 Burlington Road
Bedford, MA 01730-1433
Tel: 781-271-0022
Web: http://www.neasc.org

This organization accredits schools and degree-granting colleges and universities in Latin America and the following states: Alabama, Florida, Georgia, Kentucky, Louisiana, Mississippi, North Carolina, South Carolina, Tennessee, Texas, and Virginia.

Commission on Colleges/Southern Association of Colleges and Schools
1866 Southern Lane
Decatur, GA 30033
Tel: 404-679-4500
Web: http://www.sacscoc.org

This organization accredits schools as well as degree-granting colleges and universities in California and Hawaii and the following international regions: Guam, American Samoa, Commonwealth of the Northern Marianas Islands, the Pacific Basin, and East Asia, as well as other selected institutions.

The Accrediting Commission for Community and Junior Colleges/Western Association of Schools and Colleges
3402 Mendocino Avenue
Santa Rosa, CA 95403
Tel: 707-569-9177
Web: http://www.wascweb.org

This organization accredits public and private schools, degree-granting colleges and universities in the following states: Arkansas, Arizona, Colorado, Iowa, Illinois, Indiana, Kansas, Michigan, Minnesota, Missouri, North Dakota, Nebraska, Ohio, Oklahoma, New Mexico, South Dakota, Wisconsin, West Virginia, and Wyoming.

The Higher Learning Commission of the North Central Association of Colleges and Schools
30 North Lasalle Street, Suite 2400
Chicago, IL 60602-2504
Tel: 800-621-7440
Web: http://ncahigherlearningcommission.org

This association accredits schools and degree-granting colleges and universities in the following states: Alaska, Idaho, Montana, Nevada, Oregon, Pennsylvania, Utah, Virginia, and Washington, as well as selected international schools.

Northwest Association of Schools and Colleges
1910 University Drive
Boise, ID 83725-1060
Tel: 208-426-5727
Web: http://www2.boisestate.edu/nasc

Contact the DETC for a free Directory of Accredited Institutions, which lists nearly 80 member institutions that include high school, college, university, and military organizations.

The Accrediting Commission of the Distance Education and Training Council (DETC)
1601 18th Street, NW
Washington, DC 20009-2529
Tel: 202-234-5100
Web: http://www.detc.org

Chapter Four
TRANSFER OPTIONS

"I want to stay close to home for a while and transfer to a college in a year or so."

■

"Community college gave me a great start, but I plan to graduate from my state college."

■

"I need to save money by going to a community college this year, but I'll go away to school next year."

■

The statements above reflect typical reasons why students choose to go to community colleges only to transfer to another school later on. Students may want to transfer to a four-year college or university as a way of "stepping up" or "moving ahead." While this may be the case, many students fail to understand the need for careful planning before applying for their desired transfer.

What exactly is a transfer student and transfer program? A *transfer student* is an individual who was previously enrolled at one college and leaves to enroll at another college. The school a student leaves is called the *sending institution*. The school a student is transferring to is called the *receiving institution*.

A traditional *transfer program* is generally when a student studies at an accredited two-year college and, upon successful completion, transfers his or her credits to a four-year institution to obtain a bachelor's degree. A large number of these programs are liberal arts or professional degree programs.

However, transfer programs are becoming more varied in their configuration. Some technically oriented curriculums are referred to as *2+2 programs*, which include two years of class-oriented education followed by two years of hands-on technical training. Other programs, called *2+2+2 programs*, include the last two years of high school, followed by two years at a community college, followed by two years of a bachelor's degree program. There are even *3+1 programs.* Recently, I talked with a student who was in a music program that required her to take three years at a particular music college and finish her last year through a bachelor's degree program.

Transfer agreements can be official understandings between the sending and receiving institutions. These established transfer agreements tend to assure that, if all conditions are met, most if not all of the credits taken at one school will transfer to the new school. Some transfer agreements may include state requirements; others may be more informal agreements between two colleges.

What should a student know and do before applying for a transfer? Once again, the importance of conducting and carefully considering the results of your self-assessment should be emphasized. Next, students must decide whether they want a certificate, a two-year, bachelor's, or advanced degree, and if a transfer is needed to obtain their goal.

For some, a one- or two-year program taken at one college will do just fine. Other students may start out in a technical program and decide to transfer to a liberal arts school.

It is wise not to think too narrowly. Many students believe a one- or two-year college experience is sufficient now. But will the same be true 10 or 15 years down the road? Some students, after previously deciding on a shorter, postsecondary education, decide to transfer to a longer program, but their credits and training acquired earlier are not transferable or applicable. Therefore, hasty and poorly researched school decisions are strongly discouraged. After working at a community college for over 20 years, I have noticed that a significant percentage of my clients have either recently changed schools or plan to in the near future. This occurs at two-year colleges across the nation. It may be the student who has her sights on a bachelor's degree and readily volunteers that she is here for only a short time. Or it is the student who just enrolled for the spring semester after attending a vocational/technical school. Or perhaps it's the third-semester-freshman transferring home for a while to get his grades up. It certainly makes one wonder if transferring is popular, in part, because it gives students a sense of making progress. Granted, transferring from one college to another can be productive, especially if it is a move that has been based on careful considerations. However, many students fall prey to one or more of the following pitfalls:

1. **Failure to check credit equivalency guides or manuals.** Most two-year college counselors and advisors have access to updated credit-equivalency guides, manuals, or lists. These materials usually pair up a selected list of courses offered at a two-year college with equivalent courses at various colleges and universities and indicate the amount of credit awarded for each class. A great deal of disappointment can be avoided (as well as money saved) if more students consulted current equivalency materials before transferring schools.

2. **Failure to take basic requirements.** In order to obtain an associate or bachelor's degree, each college requires students to pass a group of core or basic courses. For example, liberal arts colleges usually require a minimum number of credits in English/communications, humanities, physical and biological sciences, and social sciences. Some students enrolled in transfer curriculums have similar course requirements and thus complete these basic classes. However, some students take classes of interest for several years, accumulating many credits but not covering the basic requirements because they never thought they would need to transfer. These students may lack the credits to transfer anywhere without having to start from the beginning. They may have to take freshman- and sophomore-level courses—at a much higher cost than what it would have cost them at their community college.

3. **Inappropriate fit due to poor research.** Too many transfer students base their reason for changing schools on what appears to be shaky grounds. For example, a student chooses to transfer to a certain college because her sister went there. Another student wants to transfer someplace warm. Yet another, after looking over a number of recruiting brochures, wants to transfer to what looks to be a large and beautiful campus. While the above may indeed be important considerations, many other factors should be considered before a final decision is made.

4. **Misunderstanding what credits will or will not transfer.** Because each college decides what courses will or will not be accepted and how much credit should be granted, it is a rare occurrence when every single credit earned at a two-year college will transfer without some adjustment. The exceptions to this are those students who have followed a formal agree-

ment curriculum in which the receiving institution guarantees that all passing courses will be accepted. It is strongly suggested that students not follow a transfer curriculum based solely on what they have read in a manual, but to verify its accuracy with a professional counselor or informed academic advisor.

These basics, along with other researched factors, should be considered before transferring to a new school. When a superficial reason motivates the change, students may be forced to make another transfer or even drop out of school because their new school is a bad fit.

Listed below is a sampling of some the many traditional bachelor's degree and pre-professional transfer curriculums.

Accounting, Art, Agriculture, Biology, Business Administration, Chemistry, Computer Science, Criminal Justice, Distributive Education, Economics, Environmental Science, English, Engineering, Foreign Language, Forestry, Geology, History, Home Economics, Journalism, Library Science, Marketing, Mathematics, Medical Technology, Music Education, Mortuary Science, Natural Resources, Nursing, Occupational Therapy, Oceanography, Optometry, Pharmacy, Photography, Physical Education, Physics, Physical Therapy, Political Science, Pre-Chiropractic, Pre-Dental, Pre-Law, Pre-Medicine, Pre-Veterinary, Psychology, Social Work, Sociology, Speech, Transportation, Teaching, Water Purification

It is strongly suggested that once students enrolled in a two-year program realize they need or want a bachelor's degree (or beyond) to advance in their most suitable career direction, they should begin their transfer preparation as early as possible. Some required courses may need to be taken during students' freshman year.

FINAL CHECKLIST FOR TRANSFER STUDENTS

____You have sent an updated transcript to your desired college, and you have verification that it has been received.

____You have read the receiving college's published transfer materials thoroughly.

____You have completed and considered your personal self-assessment when making your decision.

____If you are interested in financial aid opportunities (including scholarships), you have sent in all requested forms by the stated deadlines.

____You have checked to see if the college you are currently attending (or plan to attend) is appropriately accredited.

____Residence hall or housing arrangements have been completed and submitted by requested deadline. (Be sure any fees or deposit requested are included.)

____Your basic course requirements have already been met or will be completed in your receiving institution.

____If possible, you have visited the receiving college's campus, exploring classrooms, lecture halls, dormitories, libraries, and dining rooms.

____Application form and fee, which is usually nonrefundable, has been mailed off by the stated deadline.

____If requested, all written recommendations and essays have been submitted to the receiving college by the stated deadlines.

____You have made an appointment for (or have already had) a course credit evaluation with the admissions or registrar's office of your new school.

____You have made an appointment with a career counselor at the receiving institution to help you with career direction. This is recommended even if you have previously engaged in career development activities.

ADULT DAY CARE COORDINATORS

School Subjects **Psychology** **Sociology**	*Salary Range* **$18,000 to $31,000** **to $45,000**
Personal Skills **Helping/teaching** **Leadership/management**	*Certification or Licensing* **Required for certain** **positions**
Work Environment **Primarily indoors** **Primarily one location**	*Outlook* **Much faster than the average**

THE JOB

Adult day care coordinators direct adult day care centers. They oversee various staff members who provide care, such as nurses, physical therapists, social workers, cooks, and several aides. Coordinators are responsible for staff hiring and training as well as scheduling work shifts.

Coordinators plan daily and weekly activities for the clients and oversee meal planning and preparation. They work closely with client family members to make sure that each individual is receiving care that best fits his or her needs.

Adult day care coordinators may have other duties, such as developing and adhering to a budget. In centers licensed or certified by the state, coordinators may ensure that their centers remain in compliance with state regulations and have all necessary documentation to prove it. They may also be responsible for general bookkeeping, bill payment, and office management.

PROFESSIONAL AND PERSONAL REQUIREMENTS

Certification is available but is not required for you to become an adult day care coordinator. In some cases, however, coordinators may work for agencies licensed by the state health department. Any adult day care center that receives payment from Medicare or from other government agencies must be licensed by the state department of health. In these cases, licensing requirements may include requirements for coordinators and other staff members.

As a coordinator, you will need compassion for the elderly and disabled as well as patience and the desire to help others. You should also be organized and able to manage other workers effectively.

STARTING OUT

When looking for a position as an adult day care coordinator, you should first locate and contact all such programs in your area. Checking your local Yellow Pages under Nursing Homes, Residential Care Facilities, Aging Services, or Senior Citizens Services should provide you a list of leads. You might either send a resume and cover letter or call these potential employers directly. You should also watch for job openings listed in area newspapers and on organizations' Web sites.

Another means of finding job leads is to become affiliated with a professional association, such as the American Geriatrics Society, the American Association of Homes and Services for the Aging, the Gerontological Society of America, or the National Council on the Aging. Many such organizations have monthly or quarterly newsletters that list job opportunities. Some may even have job banks or referral services.

EARNINGS

Starting salaries for this position depend partly on the coordinator's experience and education and partly on the size and location of the day care center. Larger centers located in metropolitan areas tend to offer the highest wages.

According to the Association for Gerontology in Higher Education, beginning annual salaries range from $18,000 to $31,000 for those with a bachelor's degree and little experience. Generally, coordinators who do not have a bachelor's degree can expect to earn somewhat less. Experienced coordinators with a bachelor's degree employed in large, well-funded centers may earn from $20,000 to $45,000 annually.

In addition to salary, some coordinators are also offered a benefits package, which typically includes health insurance, paid vacation and sick days, and a retirement plan.

OUTLOOK

The employment outlook for adult day care coordinators is expected to be excellent. According to the U.S. Department of Labor, the number of human services workers is projected to grow by 54 percent between 2000 and 2010, with adult day care being one of the fastest-growing human services areas.

The senior citizen population is growing rapidly, which has led to the development of more aging-related services during the last several years. The increase in adult day care centers is one example of this trend. According to the National Adult Day Services Association, there were only approximately 300 adult day care centers in the late 1970s; today, there are more than 4,000. This growth should continue as Americans become increasingly aware of the diverse needs of the elderly and the various service options available to them.

FOR MORE INFORMATION

For career information and student resources, contact:

Gerontological Society of America
1030 15th Street, NW, Suite 250
Washington, DC 20005
Tel: 202-842-1275
Email: geron@geron.org
Web: http://www.geron.org

For facts about adult day service, contact:

National Adult Day Services Association
8201 Greensboro Drive, Suite 300
McLean, VA 22102
Tel: 866-890-7357
Email: info@nadsa.org
Web: http://www.nadsa.org

For information on certification, contact:

National Certification Council for Activity Professionals
PO Box 62589
Virginia Beach, VA 23466
Tel: 757-552-0653
Email: info@nccap.org
Web: http://www.nccap.org

AERONAUTICAL AND AEROSPACE TECHNICIANS

School Subjects	Salary Range
Physics	~~$20,000 to $53,000~~
Technical/shop	**to $56,000**
Personal Skills	*Certification or Licensing*
Mechanical/manipulative	**Recommended**
Technical/scientific	*Outlook*
Work Environment	**About as fast as the average**
Primarily indoors	
Primarily one location	

THE JOB

Aeronautical and aerospace technicians design, construct, test, operate, and maintain the basic structures of aircraft and spacecraft as well as propulsion and control systems. Many aeronautical and aerospace technicians assist engineers in preparing equipment drawings, diagrams, blueprints, and scale models. They collect information, make computations, and perform laboratory tests. They may handle problems with aerodynamics, structural design, flight-test evaluation, or propulsion. Other technicians work as manufacturers' field service technicians, write technical materials, and estimate the cost of materials and labor required to manufacture aircraft and spacecraft parts.

PROFESSIONAL AND PERSONAL REQUIREMENTS

Only a few aerospace technician positions require licensing or certification. Certification is usually required of technicians working with nuclear-powered engines, testing radioactive sources, working on aircraft in some test programs, and holding some safety-related positions.

As an aeronautical and aerospace technician, you must be able to learn basic engineering skills. You need to be proficient in mathematics and the physical sciences and able to visualize size, form, and function. You should also have an understanding of manufacturing and statistics and be able to work with computers.

STARTING OUT

The best way for you to obtain an aeronautical or aerospace technician's job is through your college's job placement office. Many aerospace manufacturers maintain recruiting relationships with schools in their area. You can also find jobs through state employment offices, newspaper advertisements, applications for government employment, and industry work-study programs offered by many aircraft companies.

EARNINGS

Aerospace technology is a broad field, so earnings vary depending on a technician's specialty, educational preparation, and work experience. Starting salaries for most aerospace technicians generally range from $20,000 to $23,000 per year, according to the U.S. Department of Labor. In 2000, the average annual salary for aerospace technicians was $53,340. For aircraft mechanics, including engine specialists, the average salary was around $40,560, with starting pay at about $25,000 and pay for more experienced mechanics at over $56,000. Avionics technicians earned salaries that ranged from $27,500 to $56,200.

Benefits depend on employers but usually include paid vacations and holidays, sick pay, health insurance, and a retirement plan. Nearly all companies offer some form of tuition reimbursement for further education. Some offer cooperative programs with local schools, combining classroom training with practical paid experience.

OUTLOOK

The *Career Guide to Industries* predicts that the civil aircraft sector of the aerospace industry will see strong growth through 2010, while the military aircraft sector is expected to decline about 4 percent during that same time period. With growth predicted in many areas and losses in others, the overall job growth for aerospace technicians should be about as fast as the average through 2010.

Cutbacks made over the last 20 years have created a shrinking pool of qualified workers for some positions, including technicians and skilled production workers, according to the Aerospace Industries Association of America (AIA). The AIA predicts aerospace companies will be looking for qualified technicians in fields such as laser optics, mission operations, hazardous materials procedures, production planning, materials testing, computer-aided design, and robotic programming.

FOR MORE INFORMATION

Contact the AIA for publications with information on aerospace technologies, careers, and space.

Aerospace Industries Association of America (AIA)
1250 Eye Street, NW, Suite 1200
Washington, DC 20005-3924
Tel: 202-371-8400
Web: http://www.aia-aerospace.org

For career information and information on student branches of this organization, contact:

American Institute of Aeronautics and Astronautics
1801 Alexander Bell Drive, Suite 500
Reston, VA 20191-4344
Tel: 800-639-2422
Web: http://www.aiaa.org

For career and scholarship information, contact:

General Aviation Manufacturers Association
1400 K Street, NW, Suite 801
Washington, DC 20005
Tel: 202-393-1500
Web: http://www.generalaviation.org

JETS offers high school students the opportunity to "try on" engineering through a number of programs and competitions.

Junior Engineering Technical Society, Inc. (JETS)
1420 King Street, Suite 405
Alexandria, VA 22314-2794
Tel: 703-548-5387
Email: jets@nae.edu
Web: http://www.jets.org

AGRIBUSINESS TECHNICIANS

School Subjects **Agriculture** **Business**	*Salary Range* **$20,000 to $38,000** **to $80,000+**
Personal Skills **Leadership/management** **Technical/scientific**	*Certification or Licensing* **None available**
Work Environment **Indoors and outdoors** **Primarily multiple locations**	*Outlook* **About as fast as the average**

THE JOB

Agribusiness technicians combine their agriculture and business backgrounds to manage farms and agricultural businesses. Agribusiness technicians, also called *agricultural business technicians,* generally work as liaisons between farms and agricultural businesses, representing either the farm or the business.

Graduates of agribusiness technician programs can find work in a variety of different areas. Agribusiness is as diverse a field as agriculture, and it involves professionals in economics, sales, marketing, commodities, science, and other areas. Technicians assist these professionals, working for a farm or for a business or organization that assists farmers. Technicians spend their hours out in the field or behind a desk. Their work may involve grain, livestock, or dairy farms.

PROFESSIONAL AND PERSONAL REQUIREMENTS

There is no certification or licensing available in this field.

To succeed as an agribusiness technician, you must be able to work well with other people, which includes being able to delegate responsibility and establish friendly relations with farmers, laborers, and company managers. You must be able to analyze management problems and make sound decisions based on your analysis. Technicians are expected to present written and oral reports, offer comments and advice clearly, and, when necessary, train other workers for a particular job. As a result, you will also need excellent oral and written communication skills.

STARTING OUT

Because agribusiness programs usually require a semester or more of employment experience, schools generally assist students with finding an internship or part-time job with agribusiness professionals. Many students are able to turn their internships into full-time work or make connections that lead to other job opportunities. Most agribusiness technician jobs are considered entry-level positions and don't require a great deal of previous experience. These jobs are often advertised in the classifieds or posted with career placement centers at community colleges.

EARNINGS

Starting salaries for agribusiness technicians range from about $20,000 to $26,000 annually. Purchasing agents who specialize in farm products earned median annual salaries of $37,560 in 2000, according to the U.S. Department of Labor. Ten percent earned less than $21,550, and 10 percent earned $80,320 or more a year.

Fringe benefits vary widely, depending upon the employer. Many employers provide such benefits as pension plans, paid vacations, insurance, and tuition reimbursement.

OUTLOOK

According to the U.S. Department of Labor, agribusiness provides employment to about 21 percent of the country's labor force. Despite the fluctuations in the agricultural industry, agribusiness professionals and technicians will continue to be in great demand in the marketing and production of food and other agricultural products.

Technicians may find more opportunities to work abroad. Agribusiness plays a large part in global trade issues and in the government's efforts to support farms and agricultural reforms in other countries. Agribusiness construction is a subfield that is developing as a result of these reforms. Technicians will be needed to assist in the planning and construction of farm-to-market roads in other countries, irrigation channels, bridges, grain silos, and other improvements.

FOR MORE INFORMATION

For more information on opportunities in the agricultural field, schooling, and these organizations, contact:

4-H
Families, 4-H & Nutrition
CSREES/USDA
1400 Independence Avenue, SW
Washington, DC 20250-2225
Tel: 202-720-2908
Web: http://www.4h-usa.org

For information on careers and chapter membership, contact:

National FFA Organization
National FFA Center
PO Box 68960
Indianapolis, IN 46268-0960
Tel: 317-802-6060
Web: http://www.ffa.org

AGRICULTURAL EQUIPMENT TECHNICIANS

School Subjects **Mathematics** **Technical/shop** *Personal Skills* **Mechanical/manipulative** **Technical/scientific** *Work Environment* **Indoors and outdoors** **Primarily multiple locations**	*Salary Range* **$17,000 to $31,000** **to $38,000+** *Certification or Licensing* **None available** *Outlook* **Little change or more slowly** **than the average**

THE JOB

Agricultural equipment technicians assemble, adjust, operate, maintain, test, and help design modern farm machinery. This machinery includes automatic animal feeding systems; milking machine systems; and tilling, planting, harvesting, and irrigating equipment. Agricultural equipment technicians work on farms or for agricultural machinery manufacturers or dealerships. They often supervise skilled mechanics and other workers who keep machines and systems operating at maximum efficiency.

Agricultural equipment technicians work in a wide variety of jobs both on and off the farm. Most agricultural equipment technicians find employment in one of three areas: equipment manufacturing, equipment sales and service, and on-farm equipment management.

PROFESSIONAL AND PERSONAL REQUIREMENTS

There is no certification or licensing available in this field.

The work of the agricultural equipment technician is similar to that of an engineer. As a result, you will need to have knowledge of physical science and engineering principles and a mathematical background. You need a working knowledge of farm crops, machinery, and all agricultural-related products. Finally, you should be detail oriented and have people skills, as you will be working closely with professionals, other technicians, and farmers.

STARTING OUT

It is possible to enter this career by starting as an inexperienced worker in a machinery manufacturer's plant or on a farm. However, this approach is becoming increasingly difficult due to the complexity of modern machinery. Because of this, some formal classroom training is usually necessary, and many people find it difficult to complete even part-time study of the field's theory and science while also working a full-time job.

Due to the high level of demand for qualified agricultural equipment technicians, managers of large farms and farm equipment companies often keep in touch with colleges offering agricultural equipment programs. In general, if you do well in your training program, you can expect employment immediately upon graduation.

EARNINGS

Agricultural technicians working for the government may be able to enter a position at the government wage level of GS-5, which was $22,737 in 2002. Those with more education and specialized experience may be able to enter at GS-8, which was $31,191. The U.S. Department of Labor reports that median hourly earnings for agricultural equipment technicians were $12.38 in 2000. Hourly pay ranged from less than $8.15 to more than $18.23. Those working on farms often receive room and board as a supplement to their annual salary.

In addition, most technicians receive fringe benefits such as health and retirement packages, paid vacations, and other benefits similar to those received by engineering technicians. Technicians employed in sales are usually paid a commission in addition to their base salary.

OUTLOOK

The *Occupational Outlook Handbook* reports that employment of agricultural equipment technicians is expected to grow more slowly than the average through 2010. However, agricultural equipment businesses now demand more expertise than ever before. A variety of complex machines and mechanical devices are steadily being produced and modified to help farmers improve the quality and productivity of their labor. These machines require trained technicians to design, produce, test, sell, and service them. Trained workers also are needed to instruct the final owners in proper repair, operation, and maintenance of the machines.

As agriculture becomes more technical, the agricultural equipment technician will assume an increasingly vital role in helping farmers solve problems that interfere with efficient production. These opportunities exist not only in the United States, but also worldwide. Inventive technicians with training in modern business principles will find expanding employment opportunities abroad.

FOR MORE INFORMATION

To read equipment sales statistics, agricultural reports, and other news of interest to agricultural equipment technicians, visit the AEM Web site.

Association of Equipment Manufacturers (AEM)
10 South Riverside Plaza, Suite 1220
Chicago, IL 60606-3710
Tel: 866-AEM-0442
Email: info@aem.org
Web: http://www.aem.org

At the FEMA Web site, you can learn about its publications and read industry news.

Farm Equipment Manufacturers Association (FEMA)
1000 Executive Parkway, Suite 100
St. Louis, MO 63141-6369
Tel: 314-878-2304
Email: info@farmequip.org
Web: http://www.farmequip.org

AIRCRAFT MECHANICS

School Subjects **Computer science** **Technical/shop**	*Salary Range* **$25,000 to $41,000** **to $56,000+**
Personal Skills **Mechanical/manipulative** **Technical/scientific**	*Certification or Licensing* **Required for certain** **positions**
Work Environment **Indoors and outdoors** **One location with travel**	*Outlook* **About as fast as the average**

THE JOB

Aircraft mechanics adjust and repair electrical wiring systems, aircraft instruments, and pneumatic and hydraulic systems. They also handle various servicing tasks, such as flushing crankcases, cleaning screens, greasing moving parts, and checking brakes.

Specific positions in this field include line maintenance mechanics, overhaul mechanics, airframe mechanics, aircraft power plant mechanics, and avionics technicians.

Mechanics may work on only one type of aircraft or on many different types, such as jets, propeller-driven planes, and helicopters. For greater efficiency, some specialize in one section of an aircraft, such as the electrical system. Among the specialists, there are airplane electricians, pneumatic testers, pressure sealer-and-testers, aircraft body repairers, bonded structures repairers, air conditioning mechanics, aircraft controls mechanics, plumbing and hydraulics mechanics, and experimental-aircraft testing mechanics.

PROFESSIONAL AND PERSONAL REQUIREMENTS

Federal Aviation Administration (FAA) certification is necessary for certain aircraft mechanic jobs and is usually required to advance beyond entry-level positions. FAA certification is granted only to aircraft mechanics with previous work experience: a minimum of 18 months for an airframe or power plant certificate and at least 30 months working with both engines and airframes for a combination certificate.

To be an aircraft mechanic, you must be able to work with precision and meet rigid standards. Your physical condition is also important, as you'll need strength for lifting heavy parts and tools and agility for reaching and climbing.

STARTING OUT

After high school, it is recommended that you enroll in an FAA-approved trade school. (Note that there are schools offering training that do not have FAA approval.) FAA-approved programs generally have placement services available for their graduates.

You can also apply directly to employers, such as companies providing air transportation or the local offices of the state employment service. However, most airlines prefer to employ people who have completed training. Finally, you can get experience in this career through joining the armed forces.

EARNINGS

Although some aircraft mechanics, especially at the entry level and at small businesses, earn little more than the minimum wage, the median annual income for aircraft mechanics was about $40,560 in 2000, according to the U.S. Department of Labor. The bottom 10 percent earned less than $25,085. Experienced mechanics can earn more than $56,000 per year. Mechanics with airframe and power plant certification earn more than those without it. Overtime, night shift, and holiday pay differentials are usually available and can greatly increase a mechanic's annual earnings.

Most major airlines are covered by union agreements. Their mechanics generally earn more than those working for other employers. Contracts usually include health insurance and often life insurance and retirement plans as well. An attractive fringe benefit for airline mechanics and their immediate families is being eligible for free or reduced ticket fares.

OUTLOOK

Employment of aircraft mechanics is likely to increase about as fast as the average through 2010, according to the U.S.

Department of Labor. The demand for air travel and the numbers of aircraft created are expected to increase due to population growth and rising incomes. However, employment growth will be affected by the use of automated systems that make the aircraft mechanic's job more efficient.

Employment opportunities will open up due to fewer young workers entering the labor force, fewer entrants from the military, and more retired workers leaving positions. But the job prospects will vary according to the type of employer. Less competition for jobs is likely to be found at smaller commuter and regional airlines, at FAA repair stations, and in general aviation. These employers pay lower wages, and fewer applicants compete for their positions. Higher-paying airline positions, which also include travel benefits, are more in demand among qualified applicants. Mechanics who keep up with technological advancements in electronics, composite materials, and other areas will be in greatest demand.

FOR MORE INFORMATION

For career books and information about high school student membership, national forums, and job fairs, contact:

Aviation Information Resources, Inc.
3800 Camp Creek Parkway, Suite 18-100
Atlanta, GA 30331
Tel: 800-JET-JOBS
Web: http://www.jet-jobs.com

Professional Aviation Maintenance Association
Ronald Reagan Washington National Airport
Washington, DC 20001
Tel: 703-417-8800
Email: hq@pama.org
Web: http://www.pama.org

ALCOHOL AND DRUG ABUSE COUNSELORS

School Subjects **Health** **Psychology**	*Salary Range* **$19,000 to $29,000** **to $43,000+**
Personal Skills **Communication/ideas** **Helping/teaching**	*Certification or Licensing* **Required by certain states**
Work Environment **Primarily indoors** **Primarily one location**	*Outlook* **Faster than the average**

THE JOB

The main goal of *alcohol and drug abuse counselors* is to help patients stop their destructive behaviors. Counselors begin by trying to learn about a patient's general background and history of drug or alcohol use. Using the information they obtain from the patient and their knowledge of substance abuse patterns, counselors formulate a program for treatment and rehabilitation. A substantial part of the rehabilitation process involves individual, group, or family counseling sessions.

Counselors monitor and assess the progress of their patients. In most cases, counselors deal with several different patients in various stages of recovery. Counselors maintain ongoing relationships with patients to help them adapt to the different recovery stages.

There is a substantial amount of administrative work in this field, including meetings with staff, other professionals, and patients' family members. There is also a great deal of paperwork involved.

PROFESSIONAL AND PERSONAL REQUIREMENTS

Certification, which is mandatory in some states, is available through state accreditation boards.

To be a successful counselor, you need to enjoy working with people. You must have compassion, good communication and listening skills, and a desire to help others. You should also be emotionally stable and able to deal with the frustrations and failures that are often a part of the job.

STARTING OUT

If you have completed a two- or four-year college degree, you can start your job search by checking with the career placement office of your college or university. If you plan to look for a position without first attending college, you might want to start by getting an entry-level or volunteer position in a treatment center or related agency. In this way, you can obtain practical experience and also make connections that might lead to full-time employment as a counselor. You should also watch the classified advertisements in local newspapers or apply directly to the personnel departments of various facilities and agencies that treat alcohol and drug abusers.

EARNINGS

Salaries of alcohol and drug abuse counselors depend on education level, amount of experience, and place of employment. Generally, the more education and experience a counselor has, the higher his or her earnings will be. Counselors who work in private treatment centers also tend to earn more than their public sector counterparts.

Alcohol and drug abuse counselors earned a median annual salary of $28,510 in 2000, according to the *Occupational Outlook Handbook*. The lowest 10 percent earned less than $18,850. The highest 10 percent earned $43,420 or more.

Almost all treatment centers provide employee benefits to their full-time counselors. Benefits usually include paid vacations and sick days, insurance, and pension plans.

OUTLOOK

Employment of alcohol and drug abuse counselors is projected to grow faster than the average for all occupations through 2010, according to the U.S. Department of Labor. There are more than 20 million alcoholics in the United States and an equal, if not greater, number of drug abusers. Because no successful method to significantly reduce drug and alcohol abuse has emerged, these numbers are not likely to decrease.

Another reason for the expected growth in counselors' jobs is that an increasing number of employers are offering employee assistance programs that provide counseling services for mental health and alcohol and drug abuse.

Finally, many job openings will arise as a result of job turnover. Because of the stress levels and the emotional demands involved in this career, there is a high burnout rate. As alcohol and drug abuse counselors leave the field, new counselors are needed to replace them.

FOR MORE INFORMATION

For more information on substance abuse and counseling careers, contact the following organizations:

American Counseling Association
5999 Stevenson Avenue
Alexandria, VA 22304-3300
Tel: 800-347-6647
Web: http://www.counseling.org

National Institute on Alcohol Abuse and Alcoholism
National Institutes of Health
6000 Executive Boulevard
Willco Building
Bethesda, MD 20892-7003
Web: http://www.niaaa.nih.gov

National Institute on Drug Abuse
National Institutes of Health
6001 Executive Boulevard, Room 5213
Bethesda, MD 20892-9561
Tel: 301-443-1124
Web: http://www.nida.nih.gov

For information on certification, contact:

National Association of Alcoholism and Drug Abuse Counselors
901 North Washington Street, Suite 600
Alexandria, VA 22314-1535
Tel: 800-548-0497
Email: naadac@naadac.org
Web: http://www.naadac.org

AUTOMOBILE COLLISION REPAIRERS

School Subjects **Computer science** **Technical/shop**	*Salary Range* **$18,000 to $31,000** **to $54,000+**
Personal Skills **Following instructions** **Mechanical/manipulative**	*Certification or Licensing* **Recommended**
Work Environment **Primarily indoors** **Primarily one location**	*Outlook* **About as fast as the average**

THE JOB

Automobile collision repairers repair, replace, and repaint damaged body parts of automobiles, buses, and light trucks. They use hand tools and power tools to straighten bent frames and body sections, replace badly damaged parts, smooth out minor dents and creases, remove rust, fill small holes and dents, and repaint surfaces damaged by accident or wear. A range of skills is needed to repair body damage to vehicles. Some collision repairers specialize in certain areas, such as painting, welding, glass replacement or air bag replacement. All repairers should know how to perform common repairs, such as realigning vehicle frames, smoothing dents, and removing and replacing panels.

A major part of the automobile collision repairer's job is assessing damage and providing an estimate on repair costs.

PROFESSIONAL AND PERSONAL REQUIREMENTS

Certification, which is offered by the National Automotive Technicians Education Foundation, is voluntary, but it is recommended. Certification assures employers that you have met industry standards.

You will be responsible for providing your own hand tools at an investment of approximately $6,000 to $20,000 or more, depending upon your specialty. You also need skill in handling both hand and power tools.

STARTING OUT

The best way to start out in the field of automobile collision repair is, first, to attend one of the many postsecondary training programs available throughout the country and, second, to obtain certification. Trade and technical schools usually provide job placement assistance for their graduates. Schools often have contacts with local employers who seek highly skilled entry-level employees. Often, employers post job openings at nearby trade schools with accredited programs.

Although postsecondary training programs are considered the best way to enter the field, you can also learn the trade on the job as an apprentice. An apprenticeship requires several years of work under the guidance of an experienced repairer. Fewer employers are willing to hire apprentices because of the time and cost it takes to train them. However, due to the current shortage of high-quality entry-level collision repair technicians, employers are hiring apprentices who can demonstrate good mechanical aptitude and a willingness to learn. Those who do learn their skills on the job will inevitably require some formal training if they wish to advance and stay in step with the changing industry.

EARNINGS

Salary ranges of collision repairers vary depending on level of experience, type of shop, and geographic location. Most earned hourly salaries between $11.12 and $20.02, with a median hourly salary of $15 in 2000, according to the U.S. Department of Labor. At the lower end of the pay scale, collision repairers with less experience and repairers who were employed by smaller shops earned about $8.49 per hour in 2000. At the high end of the pay scale, experienced repairers with management positions earned more than $26.06 an hour. In many repair shops and dealerships, collision repairers can earn more by working on commission. They typically earn 40 to 50 percent of the labor costs charged to customers.

Most repair technicians can expect health insurance and a paid vacation from employers. Other benefits may include dental and eye care, life and disability insurance, and a pension plan.

OUTLOOK

Like many service industries, the collision repair industry is facing a shortage of skilled entry-level workers in many areas of the country. Demand for collision repair services is expected to remain consistent. This demand, paired with technology that will require new skills, translates into a healthy job market for those willing to undertake the training needed.

The automobile collision repair business is not greatly affected by changes in economic conditions. Major body damage must be repaired to keep a vehicle in safe operating condition. During an economic downturn, however, people tend to postpone minor repairs until their budgets can accommodate the expense. Nevertheless, body repairers are seldom laid off. Instead, when business is bad, employers hire fewer new workers.

FOR MORE INFORMATION

For more information on careers, training, and accreditation, contact the following organizations:

Automotive Aftermarket Industry Association
4600 East-West Highway, Suite 300
Bethesda, MD 20814-3415
Tel: 301-654-6664
Email: aaia@aftermarket.org
Web: http://www.aftermarket.org

Inter-Industry Conference on Auto Collision Repair
3701 Algonquin Road, Suite 400
Rolling Meadows, IL 60008
Tel: 800-422-7872
Web: http://www.i-car.com

National Automotive Technicians Education Foundation
101 Blue Seal Drive, Suite 101
Leesburg, VA 20175
Tel: 703-669-6650
Web: http://www.natef.org

National Institute for Automotive Service Excellence
101 Blue Seal Drive, SE, Suite 101
Leesburg, VA 20175
Tel: 877-273-8324
Web: http://www.asecert.org

AUTOMOBILE SERVICE TECHNICIANS

School Subjects **Business** **Technical/shop**	*Salary Range* **$16,000 to $28,000** **to $100,000**
Personal Skills **Mechanical/manipulative** **Technical/scientific**	*Certification or Licensing* **Recommended**
Work Environment **Primarily indoors** **Primarily one location**	*Outlook* **About as fast as the average**

THE JOB

Automobile service technicians maintain and repair cars, vans, small trucks, and other vehicles. Using hand tools and specialized diagnostic test equipment, they pinpoint problems and make the necessary repairs or adjustments. They also perform a number of routine maintenance procedures, such as oil changes, tire rotation, and battery replacement. Technicians interact with customers to explain repair procedures and discuss maintenance needs.

Generally, there are two types of automobile service technicians: generalists and specialists. *Generalists* work under a broad umbrella of repair and service duties. Their work is fairly routine and basic. *Specialists* concentrate on one or two areas and learn to master them for many different car makes and models.

PROFESSIONAL AND PERSONAL REQUIREMENTS

Certification, which is currently voluntary but preferred, is available from the National Automotive Technicians Education Foundation in several different specific areas of focus.

To succeed as an automobile service technician, you must be patient and thorough in your work. A shoddy repair job can put a driver's life at risk. You must have excellent troubleshooting skills and be able to logically deduce the cause of system malfunctions.

STARTING OUT

The best way to start out in this field is to attend one of the many accredited postsecondary training programs available throughout the country. Trade and technical schools usually provide job placement assistance for their graduates. Schools often have contacts with local employers who need to hire well-trained people.

You can also break into this career by working as an intern at a local car manufacturer or independent organization.. An internship can provide you with valuable contacts who will be able to recommend future employers once you have completed your training. You may even be hired by the shop at which you intern.

EARNINGS

Salary ranges of automobile service technicians vary depending on experience, employer size, and geographic location. Generally, technicians who work in small-town, family-owned gas stations earn less than those who work at dealerships and franchises in metropolitan areas.

According to the U.S. Department of Labor, the lowest-paid automobile service technicians earned about $7.59 per hour (or $15,787 annually) in 2000. The median hourly salary for automobile service technicians was $13.70 (or $28,496 annually) in 2000. Top-paid technicians with experience and certification earned more than $23.67 per hour (or $49,234+ annually) in 2000. Technicians can earn higher incomes by working on commission. In 2001, master technicians who worked on commission were reported to have earned between $70,000 and $100,000 annually.

Most technicians can expect health insurance and paid vacation days. Additional benefits may include dental, life, and disability insurance and a pension plan.

OUTLOOK

With an estimated 189 million vehicles in operation today, automobile service technicians should feel confident that a good percentage will require servicing and repair work. Skilled and highly trained technicians will be in particular demand. Less-skilled workers will face tough competition. The U.S. Department of

Labor predicts that this field will grow as fast as the average through 2010, but in some areas, growth could be higher because of a tight labor market.

Another concern for the industry is the automobile industry's trend toward developing the "maintenance-free" car. Manufacturers are producing high-end cars that require no servicing for their first 100,000 miles. In addition, many new cars are equipped with on-board diagnostics that detect both wear and failure for many of the car's components, eliminating the need for technicians to perform extensive diagnostic tests.

FOR MORE INFORMATION

For more information on the automotive service industry, contact the following organizations:

Automotive Service Association
PO Box 929
Bedford, TX 76095-0929
Tel: 800-272-7467
Email: asainfo@asashop.org
Web: http://www.asashop.org

National Automobile Dealers Association
8400 Westpark Drive
McLean, VA 22102
Tel: 800-252-6232
Email: nadainfo@nada.org
Web: http://www.nada.org

National Automotive Technicians Education Foundation
101 Blue Seal Drive, Suite 101
Leesburg, VA 20175
Tel: 703-669-6650
Web: http://www.natef.org

For information on certification, contact:

National Institute for Automotive Service Excellence
101 Blue Seal Drive, SE, Suite 101
Leesburg, VA 20175
Tel: 877-273-8324
Web: http://www.asecert.org

BIOMEDICAL EQUIPMENT TECHNICIANS

School Subjects **Biology** **Technical/shop** *Personal Skills* **Mechanical/manipulative** **Technical/scientific** *Work Environment* **Primarily indoors** **Primarily one location**	*Salary Range* **$20,000 to $35,000** **to $44,000** *Certification or Licensing* **Recommended** *Outlook* **About as fast as the average**

THE JOB

Biomedical equipment technicians work with the complex medical equipment and instruments found in hospitals, clinics, and research facilities. This equipment is used for medical therapy and diagnosis and includes heart-lung machines, artificial-kidney machines, patient monitors, chemical analyzers, and other electrical, electronic, mechanical, or pneumatic devices.

The technician's main duties are to inspect, maintain, repair, and install this equipment. Technicians take equipment apart to locate malfunctioning components, repair or replace defective parts, and reassemble the equipment, adjusting the parts to ensure that it operates according to manufacturers' specifications. Other duties of biomedical equipment technicians include modifying equipment according to the directions of medical personnel and safety-testing equipment to ensure that patients, equipment operators, and other staff members are safe from electrical or mechanical hazards. Biomedical equipment technicians work with hand tools, power tools, measuring devices, and manufacturers' manuals.

PROFESSIONAL AND PERSONAL REQUIREMENTS

Although certification is not required for employment, it is highly recommended. Technicians with certification (offered by the Association for the Advancement of Medical Instrumentation) demonstrate that they have attained an overall knowledge of the field and are dedicated to their profession. Many employers prefer to hire technicians who have this certification.

You will need mechanical ability and should enjoy working with tools to succeed as a biomedical equipment technician. Because this job demands quick decision-making and prompt repairs, you should work well under pressure. You also should have good communication skills and be extremely precise and accurate in your work.

STARTING OUT

Most schools offering programs in biomedical equipment technology work closely with local hospitals and industries. As a result, your school's placement officer should be informed about job openings as they become available. In some cases, recruiters may visit schools periodically to conduct interviews. While in school, try to get a part-time hospital job to gain practical experience. You may be able to return to the hospital for full-time employment after graduation.

Another effective method of finding employment is to write and apply directly to hospitals, research institutes, or biomedical equipment manufacturers. Other good sources of leads for job openings include your state's employment office and newspaper want ads.

EARNINGS

Salaries for biomedical equipment technicians vary in different institutions and localities and according to the experience, training, certification, and type of work done by the technician. According to the U.S. Department of Labor, the median hourly wage for medical equipment repairers was $16.99, or approximately $35,340 a year, in 2000.

A survey by the Association for the Advancement of Medical Instrumentation reports that graduates of two-year biomedical equipment training programs earned an average annual salary

of $28,200 in 2000. At the low end of the salary ranges, gradu-
ates had yearly earnings of $20,000; at the high end, graduates
reported earnings of $44,000.

In general, technicians who work for manufacturers have
higher earnings than those who work for hospitals. Naturally,
those in supervisory or senior positions also command higher
salaries. Benefits, such as health insurance and vacation days,
vary with the employer.

OUTLOOK

Because of the increasing use of electronic medical devices and
other sophisticated biomedical equipment, there is a steady
demand for skilled and trained biomedical equipment technicians. The U.S. Department of Labor predicts employment for
this group to grow about as fast as the average through 2010.

In hospitals, the need for more biomedical equipment technicians exists not only because of the increasing use of biomedical
equipment, but also because hospital administrators realize that
these technicians can help hold down costs by maintaining the
very expensive equipment and taking over some routine activities of other hospital staff.

For the many biomedical equipment technicians who work
for companies that build, sell, lease, or service biomedical
equipment, job opportunities should also continue to grow.

FOR MORE INFORMATION

*For information on student memberships, biomedical technology pro-
grams, and certification, contact:*

**Association for the Advancement of Medical
Instrumentation**
1110 North Glebe Road, Suite 220
Arlington, VA 22201-4795
Tel: 800-332-2264
Web: http://www.aami.org

BROADCAST ENGINEERS

School Subjects **Computer science** **Mathematics** *Personal Skills* **Mechanical/manipulative** **Technical/scientific** *Work Environment* **Indoors and outdoors** **Primarily multiple locations**	*Salary Range* **$14,000 to $27,000** **to $63,000+** *Certification or Licensing* **Recommended** *Outlook* **About as fast as the average**

THE JOB

Broadcast engineers, also referred to as *broadcast technicians* or *broadcast operators,* operate and maintain the electronic equipment used to transmit the audio for radio signals and the audio and visual images for television signals. They work on both live and recorded broadcasts, usually transmitting directly from the radio or TV station. They are also capable of transmitting signals on location from specially designed, mobile equipment.

The specific tasks of the broadcast engineer depend on the size of the TV or radio station. In small stations, engineers have a wide variety of responsibilities. Larger stations are able to hire a greater number of engineers and delegate different responsibilities to each engineer. These larger stations often employ a chief and assistant chief engineer, maintenance technicians, and video technicians.

PROFESSIONAL AND PERSONAL REQUIREMENTS

The Federal Communications Commission licenses and permits are no longer required of broadcast engineers. However, certification from the Society of Broadcast Engineers is recommended. Certified engineers consistently earn higher salaries than uncertified engineers.

Broadcast engineers must have both an aptitude for working with highly technical electronic and computer equipment and great attention to detail. You should enjoy both the technical and artistic aspects of working in the radio or television industry. You should also be able to communicate with a wide range of people with various levels of technical expertise.

STARTING OUT

Many towns and cities have public-access cable television stations and public radio stations. This is a great place to get experience in an internship. Once you begin looking for a full-time job, you should be flexible about your job location. Most technicians begin their careers at small stations and with experience may advance to larger-market stations.

EARNINGS

Most larger stations pay higher wages than smaller stations, television stations tend to pay more than radio stations, and commercial stations usually pay more than public broadcasting stations. According to the U.S. Department of Labor, the median annual salary for broadcast technicians was $26,950 in 2000. The lowest-paid 10 percent earned less than $13,860 and the highest-paid 10 percent earned more than $63,340. Experience, job location, and educational background are all factors that influence a technician's pay.

OUTLOOK

According to the U.S. Department of Labor, the overall employment of broadcast technicians is expected to grow about as fast as the average through 2010. There will be strong competition for jobs in metropolitan areas. In addition, the slow growth in the number of new radio and television stations may mean few new job opportunities in the field. Technicians who are able to install transmitters should have better work prospects as television stations switch from their old analog equipment to digital transmitters. Job openings will also result from the need to replace existing engineers who often leave the industry for other jobs in electronics.

FOR MORE INFORMATION

For information on its summer internship program, contact:

Association of Local Television Stations
1320 19th Street, NW, Suite 300
Washington, DC 20036
Tel: 202-887-1970
Web: http://www.altv.com

For education, support, and scholarship information, contact:

National Association of Broadcasters
1771 N Street, NW
Washington, DC 20036-2891
Tel: 202-429-5300
Email: nab@nab.org
Web: http://www.nab.org

For a booklet on careers in cable, contact:

National Cable and Telecommunications Association
1724 Massachusetts Avenue, NW
Washington, DC 20036
Tel: 202-775-3550
Web: http://www.ncta.com

For general information on membership, scholarships, and certification, contact:

Society of Broadcast Engineers
9247 North Meridian Street, Suite 305
Indianapolis, IN 46260
Tel: 317-846-9000
Web: http://www.sbe.org

CARDIOVASCULAR TECHNOLOGISTS

School Subjects **Biology** **Health**	*Salary Range* **$20,000 to $33,000** **to $53,000+**
Personal Skills **Communication/ideas** **Technical/scientific**	*Certification or Licensing* **Voluntary**
Work Environment **Primarily indoors** **Primarily one location**	*Outlook* **Faster than the average**

THE JOB

Cardiovascular technologists assist physicians in diagnosing and treating heart and blood vessel ailments. Depending on their specialty, they operate electrocardiograph (EKG) machines, perform stress tests, and assist in cardiac catheterization procedures and ultrasound testing. They help the physicians diagnose heart disease and monitor progress during treatment.

Specific jobs within this field include EKG technologists, stress test technologists, cardiology technologists, vascular technologists, echocardiographers, and cardiac monitor technicians.

Cardiovascular technologists perform one or more of a wide range of procedures in cardiovascular medicine, including invasive, noninvasive, peripheral vascular, or echocardiography (ultrasound) procedures. They often use equipment that is among the most advanced in the medical field. Technologists' services may be required when the patient's condition is first being explored, before surgery, during surgery, or during rehabilitation. Some of the work is performed on an outpatient basis.

PROFESSIONAL AND PERSONAL REQUIREMENTS

Right now, certification or licensing for cardiovascular technologists is voluntary, but the move to state licensing is expected in the near future. Many credentialing bodies for cardiovascular and pulmonary positions exist, including American Registry of Diagnostic Medical Sonographers, and the Cardiovascular

Credentialing International, and there are more than a dozen possible credentials for cardiovascular technologists.

As a technician, you must be able to put patients at ease about the procedure they are to undergo. You should be patient and alert, and your manner should be reassuring and confident.

STARTING OUT

Because most cardiovascular technologists receive their initial training on their first job, great care should be taken in finding your first employer. Pay close attention to not only the pay and working conditions, but also to the kind of on-the-job training that is provided. High school counselors may be able to tell you which hospitals have good reputations for training programs.

If you graduate from a one- or two-year training program, finding your first job should be easier. First, employers are eager to hire people who are already trained. Second, you can be less concerned about the training programs offered. Third, you should find that your teachers and guidance counselors can be excellent sources of information about job possibilities in the area. If your training program includes practical experience, you may find that the hospital in which you trained or worked before graduation is willing to hire you after graduation.

EARNINGS

The median salary for cardiovascular technologists was $33,350 in 2000, according to the U.S. Department of Labor. The lowest-paid 10 percent earned less than $19,540, and the highest-paid 10 percent earned more than $52,930 annually. Earnings can vary by size and type of employer. For example, technologists working in physicians' offices had a median annual income of $33,100, while those in hospitals earned a median of $32,860. Those with formal training earn more than those who trained on the job, and those who are able to perform more sophisticated tests, such as stress testing, earn more than those who perform only the basic electrocardiograph tests.

Technologists working in hospitals receive the same fringe benefits as other hospital workers, including medical insurance, paid vacations, and sick leave. In some cases, benefits also include educational assistance, retirement plans, and uniform allowances.

OUTLOOK

Employment of cardiovascular technologists and technicians should grow faster than the average through 2010, according to the U.S. Department of Labor. Growth will be primarily due to the increasing numbers of older people who have a higher incidence of heart problems. The labor department, however, projects employment for EKG technicians to decline during this same period as hospitals train other health care personnel to perform basic EKG procedures.

FOR MORE INFORMATION

For information on careers, contact:

Alliance of Cardiovascular Professionals
4456 Corporation Lane, #164
Virginia Beach, VA 23462
Tel: 757-497-1225
Web: http://www.acp-online.org

For information on accredited medical programs, contact:

American Medical Association
515 North State Street
Chicago, IL 60610
Tel: 312-464-5000
Web: http://www.ama-assn.org

For information on certification or licensing, contact:

American Registry of Diagnostic Medical Sonographers
51 Monroe Street
Plaza East One
Rockville, MD 20850-2400
Tel: 800-541-9754
Web: http://www.ardms.org

For information on credentials, contact:

Cardiovascular Credentialing International
4456 Corporation Lane, Suite 120
Virginia Beach, VA 23462
Tel: 800-326-0268
Web: http://cci-online.org

CARPENTERS

School Subjects **Mathematics** **Technical/shop**	*Salary Range* **$20,000 to $33,000** **to $56,000+**
Personal Skills **Following instructions** **Mechanical/manipulative**	*Certification or Licensing* **Voluntary**
Work Environment **Indoors and outdoors** **Primarily multiple locations**	*Outlook* **Little change or more slowly** **than the average**

THE JOB

Carpenters cut, shape, level, and fasten together pieces of wood and other construction materials, such as wallboard, plywood, and insulation. Many carpenters work on constructing, remodeling, or repairing houses and other kinds of buildings. Other carpenters work at construction sites where roads, bridges, docks, boats, mining tunnels, and wooden vats are built. Those who specialize in building the rough framing of a structure are often called *rough carpenters.* Those specializing in the finishing details of a structure, such as the trim around doors and windows, are called *finish carpenters.*

PROFESSIONAL AND PERSONAL REQUIREMENTS

The United Brotherhood of Carpenters and Joiners of America (UBC), the national union for the industry, offers voluntary certification courses in a variety of specialty skills. These courses teach the ins and outs of advanced skills, such as scaffold construction, that help to ensure worker safety. Obtaining certification can also give workers a way to enhance their abilities and qualify for better jobs. Some job sites require all workers to undergo training in safety techniques and guidelines specified by the Occupational Safety and Health Administration. Workers who have not passed these courses are considered ineligible for jobs at these sites.

You will need to have manual dexterity, good hand-eye coordination, and a good sense of balance to work as a carpenter. You also need to be in good physical condition, as the work involves a great deal of physical activity. Stamina is much more important than physical strength. On the job, you may have to climb, stoop, kneel, crouch, and reach as well as deal with the challenges of weather.

STARTING OUT

Information about available apprenticeships can be obtained by contacting your state's employment service, local contractors that hire carpenters, or your local office of the UBC. Helper jobs that can be filled by beginners without special training in carpentry may be advertised in newspaper classified ads. You also might consider contacting potential employers directly.

EARNINGS

According to the U.S. Bureau of Labor Statistics, carpenters had median hourly earnings of $15.69 in 2000, or roughly $32,635 a year. The lowest-paid 10 percent of carpenters earned less than $9.48 per hour (or approximately $19,720 per year), and the highest-paid 10 percent made more than $26.73 hourly ($55,600 annually). It is important to note that the estimated yearly salaries are based on full-time work. Many carpenters, like others in the building trades, have periods of unemployment during the year, and their incomes may be less than that listed.

Starting pay for apprentices is approximately 40 percent of the experienced worker's median, or roughly $13,000 a year. The wage is increased periodically so that by the fourth year of training, apprentice pay is 80 percent of the experienced carpenter.

Benefits, such as health insurance, pension funds, and paid vacations, are available to most workers in this field and vary with local union contracts. In general, benefits are more likely to be offered on jobs staffed by union workers.

OUTLOOK

Although the U.S. Department of Labor predicts employment growth for carpenters to increase more slowly than the average through 2010, job opportunities should be plentiful. This is mainly due to high turnover in the field. Replacement workers are needed for the large number of both experienced and beginning carpenters who leave the field every year for work that is less strenuous. In addition, replacements are needed for carpenters who retire. Home modifications for the growing elderly population, two-income couples' desire for larger homes, and the growing population of all ages should contribute to the demand for carpenters.

Factors that may hold down employment growth in the field include the use of more prefabricated building parts and improved tools that make construction easier and faster. In addition, a weak economy has a major impact on the building industry, causing companies and individuals to put off expensive building projects until economic conditions look better. Carpenters with good all-around skills, such as those who have completed apprenticeships, will have the best job opportunities, even in difficult times.

FOR MORE INFORMATION

For information on activities and student chapters, contact:

Associated General Contractors of America
333 John Carlyle Street, Suite 200
Alexandria, VA 22314
Tel: 703-548-3118
Web: http://www.agc.org

Habitat for Humanity is a nonprofit organization dedicated to the elimination of poverty housing. For information, contact:

Habitat for Humanity International
121 Habitat Street
Americus, GA 31709
Tel: 229-924-6935, ext. 2551
Web: http://www.habitat.org

For information on training programs, contact:

Home Builders Institute
1201 15th Street, NW, Sixth Floor
Washington, DC 20005
Tel: 202-371-0600
Web: http://www.hbi.org

For information on certification, publications, apprenticeships, and local chapters, visit the following Web site:

United Brotherhood of Carpenters and Joiners of America
Web: http://www.carpenters.org

CARTOONISTS AND ANIMATORS

School Subjects	Salary Range
Art	$23,000 to $31,000
Computer science	to $71,000+
Personal Skills	*Certification or Licensing*
Artistic	None available
Communication/ideas	*Outlook*
Work Environment	About as fast as the average
Primarily indoors	
Primarily one location	

THE JOB

Cartoonists draw illustrations for newspapers, books, magazines, greeting cards, movies, television shows, organizations, and private businesses. Cartoons most often are associated with newspaper comics or with children's television, but they are also used to highlight and interpret information in publications as well as in advertising. Cartoons can be used to relate directly to the news of the day, the content of a magazine article, or a new product. After cartoonists come up with ideas, they discuss them with their employers, who may be editors, producers, or creative directors at advertising agencies. Next, cartoonists sketch drawings and submit these for approval.

Animators, or *motion cartoonists*, also draw individual pictures, but they draw series of them for a moving cartoon. Each picture varies only slightly from the one before and after it in a series. These drawings are photographed in sequence and then projected at high speed, causing the cartoon images to appear to be moving. Animators today also work a great deal with computers.

PROFESSIONAL AND PERSONAL REQUIREMENTS

There is no certification or licensing available in this field.

You need to be highly creative to work as a cartoonist or animator. You should have a good sense of humor and an observant eye to detect people's distinguishing characteristics as well as society's interesting attributes or incongruities. You should also

be flexible and be able to take suggestions and rejections grace-
fully. Because cartoonists' and animators' art is commercial, they
must be willing to accommodate their employers' desires if they
are to build a broad clientele and earn a decent living.

STARTING OUT

A few places, such as the Walt Disney studios, offer apprenticeships. To enter these programs, you must have attended an
accredited art school for two or three years.

Formal entry-level positions for cartoonists and animators are
rare, but there are several ways for you to enter the cartooning
field. Most cartoonists and animators begin by working as freelancers, selling cartoons to small publications, such as community newspapers, that buy cartoons. Others assemble a portfolio
of their best work and apply to publishers or the art departments of advertising agencies.

EARNINGS

Freelance cartoonists may earn anywhere from $100 to $1,200 or
more per drawing, but top dollar generally goes only for big,
full-color projects such as magazine cover illustrations.

The U.S. Department of Labor reports a median annual
income of $41,130 for salaried multimedia artists and animators
in 2000. Incomes ranged from the lowest-paid 10 percent earning less than $23,740 to the highest-paid 10 percent making more
than $70,560 that same year. Comic strip artists are usually paid
according to the number of publications that carry their strip.
Although the Department of Labor does not give specific information regarding cartoonists' earnings, it does note that the
median earnings for salaried fine artists were $31,190 in 2000.
Salaried cartoonists, who are related workers, may have earnings similar to this figure.

Self-employed artists do not receive fringe benefits such as
paid vacations, sick leave, health insurance, or pension benefits.
Those who are salaried employees of companies, agencies, newspapers, and the like do typically receive these fringe benefits.

OUTLOOK

Employment for artists and related workers is expected to grow
at a rate about as fast as the average through 2010, according to

the U.S. Department of Labor. Because so many creative and talented people are drawn to this field, however, competition for jobs will be strong.

Cartoons are not just for children anymore. Much of the animation today is geared for an adult audience. Interactive games, animated films, network and cable television, and the Internet provide many employment opportunities for talented cartoonists and animators. More than half of all visual artists are self-employed, but freelance work can be hard to come by, and many freelancers earn little until they acquire experience and establish a good reputation. Individuals with an undergraduate or advanced degree in art or film will be in demand. Experience in action drawing and computers is crucial.

The growing trend toward sophisticated special effects in motion pictures should create opportunities at industry effects houses such as Sony Pictures Imageworks, DreamQuest Software, Industrial Light & Magic, and DreamWorks SKG.

FOR MORE INFORMATION

For membership and scholarship information, contact:

International Animated Film Society
721 South Victory Boulevard
Burbank, CA 91502
Tel: 818-842-8330
Email: info@asifa-hollywood.org
Web: http://www.asifa-hollywood.org

For an art school directory, a scholarship guide, or general information, contact:

National Art Education Association
1916 Association Drive
Reston, VA 20191-1590
Tel: 703-860-8000
Email: naea@dgs.dgsys.com
Web: http://www.naea-reston.org

For education and career information, contact:

National Cartoonists Society
PO Box 713
Suffield, CT 06078
Web: http://www.reuben.org

CATERERS

School Subjects	Salary Range
Business	**$15,000 to $35,000**
Family and consumer science	**to $75,000+**
Personal Skills	*Certification or Licensing*
Artistic	**Voluntary (certification)**
Helping/teaching	**Required by certain states (licensing)**
Work Environment	
Primarily indoors	*Outlook*
Primarily multiple locations	**About as fast as the average**

THE JOB

Caterers plan, coordinate, and supervise food service at parties and other social functions. Working with their clients, they purchase appropriate supplies, plan menus, supervise food preparation, direct serving of food and refreshments, and ensure the overall smooth functioning of the event. The caterer must be in frequent contact with all parties involved in the affair, making sure, for example, that the food is delivered on time, the flowers are fresh, and the entertainment shows up and performs as promised. As entrepreneurs, they are also responsible for budgeting, bookkeeping, and other administrative tasks.

Caterers need to be flexible in their approach to food preparation, that is, able to prepare food both on- and off-premises, as required by the client. The caterer and client work together to establish a budget, develop a menu, and determine the desired atmosphere. Clients always want their affairs to be special, and the caterer's ability to meet or exceed the clients' expectations will ensure customer satisfaction and future business.

PROFESSIONAL AND PERSONAL REQUIREMENTS

As a measure of professional status, many caterers become certified through the National Association of Catering Executives or the International Food Service Executives. Applicants must meet certain educational requirements and pass a written test in order to become certified.

Most states require caterers to be licensed. Inspectors may make periodic visits to catering operations to ensure that local health and safety regulations are being maintained in food preparation, handling, and storage.

Because caterers run their own businesses, you will need to be organized, able to work on tight schedules, and conscientious about keeping accurate records. You should enjoy working with people and also have an artistic eye with the ability to arrange food and settings in an appealing manner.

STARTING OUT

Some caterers enter the profession as a matter of chance after helping a friend or relative prepare a large banquet or volunteering to coordinate a group function. Most caterers, however, begin their careers after graduating from college with a degree in home economics or after finishing a culinary training program at a vocational school or community college.

You can begin working as a manager for a large catering firm or as a manager for a hotel or country club or banquet service. In order to start your own catering service, you need extensive experience and sufficient finances to purchase equipment and cover other start-up costs.

EARNINGS

Earnings vary widely, depending on the size and location of the catering operation and the skill and motivation of the individual entrepreneur. Many caterers charge according to the number of guests attending a function. In many cases, the larger the event, the larger the profit.

According to the U.S. Department of Labor, a caterer who is employed as a manager for a company cafeteria or other industrial client may earn between $19,000 and $50,000 per year, with vacation, health insurance, and other benefits usually included.

Self-employed caterers can earn between $15,000 and $60,000 per year, depending on skill, reputation, and experience. An extremely successful caterer can easily earn more than $75,000 annually. However, a part-time caterer may earn closer to $7,000 to $15,000 per year.

OUTLOOK

The U.S. Department of Labor projects that employment opportunities in food service should continue to grow at an average rate through 2010. Opportunities will be good for individuals who handle special events, such as weddings, bar and bat mitzvahs, and other festive occasions less affected by downswings in the economy. On the other hand, events such as business functions may offer fewer catering opportunities during times of recession and cutbacks.

Competition is keen as many hotels and restaurants branch out to offer catering services. However, despite competition and fluctuating economic conditions, highly skilled and motivated caterers should be in demand throughout the country, especially in and around large metropolitan areas.

FOR MORE INFORMATION

For information on scholarships, student branches, certification, and industry news, contact:

International Food Service Executives Association
836 San Bruno Avenue
Henderson, NV 89015-9006
Tel: 888-234-3732
Web: http://www.ifsea.org

For information on certification programs and catering publications, contact:

National Association of Catering Executives
5565 Sterrett Place, Suite 328
Columbia, MD 21044
Tel: 410-997-9055
Web: http://www.nace.net

For more information on programs and chapters, contact:

National 4-H Council
7100 Connecticut Avenue
Chevy Chase, MD 20815
Tel: 301-961-2800
Email: info@fourhcouncil.edu
Web: http://www.fourhcouncil.edu

CHEMICAL TECHNICIANS

School Subjects **Chemistry** **Mathematics** *Personal Skills* **Following instructions** **Technical/scientific** *Work Environment* **Primarily indoors** **Primarily one location**	*Salary Range* **$17,000 to $35,000** **to $43,000** *Certification or Licensing* **None available** *Outlook* **About as fast as the average**

THE JOB

Most *chemical technicians* work in the chemical industry and are involved in the development, testing, and manufacturing of plastics, paints, detergents, synthetic fibers, industrial chemicals, and pharmaceuticals. Others work in the petroleum, aerospace, metals, electronics, automotive, and construction industries. Some chemical technicians work in universities and government laboratories.

Chemical technicians may specialize in a subfield of chemistry, such as analytical chemistry, inorganic or organic chemistry, and biochemistry. Technicians work in research and development, design and production, and quality control. Technicians often determine the chemical composition, concentration, stability, and level of purity of a wide range of materials. They assist chemists with experiments, perform analyses, and report test results.

PROFESSIONAL AND PERSONAL REQUIREMENTS

There is no certification or licensing available in this field.

Working as a chemical technician, you must be capable of precise, detailed work. To do this, you will need good eyesight, color perception, and eye-hand coordination. You should also have a good supply of patience because experiments must frequently be repeated several times. Excellent organizational and communications skills, mechanical aptitude, and an ability to follow directions closely are also a must.

STARTING OUT

Graduates of chemical technology programs often find jobs during the last term of their two-year programs. Some company recruiters regularly visit colleges where chemical technology programs are offered. Some recruiters also go to four-year colleges and look for chemists with bachelor's degrees. Because these companies hire locally and work closely with technical schools, your college's placement office is usually a good place to start.

Internships and co-op work are highly regarded by employers and are good ways to get a foot in the door. Many two- and four-year schools have co-op programs in which full-time students work about 20 hours a week for a local company.

EARNINGS

Earnings for chemical technicians vary based on their education, experience, employer, and location. The U.S. Department of Labor reports that the median hourly wage for chemical technicians was $17.05, or approximately $35,465 a year, in 2000. Science technicians (a category including chemical technicians) working for the federal government had starting salaries ranging from $17,483 to $22,251 in 2001. Physical science technicians working for the federal government earned an average of $42,657 a year. Salaries tend to be highest in private industry and lowest in colleges and universities.

Benefits depend on the employer, but they usually include paid vacations and holidays, insurance, and tuition refund plans. Technicians normally work a five-day, 40-hour week, but occasional overtime may be necessary.

OUTLOOK

The U.S. Department of Labor expects employment for all science technicians to grow at a rate about as fast as the average through 2010. Chemical technicians will be in demand as the chemical and drug industries work to improve and produce new medicines and personal care products. Chemical technicians will also be needed in businesses providing environmental services and "earth-friendly" products, analytical development and services, custom or niche products and services, and quality control.

Graduates of chemical technology programs will continue to face competition from bachelor's-level chemists. The chemical and chemical-related industries will continue to become increasingly sophisticated in both their products and their manufacturing techniques. Technicians trained to deal with automation and complex production methods will have the best employment opportunities.

FOR MORE INFORMATION

For listings of chemical technology programs, internships, and summer job opportunities, contact:

American Chemical Society
1155 16th Street, NW
Washington, DC 20036
Tel: 800-227-5558
Email: help@acs.org
Web: http://www.chemistry.org

For information on awards, student chapters, and careers, contact:

American Institute of Chemical Engineers
3 Park Avenue
New York, NY 10016-5991
Tel: 800-242-4363
Email: xpress@aiche.org
Web: http://www.aiche.org

For information about programs, products, and careers, contact:

Junior Engineering Technical Society
1420 King Street, Suite 405
Alexandria, VA 22314-2794
Tel: 703-548-5387
Email: jetsinfo@jets.org
Web: http://www.jets.org

For fun and educational information on the field of chemistry, check out the following Web site:

Chem 4 Kids
Web: http://www.chem4kids.com

CIVIL ENGINEERING TECHNICIANS

School Subjects **Mathematics** **Physics** *Personal Skills* **Following instructions** **Technical/scientific** *Work Environment* **Indoors and outdoors** **Primarily multiple locations**	*Salary Range* **$22,000 to $36,000** **to $55,000+** *Certification or Licensing* **Recommended** *Outlook* **About as fast as the average**

THE JOB

Civil engineering technicians help civil engineers design, plan, and build public and private works to meet a community's needs. They are employed in a wide range of projects, such as highways, drainage systems, water and sewage facilities, railroads, subways, airports, dams, bridges, and tunnels. State highway departments as well as railroad and airport facilities hire civil engineering technicians to collect data, design and draw plans, and supervise the construction and maintenance of roadways, railways, and airport runways.

Some technicians specialize in certain types of construction projects, such as highway technicians, rail and waterway technicians, and assistant city engineers. Other technicians specialize in certain phases of the construction process, such as construction materials testing technicians, research engineering technicians, and photogrammetric technicians.

PROFESSIONAL AND PERSONAL REQUIREMENTS

To advance in professional standing, civil engineering technicians need to become certified. The National Institute for Certification in Engineering Technologies and the American Society of Certified Engineering Technicians offer voluntary certification programs for engineering technicians. To achieve certification, typically a candidate must graduate from an accredited program, pass a written exam, and have some work experience. There is no licensing requirement for this job.

Civil engineering projects are often complex and long term, requiring a variety of specialized skills. As a result, you will need the ability to think and plan ahead, as well as patience and great attention to detail, to succeed in this line of work.

STARTING OUT

A good place to start looking for jobs is through your school's placement office. There you should be able to get help preparing your resume of relevant school and work experiences and possibly even set up an interview with prospective employers. If available at your school, take advantage of any cooperative work-study programs with local employers or government agencies. These programs may offer you full-time employment after graduation.

EARNINGS

The U.S. Department of Labor reports that the median annual salary for civil engineering technicians was $35,990 in 2000. The highest-paid 10 percent earned more than $54,770, while the lowest-paid 10 percent earned less than $21,830. Technicians working for local governments earned a median salary of $39,080; for engineering and architectural services, $36,670; and for state governments, $32,160.

The incomes of many civil engineering technicians who operate their own construction, surveying, or equipment businesses are excellent. Some of these companies can earn millions of dollars each year.

Paid vacations, pension plans, and insurance are normal parts of the benefits paid to civil engineering technicians. Many companies pay a bonus if a job is completed ahead of schedule or if the job is completed for less than the estimated cost. These bonuses sometimes amount to more than the employee's regular annual salary.

OUTLOOK

The outlook for civil engineering technicians is generally favorable. The U.S. Department of Labor predicts employment for all engineering technicians to grow about as fast as the average through 2010. As in most industries, those with certification and the most education have the best employment prospects. Construction is, however, one of the industries most likely to feel the effects of economic recessions, so civil engineering technicians must be prepared for occasional slowdowns in business.

FOR MORE INFORMATION

For career and educational information and links to additional resources, contact:

American Society for Engineering Education
1818 N Street, NW, Suite 600
Washington, DC 20036-2479
Tel: 202-331-3500
Web: http://www.asee.org

For information on training and scholarships, contact the following organizations:

American Society of Certified Engineering Technicians
PO Box 1348
Flowery Branch, GA 30542
Tel: 770-967-9173
Email: General_Manager@ascet.org
Web: http://www.ascet.org

American Society of Civil Engineers
1801 Alexander Bell Drive
Reston, VA 20191
Tel: 800-548-2723
Web: http://www.asce.org

For certification information, contact:

National Institute for Certification in Engineering Technologies
1420 King Street
Alexandria, VA 22314-2794
Tel: 888-476-4238
Web: http://www.nicet.org

COMPUTER AND OFFICE MACHINE SERVICE TECHNICIANS

School Subjects **Computer science** **Technical/shop** *Personal Skills* **Mechanical/manipulative** **Technical/scientific** *Work Environment* **Primarily indoors** **Primarily multiple locations**	*Salary Range* **$20,000 to $31,000** **to $49,000+** *Certification or Licensing* **Recommended** *Outlook* **About as fast as the average**

THE JOB

Computer and office machine service technicians install, calibrate, maintain, troubleshoot, and repair equipment such as computers and their attachments, office equipment, and specialized electronic equipment used in many factories, hospitals, airplanes, and numerous other businesses. A large part of their work is the maintenance, diagnostic work, and repair of computer equipment. They may also be responsible for training employees on how to use the machinery. Other duties may include presenting company products and services to potential clients and bidding for maintenance contracts. Many service technicians are required to carry pagers and be prepared to respond to unexpected situations 24 hours a day. Traveling is also a common requirement of employees in this field, sometimes amounting to 80 percent of a technician's work hours.

PROFESSIONAL AND PERSONAL REQUIREMENTS

Most employers require certification, which is considered by many as a measure of industry knowledge. A variety of certification programs are available, such as those offered by the International Society of Certified Electronics Technicians and the Institute for Certification of Computing Professionals. After the successful completion of study and examination, you may be certified in fields such as computer, industrial, and electronic equipment. There is no licensing requirement for the job.

You will need a strong technical background, manual dexterity, and an aptitude for learning about new technologies to do this sort of work. You should be task oriented, organized, and personable and be able to convey technical terms in writing and in communicating with others.

STARTING OUT

If your school offers placement services, take advantage of them. Many times, school placement and counseling centers are aware of job openings before they are advertised in the newspaper. Make sure your counselors know of any important preferences, such as location, specialization, and other requirements, so they can best match you to an employer. Don't forget to supply them with an updated resume.

There are also other avenues to take when searching for a job in this industry. Many jobs are advertised in the classified section of your local newspaper. Look under "Computers" or "Electronics." Also, inquire directly with the personnel departments of companies that appeal to you and fill out an application. Professional association Web sites are good sources of job leads; many will post employment opportunities as well as allow you to post your resume. (See the end of the article for contact information.)

EARNINGS

The U.S. Department of Labor reports the median hourly rate for technicians working for computer and data processing services was $15.05 in 2000, or approximately $31,300 a year. The lowest-paid 10 percent of all computer and office machine service technicians (regardless of employer) earned less than $9.50 per hour ($19,760 annually). At the other end of the pay scale, 10 percent earned more than $23.42 per hour ($48,710 annually). Those with certification are typically paid more than those without.

Standard benefits for full-time technicians include health and life insurance, paid vacation and sick time, and a retirement plan. Most technicians are given travel stipends, and some receive company cars.

OUTLOOK

According to the U.S. Department of Labor, employment for service technicians working with computer and office equipment should grow about as fast as the average through 2010. As corporations, government agencies, hospitals, and universities worldwide continue their reliance on computers to help manage their daily business, demand for qualified and skilled technicians will be strong. Opportunities are expected to be best for those with knowledge of electronics and those working in computer repairs. Technicians working on office equipment, such as digital copiers, should also find a demand for their services to repair and maintain increasingly technically sophisticated office machines.

FOR MORE INFORMATION

For information on internships, student membership, and the magazine, Crossroads, *contact:*

Association for Computing Machinery
1515 Broadway
New York, NY 10036
Tel: 800-342-6626
Email: sigs@acm.org
Web: http://www.acm.org

For industry and certification information, contact the following organizations:

Institute for Certification of Computing Professionals
2350 East Devon Avenue, Suite 115
Des Plaines, IL 60018-4610
Tel: 800-843-8227
Email: office@iccp.org
Web: http://www.iccp.org

International Society of Certified Electronics Technicians
3608 Pershing Avenue
Fort Worth, TX 76107-4527
Tel: 817-921-9101
Email: info@iscet.org
Web: http://www.iscet.org

COMPUTER PROGRAMMERS

School Subjects **Computer science** **Mathematics**	*Salary Range* **$35,000 to $58,000** **to $93,000+**
Personal Skills **Communication/ideas** **Technical/scientific**	*Certification or Licensing* **Voluntary**
Work Environment **Primarily indoors** **Primarily one location**	*Outlook* **About as fast as the average**

THE JOB

Computer programmers work in the field of electronic data processing. They write instructions that tell computers what to do in a computer language (often called code) that the computer understands. Broadly speaking, there are two types of computer programmers: systems programmers and applications programmers.

Systems programmers maintain the instructions, called programs or software, that control the entire computer system, including both the central processing unit and the equipment with which it communicates, such as terminals, printers, and disk drives.

Applications programmers write the software to handle specific jobs and may specialize as engineering and scientific programmers or as business programmers. Some of the latter specialists may be designated *chief business programmers,* who supervise the work of other business programmers.

Other specific positions in the field include programmer-analysts, information system programmers, process control programmers, and numerical control tool programmers.

PROFESSIONAL AND PERSONAL REQUIREMENTS

Students who choose to obtain a two-year degree might consider becoming certified by the Institute for Certification of

Computing Professionals (see sources at the end of this article). Although it is not required, certification may boost an individual's attractiveness to employers during the job search. There is no licensing requirement in computer programming.

You should have a high degree of reasoning ability, patience, persistence, and an aptitude for mathematics to work as a computer programmer. If you plan to specialize, you should have a solid background in that area in addition to computer programming. Engineering firms, for example, prefer young people with an engineering background and are willing to train them in some programming techniques.

STARTING OUT

You can look for an entry-level programming position in the same way as most other jobs. If you have the necessary qualifications, you can apply directly to companies, agencies, or industries that have announced job openings through school placement offices, employment agencies, or classified ads.

You should work closely with your schools' placement center, since major local employers often list job openings exclusively with these offices.

If the market for programmers is particularly tight, you may want to obtain an entry-level job with a large corporation or computer software firm, even if the job does not include programming. As jobs in the programming department open up, current employees in other departments are often the first to know, and they are often favored over nonemployees during the interviewing process. Getting a foot in the door in this way has proven to be successful for many programmers.

EARNINGS

The U.S. Department of Labor reports that the median annual salary for computer programmers was $57,590 in 2000. The lowest-paid 10 percent of programmers earned less than $35,020 annually, and at the other end of the pay scale, the highest-paid 10 percent earned more than $93,210. Programmers in the West and the Northeast are generally paid more than those in the South and Midwest. This is because most big computer companies are located in the Silicon Valley in California or in the state of Washington, where Microsoft, a major employer of programmers, has its headquarters.

Most programmers receive the customary paid vacation and sick leave and are included in such company benefits as group insurance and retirement benefit plans.

OUTLOOK

The employment rate for computer programmers is expected to increase about as fast as the average through 2010, according to the U.S. Department of Labor. One factor that has resulted in slower job growth in this area compared to other computer professions is the emergence of new technologies that eliminate the need for some routine programming work of the past.

Job applicants with the best chances of employment will be college graduates with a knowledge of several programming languages, especially newer ones used for computer networking and database management. Applicants with the most promising prospects will also have some training or experience in an applied field such as accounting, science, engineering, or management. Since this field is constantly changing, programmers should stay abreast of the latest technology to remain competitive.

FOR MORE INFORMATION

For information about careers in computer programming, contact:

Association for Computing Machinery
1515 Broadway
New York, NY 10036
Tel: 800-342-6626
Email: sigs@acm.org
Web: http://www.acm.org

For information on certification programs, contact:

Institute for Certification of Computing Professionals
2350 East Devon Avenue, Suite 115
Des Plaines, IL 60018-4610
Tel: 800-843-8227
Web: http://www.iccp.org

COMPUTER SUPPORT SERVICE OWNERS

School Subjects **Business** **Computer science** *Personal Skills* **Helping/teaching** **Technical/scientific** *Work Environment* **Primarily indoors** **Primarily multiple locations**	*Salary Range* **$35,000 to $60,000** **to $150,000+** *Certification or Licensing* **Voluntary** *Outlook* **Much faster than the average**

THE JOB

Computer support service owners help businesses and individuals install and maintain computer hardware and software. They teach the computer operators, either one-on-one or in group training sessions, how to use new systems. Many computer consultants also offer their expertise in Web design and desktop publishing to help clients upload Web pages or prepare presentations. Some computer consultants are involved in issues of programming. Though some of their assistance is offered over the phone, much of their work is performed on site.

In addition to the technical work, computer support service owners must handle all the details of running their businesses. They answer the phone, handle the bookkeeping, and organize client records. They must also research new technologies and keep up to date on advanced technical skills.

PROFESSIONAL AND PERSONAL REQUIREMENTS

There are many different kinds of certifications available to people working in computer support and consulting. No one certification, however, serves all the varying needs of computer professionals. The Institute for Certification of Computer Professionals offers a Certified Computer Professional exam, which tests knowledge of business information systems, data resource management, software engineering, and other subjects. There is no licensing requirement for this job.

You will need good business and money management skills to work as a computer support service owner. Though computer skills are very important, you can't just be a computer "geek"—you need good people skills to maintain customer relations. Teaching skills are also important, as training people in how to use their systems is part of the job.

STARTING OUT

You first need to work with an established company for some time after school in order to gain experience and make contacts in computer support. After you have cultivated your skills and knowledge in this area, you can start doing outside consulting work. Many start working for friends, family, and past business contacts.

As with many start-up companies, it's good for you to focus your talents. Decide on a niche, such as networking or client customization, and then promote those specific services. Good marketing techniques, which includes careful attention to image, is crucial to making a name for yourself and attracting new clients.

EARNINGS

According to Robert Half Technology, the median annual earnings for computer consultants ranges from about $57,000 to $77,000. In the first few years of a business, a consultant will make about $35,000 or less, depending on location. Those working in large cities like New York and Los Angeles average more than those in the Midwest, the Southwest, and the Northwest. Someone in New York with more than 10 years of experience can average over $90,000 a year, while a consultant with similar experience in the Southwest may make closer to $65,000 a year. Some very experienced, business-minded consultants can make $150,000 a year or more.

OUTLOOK

According to the U.S. Department of Labor, the industry is expected to grow quickly as computer systems become more important to more businesses. Lower prices on computer hardware and software will inspire businesses to expand their systems and to invest in the services needed to keep them up and running. As computer programs become more sophisticated and are able to perform more complex operations, consultants will be needed to help clients operate these programs. With companies relying more on complex computer systems, they'll be less likely to take risks in the installation of hardware and software. To stay at the top of the industry, consultants will have to keep up on technological developments and take continuing education courses.

FOR MORE INFORMATION

To subscribe to a free electronic newsletter, and to check out an extensive list of related Web links, visit the ACSS Web page. To learn more about membership and its career training courses, contact:

Association of Computer Support Specialists (ACSS)
218 Huntington Road
Bridgeport, CT 06608
Tel: 203-332-1524
Email: hhr@acss.org
Web: http://www.acss.org

To learn about membership benefits, contact:

Independent Computer Consultants Association
11131 South Towne Square, Suite F
St. Louis, MO 63123
Tel: 800-774-4222
Email: info@icca.org
Web: http://www.icca.org

For information on certification programs, contact:

Institute for Certification of Computing Professionals
2350 East Devon Avenue, Suite 115
Des Plaines, IL 60018-4610
Tel: 800-843-8227
Email: office@iccp.org
Web: http://www.iccp.org

For resume and cover letter advice, salary statistics, and other career information in information technology, check out the following Web site:

Robert Half Technology
Web: http://www.roberthalftechnology.com

COMPUTER-AIDED DESIGN DRAFTERS AND TECHNICIANS

School Subjects **Computer science** **Technical/shop**	*Salary Range* **$23,000 to $35,000** **to $54,000+**
Personal Skills **Mechanical/manipulative** **Technical/scientific**	*Certification or Licensing* **Voluntary**
Work Environment **Primarily indoors** **Primarily one location**	*Outlook* **About as fast as the average**

THE JOB

Computer-aided design drafters and technicians use computers to produce and revise technical illustrations needed in the design and development of machines, products, buildings, manufacturing processes, and other work. Also called *CAD technicians* or *CAD designers,* these professionals create design concepts so that they are feasible to produce and use in the real world. They use a keyboard, touch screen, mouse, joystick, or other electronic methods to move, rotate, or zoom in on any aspect of the drawing. Starting from two-dimensional sketches, technicians are able to project these drawings as three-dimensional images on the computer screen. Compared to traditional drafting and design techniques, CAD offers virtually unlimited freedom to explore design alternatives, and in far less time.

PROFESSIONAL AND PERSONAL REQUIREMENTS

Voluntary certification is available from the American Design and Drafting Association. The examination, called the Drafter Certification Test, covers basic drafting skills but does not include testing of CAD drafting. Applicants are tested on geometric construction, architectural terms and regulations, and working sketches.

Licensing requirements vary. Licensing may be required for specific projects, such as a construction project, when the client requires it.

As a CAD technician or drafter, you will need to think logically, have good analytical skills, and be methodical, accurate, and detail oriented in all your work. You should be able to work as part of a team, as well as independently, and be willing to spend long periods of time in front of a computer monitor.

STARTING OUT

Probably the most reliable method for entering this field is through your school's placement office. This is especially true if you plan on attending a two-year college or technical institute. Recruiters from companies employing CAD technicians often visit such schools, and placement office personnel can help you meet with these recruiters.

You can conduct your own job search by contacting architects, building firms, manufacturers, high-technology companies, and government agencies. State or private employment agencies may also be helpful, and classified ads in newspapers and professional journals may provide additional leads.

EARNINGS

The U.S. Department of Labor reports the median hourly wage for civil and architectural drafters was $16.93 in 2000. A drafter earning this wage and working full-time would have a yearly income of approximately $35,215. The lowest-paid 10 percent of these drafters made less than $11.18 per hour (approximately $23,255 annually); the highest-paid 10 percent made more than $26.13 per hour (approximately $54,350 annually).

According to a 2001 salary survey by the Web site, JustCADJobs.com, CAD designers/drafters with one to two years of experience averaged $35,617 annually. Those with four to six years of experience averaged $41,562 per year.

Actual salaries vary widely depending on geographic location, exact job requirements, and the training needed to obtain those jobs. With increased training and experience, technicians can earn higher salaries, and some technicians with special skills, extensive experience, or added responsibilities may earn more.

Benefits usually include insurance, paid vacations and holidays, pension plans, and sometimes stock-purchase plans.

OUTLOOK

By some estimates, there will be as many as a million jobs available for technically trained personnel in the field of CAD technology in the next few years. Many companies in the near future will feel pressure to increase productivity in design and manufacturing activities, and CAD technology provides some of the best opportunities to improve that productivity. Another factor that will create a demand for CAD drafters and technicians is the continued focus on safety and quality throughout manufacturing and industrial fields. Companies are scrutinizing their current designs more carefully than ever, requiring more CAD work for new concepts and alterations that will create a better product.

Any economic downturn could adversely affect CAD technicians because many of the industries that they serve, such as auto manufacturing or construction, fluctuate greatly with economic swings. In any event, the best opportunities will be for drafters and technicians proficient in CAD technology who continue to learn, both in school and on the job.

FOR MORE INFORMATION

For information about certification, student drafting contests, and job postings, contact:

American Design and Drafting Association
PO Box 11937
Columbia, SC 29211
Tel: 803-771-0008
Email: national@adda.org
Web: http://www.adda.org

For information about the electrical field or to find the student branch nearest you, contact:

Institute of Electrical and Electronics Engineers, Inc.
1828 L Street, NW, Suite 1202
Washington, DC 20036
Tel: 202-785-0017
Email: ieeeusa@ieee.org
Web: http://www.ieeeusa.org

COOKS AND CHEFS

School Subjects **Family and consumer science** **Mathematics** *Personal Skills* **Artistic** **Following instructions** *Work Environment* **Primarily indoors** **Primarily one location**	*Salary Range* **$13,000 to $25,000** **to $47,000+** *Certification or Licensing* **Required by certain states** *Outlook* **About as fast as the average**

THE JOB

Cooks and *chefs* are primarily responsible for the preparation and cooking of foods. They order food from various suppliers and check it for quantity and quality when it arrives. They measure and mix ingredients and prepare foods for baking, roasting, broiling, and steaming. They may use blenders, mixers, grinders, slicers, or tenderizers to prepare the food and ovens, broilers, grills, roasters, or steam kettles to cook it. Cooks and chefs rely on their judgment and experience to add seasonings. They constantly taste and smell food as they prepare it and must know when it is cooked and seasoned properly.

Specific jobs within this field include broiler cooks, prep cooks, cafeteria and mess cooks, pastry chefs, executive chefs, sous chefs, barbecue cooks, pizza bakers, and short-order cooks.

PROFESSIONAL AND PERSONAL REQUIREMENTS

The American Culinary Federation offers voluntary certification at a variety of levels, such as executive chef and sous chef. In addition to educational and experience requirements, certification candidates must also pass written tests.

In most states, chefs and cooks are required by law to possess a health certificate and be examined by a physician periodically to protect the public's health. These examinations, usually given by the state board of health, make certain that the individual is free from communicable diseases and skin infections.

If you want to succeed as a chef or cook, you should be able to work as part of a team and to work under pressure during rush hours, in close quarters, and with a certain amount of noise and confusion. Cooks and chefs need an even temperament and patience to contend with the public daily and to work closely with many other kinds of employees.

STARTING OUT

Apprenticeship programs are one method of entering the trade. These programs can offer you sound basic training and a regular salary. Upon completion of the apprenticeship, you may be hired full-time in your place of training or be assisted in finding employment with another establishment.

In general, cooks are hired as chefs only after they have acquired a number of years of experience. You may have to start out in a small restaurant, perhaps working as a short-order cook, grill cook, or sandwich or salad maker, and transfer to a larger establishment as you gain experience.

Small restaurants, school cafeterias, and other eating places with simple food preparation will provide the greatest number of starting jobs for cooks. Job applicants who have had courses in commercial food preparation will have an advantage in large restaurants and hotels, where hiring standards are often high.

EARNINGS

The salaries earned by chefs and cooks are widely divergent and depend on many factors, such as the size, type, and location of the establishment and the skill, experience, training, and specialization of the worker.

The U.S. Department of Labor reports the following earnings for cooks and chefs in a variety of positions. In 2000, the median hourly wage for head cooks and chefs was $12.07, or approximately $25,105 a year if employed full-time. The highest-paid 10 percent of head cooks and chefs earned more than $22.77 per hour ($47,360 per year). Restaurant cooks had a median hourly wage of $8.72 ($18,135 per year). Cooks working at institutions or cafeterias had a median of $8.22 per hour ($17,098 per year). Short-order cooks earned a median hourly wage of $7.55 ($15,700 per year). Cooks at fast-food restaurants were at the bottom of the pay scale, earning a median of $6.53 per hour ($13,580 per year).

Chefs and cooks usually receive their meals free during working hours and are furnished with any necessary job uniforms. Those working full-time usually receive standard benefits, such as health insurance and vacation and sick days.

OUTLOOK

The overall employment of cooks and chefs is expected to increase as fast as the average for all occupations through 2010, according to the U.S. Department of Labor. While some areas (such as cooks in fast food) may not see much growth in number of new jobs, turnover rates are high, and the need to find replacement cooks and chefs will mean many job opportunities in all areas. The need for cooks and chefs will also grow as the population increases and lifestyles change. As people earn higher incomes and have more leisure time, they dine out more often and take more vacations. In addition, more working parents and their families are dining out frequently as a convenience.

FOR MORE INFORMATION

For information on careers in baking and cooking, education, and certification, contact the following organizations:

American Culinary Federation, Inc.
10 San Bartola Drive
St. Augustine, FL 32086
Tel: 800-624-9458
Email: acf@acfchefs.net
Web: http://www.acfchefs.org

Culinary Institute of America
1946 Campus Drive
Hyde Park, NY 12538-1499
Tel: 845-452-9600
Web: http://www.ciachef.edu

National Restaurant Association Educational Foundation
175 West Jackson Boulevard, Suite 1500
Chicago, IL 60604-2702
Tel: 800-765-2122
Web: http://www.nraef.org

CORRECTIONS OFFICERS

School Subjects	Salary Range
Government	**$20,000 to $37,000**
Physical education	**to $49,000+**
Personal Skills	*Certification or Licensing*
Communication/ideas	**Required by certain states**
Helping/teaching	*Outlook*
Work Environment	**Faster than the average**
Primarily indoors	
Primarily one location	

THE JOB

Corrections officers guard people who have been arrested and are awaiting trial or people who have been tried, convicted, and sentenced to serve time in a penal institution. They search prisoners and their cells for weapons, drugs, and other contraband; inspect windows, doors, locks, and gates for signs of tampering; observe the conduct and behavior of inmates to prevent disturbances or escapes; and make verbal or written reports to superior officers. Corrections officers assign work to inmates and supervise their activities. They guard prisoners who are being transported between jails, courthouses, mental institutions, and other destinations and supervise prisoners receiving visitors. When necessary, these workers use weapons or force to maintain discipline and order.

PROFESSIONAL AND PERSONAL REQUIREMENTS

Though there are no certification requirements, a few states require that aspiring corrections officers pass a written examination. Officers who work for the federal government and most state governments are covered by civil service systems or merit boards and may be required to pass a competitive exam for employment. Many states require random or comprehensive drug testing of their officers, either during hiring procedures or while employed at the facility.

If you are interested in this line of work, keep in mind that you need to be in good physical condition to handle some of the more physical aspects of the job. Many states have set minimum height, vision, and hearing standards, as sound judgment and the ability to think and act quickly are important qualities for this work. You also must have a clean police record. The ability to speak foreign languages is often a plus when applying for corrections jobs.

STARTING OUT

To apply for a job as a corrections officer, contact federal or state civil service commissions, state departments of correction, or local correctional facilities, and ask about entrance requirements, training, and job opportunities. Private contractors and other companies are also a growing source of employment opportunities. Many officers enter this field from social work areas and parole and probation positions.

EARNINGS

Wages for corrections officers vary considerably depending on their employers and their level of experience. According to the U.S. Department of Labor, the median annual salary for corrections officers employed by the federal government was $37,430 in 2000. That same year, those employed by state governments earned $31,860; in local governments, they earned $29,240; and in private facilities, they earned $21,600. The U.S. Department of Labor reports that the lowest-paid 10 percent of corrections officers earned less than $20,010 per year, and the highest-paid 10 percent earned more than $49,310.

Overtime, night shift, weekend, and holiday pay differentials are generally available at most institutions. Fringe benefits may include health and life insurance, uniforms, and sometimes meals and housing. Some corrections officers also receive retirement and pension plans.

OUTLOOK

Employment in this field is expected to increase faster than the average through 2010, according to the U.S. Department of Labor. The ongoing war on illegal drugs, new tough-on-crime legislation, and increasing mandatory sentencing policies will create a need for more prison beds and more corrections officers.

In addition, many job openings will occur from a characteristically high turnover rate, as well as from the need to fill vacancies caused by the retirement of older workers.

Because security must be maintained at correctional facilities at all times, corrections officers can depend on steady employment. They are not usually affected by poor economic conditions or changes in government spending. Corrections officers are rarely laid off, even when budgets need to be trimmed. Instead, because of high turnovers, staffs can be cut simply by not replacing those officers who leave.

Most jobs will be found in relatively large institutions located near metropolitan areas, although opportunities for corrections officers exist in jails and other smaller facilities throughout the country.

FOR MORE INFORMATION

For information on training, conferences, and membership, contact the following organizations:

American Correctional Association
4380 Forbes Boulevard
Lanham, MD 20706
Tel: 301-918-1800
Web: http://www.aca.org

American Probation and Parole Association
PO Box 11910
Lexington, KY 40578
Tel: 859-244-8203
Web: http://www.appa-net.org

For information on careers at the federal level, contact:

Federal Bureau of Prisons
320 First Street, NW
Washington, DC 20534
Tel: 202-307-3198
Web: http://www.bop.gov

This Web site bills itself as the "Largest Online Resource for News and Information in Corrections."

The Corrections Connection
Web: http://www.corrections.com

COURT REPORTERS

School Subjects **English** **Foreign language**	*Salary Range* **$19,000 to $40,000** **to $69,000+**
Personal Skills **Communication/ideas** **Following instructions**	*Certification or Licensing* **Required by certain states**
Work Environment **Primarily indoors** **Primarily multiple locations**	*Outlook* **About as fast as the average**

THE JOB

Court reporters record every word at hearings, trials, depositions, and other legal proceedings by taking shorthand notes with a stenotype machine. This machine looks like a miniature typewriter, having only 24 keys on its keyboard. Each key prints a single symbol, each of which represents a different sound, word, or phrase. Court reporters must record testimony word for word as quickly as possible. Accuracy is imperative, as the reporter's record becomes the official transcript for the entire proceeding. If a court reporter misses a word or phrase, he or she must interrupt the proceedings to have the words repeated.

After the trial or hearing, the court reporter uses a computer program to translate the stenotype notes into English. This rough translation is then edited, printed, and bound.

PROFESSIONAL AND PERSONAL REQUIREMENTS

The National Court Reporters Association offers several levels of certification. Currently, 42 states grant licenses in either shorthand reporting or court reporting, although not all of these states require licensure to work as a court reporter.

To be successful at this type of work, you need to be able to work well under pressure, meet deadlines with accuracy, and pay close attention to detail. You must also be familiar with a wide range of medical and legal terms and must be assertive enough to ask for clarification when necessary.

STARTING OUT

After completing the required training, court reporters usually work for a freelance reporting company that provides short-hand services for business meetings and courtroom proceedings on a temporary basis. You can contact these freelance reporting companies on your own to inquire about job opportunities.

You may be able to find a job directly out of school as a court-room official, but ordinarily only those with several years of experience are hired for full-time judiciary work. To gain experience, you can start out working as a medical transcriptionist or other specific reporter. Job placement counselors at your college can be helpful in finding that first job.

EARNINGS

Earnings vary according to the skill, speed, experience, and location of the court reporter. Those who are employed by large court systems generally earn more than their counterparts in smaller communities. The median annual income for all court reporters was $39,660 in 2000, according to the U.S. Department of Labor. Ten percent of reporters earned less than $18,750 annually, and 10 percent earned more than $69,060. Official court reporters earn not only a salary, but also a per-page fee for transcripts. Freelance court reporters are paid by the job and also per page for transcripts.

Those working for the government or full-time for private companies usually receive health insurance and other benefits, such as paid vacations and retirement pensions. Freelancers may or may not receive health insurance or other benefits, depending on the policies of their agencies.

OUTLOOK

The U.S. Department of Labor predicts that employment of court reporters should grow at a rate about as fast as the average through 2010. The rising number of criminal court cases and civil lawsuits will cause both state and federal court systems to expand. Job opportunities should be greatest in and around large metropolitan areas, but qualified court reporters should be able to find work in most parts of the country. Court reporters can also find work using their skills to produce captioning for television programs, which is a federal requirement for all new television programming by 2006.

As always, job prospects will be best for those with the most training and experience. Because of the reliance on computers in many aspects of this job, computer experience and training are important. Court reporters who are certified will have the most opportunities to choose from.

FOR MORE INFORMATION

For information on certification and court reporting careers, contact:

National Court Reporters Association
8224 Old Courthouse Road
Vienna, VA 22182-3808
Tel: 800-272-6272
Email: msic@ncrahq.org
Web: http://www.verbatimreporters.com

Information on the Frank Sarli Memorial Scholarship and the Santo J. Aurelio Award for Altruism is available from:

National Court Reporters Foundation
8224 Old Courthouse Road
Vienna, VA 22182-3808
Tel: 800-272-6272
Web: http://www.verbatimreporters.com/ncrf

For tips on preparing for the certification exams, and for other career information, contact:

National Verbatim Reporters Association
2729 Drake Street
PMB130
Fayetteville, AR 72703
Tel: 479-582-2200
Email: nvra@aol.com
Web: http://www.nvra.org

DENTAL ASSISTANTS

School Subjects **Business** **Health**	*Salary Range* **$17,000 to $26,000** **to $39,000**
Personal Skills **Helping/teaching** **Technical/scientific**	*Certification or Licensing* **Recommended**
Work Environment **Primarily indoors** **Primarily one location**	*Outlook* **Much faster than the average**

THE JOB

Dental assistants perform a variety of duties in dental offices. They assist the dentist by preparing patients for dental exams, handing the dentist the proper instruments, taking and processing X rays, preparing materials for making impressions and restorations, and instructing patients in oral health care. They also perform administrative and clerical tasks so that the office runs smoothly and the dentist's time is available for working with patients.

PROFESSIONAL AND PERSONAL REQUIREMENTS

The Dental Assisting National Board offers the designation Certified Dental Assistant (CDA). Though not required by most employers, certification shows that an assistant meets certain standards of professional competence. In 21 states, dental assistants are allowed to take X rays (under a dentist's direction) only after completing a training program and passing a test. Completing the program for CDA certification fulfills this requirement. To keep their CDA credentials, assistants must either prove their skills through retesting or acquire further education.

When working as a dental assistant, you need a clean, well-groomed appearance and a pleasant personality. Manual dexterity and the ability to follow directions are also important.

STARTING OUT

High school guidance counselors, family dentists, dental schools, dental placement agencies, and dental associations can provide you with leads about job openings. Students in formal training programs often learn of jobs through school placement services.

EARNINGS

Dental assistants' salaries are determined by their level of responsibility and the size and location of their employer. The median hourly earnings for dental assistants were $12.49 in 2000, according to the *Occupational Outlook Handbook*. The highest 10 percent earned more than $18.57 an hour, while the lowest 10 percent earned less than $8.26 an hour.

OUTLOOK

According to the U.S. Department of Labor, employment for dental assistants is expected to grow much faster than the average through 2010. As the population grows, more people will seek dental services for preventive care and cosmetic improvements.

In addition, dentists who earned their dental degrees since the 1970s are more likely than other dentists to hire one or more assistants. Also, as dentists increase their knowledge of innovative procedures, they generally delegate more routine tasks to dental assistants so they can make the best use of their time and increase profits.

FOR MORE INFORMATION

For continuing education information and career services, contact:

American Dental Assistants Association
203 North LaSalle Street, Suite 1320
Chicago, IL 60601
Tel: 312-541-1550
Email: adaa1@aol.com
Web: http://www.dentalassistant.org

For education information, contact:

American Dental Association
211 East Chicago Avenue
Chicago, IL 60611
Tel: 312-440-2500
Web: http://www.ada.org

For publications, information on dental schools, and scholarship information, contact:

American Dental Education Association
1625 Massachusetts Avenue, NW, Suite 600
Washington, DC 20036-2212
Tel: 202-667-9433
Email: adea@adea.org
Web: http://www.adea.org

For information on voluntary certification for dental assistants, contact:

Dental Assisting National Board
676 North Saint Clair, Suite 1880
Chicago, IL 60611
Tel: 800-367-3262
Email: danbmail@dentalassisting.com
Web: http://www.dentalassisting.com

DENTAL HYGIENISTS

School Subjects **Biology** **Health**	*Salary Range* **$32,000 to $51,000** **to $74,000**
Personal Skills **Helping/teaching** **Mechanical/manipulative**	*Certification or Licensing* **Required**
Work Environment **Primarily indoors** **Primarily one location**	*Outlook* **Much faster than the average**

THE JOB

Dental hygienists help prevent gum diseases and cavities by removing deposits from patients' teeth and applying sealants and fluoride to prevent tooth decay. They remove tartar, stains, and plaque from teeth; take X rays and run other diagnostic tests; place and remove temporary fillings; take health histories; remove sutures; polish amalgam restorations; and examine head, neck, and oral regions for disease. Hygienists also provide nutritional counseling and screen patients for oral cancer and high blood pressure.

Their tools include hand and rotary instruments to clean teeth, syringes to administer local anesthetic (such as Novocain), teeth models to demonstrate home care procedures, and X-ray machines that take pictures of the oral cavity to detect signs of decay or oral disease.

PROFESSIONAL AND PERSONAL REQUIREMENTS

After graduating from an accredited school, you must pass state licensing examinations before beginning to practice. Depending on your program, you may be required to take aptitude tests sponsored by the American Dental Hygienists' Association that assess your level of skill and knowledge.

In addition to becoming licensed, you will need skill in handling delicate instruments, a sensitive touch, and depth perception. You should be neat, clean, and personable to attract and maintain your clients.

STARTING OUT

Once you have passed your school and licensing exams, you must decide on an area of work. Most dental hygiene schools maintain placement services for the assistance of their graduates, and finding a satisfactory position is usually not too difficult.

EARNINGS

Earnings for dental hygienists are influenced by education, experience, location, and type of employer. Most dental hygienists who work in private dental offices are salaried employees, although some are paid based on work performed.

According to the U.S. Department of Labor, the average earnings of full-time hygienists ranged between $42,500 and $61,800 a year in 2000. The median hourly wage for full-time hygienists was $24.68, but ranged from $15.53 to $35.39 an hour. Salaries in large metropolitan areas are generally somewhat higher than in small cities and towns. In addition, dental hygienists in research, education, or administration may earn higher salaries.

A salaried dental hygienist in a private office typically receives paid vacation and health benefits. Part-time or commissioned dental hygienists in private offices usually do not receive vacation time or benefits.

OUTLOOK

The U.S. Department of Labor projects that employment of dental hygienists will grow much faster than the average through 2010. The demand for dental hygienists is expected to grow as younger generations that grew up receiving better dental care continue to maintain their teeth throughout adulthood.

Population growth, increased public awareness of proper oral home care, and the availability of dental insurance should create more dental hygiene jobs. Moreover, as the population ages, there will be a special demand for hygienists to work with older people, especially those who live in nursing homes.

Because of increased awareness about caring for animals in captivity, hygienists are also among a small number of dental professionals who can volunteer to help care for animals' teeth and perform annual examinations. Dental professionals are not licensed to treat animals, however, and they must work under the supervision of veterinarians.

FOR MORE INFORMATION

For education information, contact:

American Dental Association
211 East Chicago Avenue
Chicago, IL 60611
Tel: 312-440-2500
Web: http://www.ada.org

For publications, information on dental schools, and scholarship information, contact:

American Dental Education Association
1625 Massachusetts Avenue, NW, Suite 600
Washington, DC 20036-2212
Tel: 202-667-9433
Email: adea@adea.org
Web: http://www.adea.org

For career information and tips for dental hygiene students on finding a job, contact:

American Dental Hygienists' Association
444 North Michigan Avenue, Suite 3400
Chicago, IL 60611
Tel: 312-440-8900
Email: mail@adha.net
Web: http://www.adha.org

DESKTOP PUBLISHING SPECIALISTS

School Subjects **Computer science** **English**	*Salary Range* **$18,000 to $31,000** **to $51,000+**
Personal Skills **Artistic** **Communication/ideas**	*Certification or Licensing* **Voluntary**
Work Environment **Primarily indoors** **Primarily one location**	*Outlook* **Much faster than the average**

THE JOB

Desktop publishing specialists prepare reports, brochures, books, cards, Web publications, or other documents for printing or reading online. They work with files that others have created, or they create original text and graphics for their clients. They work either as freelancers or for corporations, service bureaus, and advertising agencies. Desktop publishing specialists use computers to convert and prepare files for printing presses and other media, such as the Internet and CD-ROM. Much of desktop publishing is considered prepress work, which means that these specialists typeset, or arrange and transform, text and graphics before it goes to the printer or can be read online.

PROFESSIONAL AND PERSONAL REQUIREMENTS

Certification is not mandatory, and currently there is only one certification program offered in desktop publishing. The Association of Graphic Communications has an Electronic Publishing Certificate designed to set industry standards and measure the competency levels of desktop publishing specialists. The examination is divided into a written test and a practical test. The Printing Industries of America is in the process of developing industry standards in the prepress and press industries and may eventually design a certification program in desktop publishing or electronic prepress operation.

If you want to work as a desktop publishing specialist, you must be detail oriented, have a good control of language, and have a sense of design and artistic skills. Other helpful qualities include patience, flexibility, an aptitude for computers, and the ability to type quickly and accurately.

STARTING OUT

To start your own business, you must have a great deal of experience with design and page layout and a careful understanding of the computer design programs you'll be using. Before striking out on your own, you may want to gain experience as a full-time staff member of a large business. Most desktop publishing specialists enter the field through the production or editorial side of the industry. Printing houses and design agencies are places to check for production artist opportunities. Publishing companies often hire desktop publishing specialists to work in-house or as freelance employees.

EARNINGS

There is limited salary information available for desktop publishing specialists, most likely because the job duties of desktop publishing specialists can vary and often overlap with other jobs. The average wage of desktop publishing specialists in the prepress department generally ranges from $15 to $50 an hour. Entry-level desktop publishing specialists with little or no experience generally earn minimum wage. Freelancers can earn from $15 to $100 an hour.

According to the *Occupational Outlook Handbook,* median annual earnings of desktop publishing specialists were $30,600 in 2000. Salaries ranged from less than $17,800 to more than $50,920 a year. Wage rates vary depending on experience, training, region, and size of the company.

OUTLOOK

According to the U.S. Department of Labor, employment for desktop publishing specialists is projected to grow much faster than the average through 2010, even though overall employment in the printing industry is expected to decline slightly. This is in part because electronic processes are replacing many of the manual processes involved in printing, which eliminates some jobs.

Despite this fact, the ability to create and publish documents will become easier and faster, thus influencing more businesses to produce printed materials. Desktop publishing specialists will be needed to satisfy typesetting, page layout, design, and editorial demands. With new equipment, commercial printing shops will be able to shorten the turnaround time on projects and in turn can increase business and accept more jobs. QuarkXPress, Adobe PageMaker, Macromedia FreeHand, Adobe Illustrator, and Adobe Photoshop are some programs often used in desktop publishing. Specialists with experience in these and other software will be in demand.

FOR MORE INFORMATION

For information on the Electronic Publishing Certificate, contact:

Association of Graphic Communications
330 Seventh Avenue, 9th Floor
New York, NY 10001-5010
Tel: 212-279-2100
Email: info@agcomm.org
Web: http://www.agcomm.org

For career brochures and other information about grants, scholarships, and educational programs, contact the following organizations:

Graphic Arts Technical Foundation
200 Deer Run Road
Sewickley, PA 15143
Tel: 412-741-6860
Email: info@gatf.org
Web: http://www.gain.net

Printing Industries of America
100 Daingerfield Road
Alexandria, VA 22314
Tel: 703-519-8100
Email: gain@printing.org
Web: http://www.gain.net

DIAGNOSTIC MEDICAL SONOGRAPHERS

School Subjects **Biology** **Chemistry** *Personal Skills* **Helping/teaching** **Technical/scientific** *Work Environment* **Primarily indoors** **Primarily one location**	*Salary Range* **$32,000 to $45,000** **to $59,000+** *Certification or Licensing* **Recommended** *Outlook* **Faster than the average**

THE JOB

Diagnostic medical sonographers use high-frequency sound waves to produce two-dimensional images of internal body organs to be analyzed by physicians or radiologists.

Sonographers are responsible for the proper setup and selection of the ultrasound equipment for each specific exam. They explain the procedure to patients and record any additional information that may be of later use to the physician. When the patient is properly positioned, the sonographer applies a gel to the skin that improves the diagnostic image. The sonographer positions the transducer, a microphone-shaped device that directs high-frequency sound waves into the area to be imaged, and adjusts equipment controls. Sonographers must master the exact location of human anatomy to get a clear picture and be able to clearly differentiate between healthy and diseased organs.

When a clear image is obtained, the sonographer activates equipment that records individual photographic pictures or records real-time images of the affected area. After recording, the sonographer removes the film and prepares it for analysis by the physician or radiologist.

PROFESSIONAL AND PERSONAL REQUIREMENTS

After completing a degree, sonographers can become certified by the American Registry of Diagnostic Medical Sonographers. Although optional, certification is frequently required by employers. In order to stay certified, sonographers must fill continuing education requirements to keep them at the forefront of current technology and diagnostic theory. Licensing requirements may also exist at the state level but vary greatly.

As a prospective sonographer, you need to be technically adept, detail oriented, and precision minded. You need to enjoy helping others and working with a variety of professionals as part of a team. You must be able to follow physician instructions and keep a professional demeanor while still expressing empathy, patience, and understanding in order to reassure patients.

STARTING OUT

To become a sonographer, you must complete a sonographic educational program such as one offered by teaching hospitals, colleges and universities, technical schools, and the armed forces. You should be sure to enroll in an accredited educational program for the best employment opportunities.

Methods of entering the field include responding to job listings in sonography publications, registering with employment agencies specializing in the health care field, contacting headhunters, or applying to the personnel offices of health care employers.

EARNINGS

According to the U.S. Department of Labor, diagnostic medical sonographers earned a median annual income of $44,820 in 2000. The lowest-paid 10 percent of this group, which included those just beginning in the field, made approximately $32,470. The highest-paid 10 percent earned more than $59,310 annually. Median earnings for those who worked in hospitals were $43,950, and earnings for those employed in offices and clinics of medical doctors were $46,190.

Beyond base salaries, sonographers can expect to enjoy many fringe benefits, including paid vacation, sick and personal days, and health and dental insurance.

OUTLOOK

The U.S. Department of Labor predicts employment of diagnostic medical sonographers to grow faster than the average through 2010. One reason for this growth is that sonography is a safe, nonradioactive imaging process. Sonography has proved successful in detecting life-threatening diseases and in analyzing previously nonimageable internal organs. As a result, sonography will play an increasing role in the fields of obstetrics/gynecology and cardiology. Furthermore, the aging population will create high demand for qualified technologists to operate diagnostic machinery. Demand for qualified sonographers exceeds the current supply in some areas of the country, especially rural communities, small towns, and some retirement areas. Those flexible about location and compensation will enjoy the best opportunities in current and future job markets.

FOR MORE INFORMATION

For information about available jobs and credentials, contact:

American Registry of Diagnostic Medical Sonographers
51 Monroe Street, Plaza East One
Rockville, MD 20850-2400
Tel: 800-541-9754
Web: http://www.ardms.org

For information on accredited programs of sonography, contact:

Commission on Accreditation of Allied Health Education Programs
35 East Wacker Drive, Suite 1970
Chicago, IL 60601-2208
Tel: 312-553-9355
Email: caahep@caahep.org
Web: http://www.caahep.org

For information regarding a career in sonography or to subscribe to the Journal of Diagnostic Medical Sonography, *contact:*

Society of Diagnostic Medical Sonography
2745 Dallas Parkway, Suite 350
Plano, TX 75093-4706
Tel: 800-229-9506
Web: http://www.sdms.org

DIALYSIS TECHNICIANS

School Subjects **Biology** **Chemistry**	Salary Range **$29,000 to $35,000** **to $40,000+**
Personal Skills **Helping/teaching** **Technical/scientific**	Certification or Licensing **Required by certain states**
Work Environment **Primarily indoors** **Primarily one location**	Outlook **About as fast as the average**

THE JOB

Dialysis technicians, also called *nephrology technicians* or *renal dialysis technicians,* set up and operate hemodialysis artificial kidney machines for patients with chronic renal failure (CRF). CRF is a condition where a patient's kidneys cease to function normally. Many people, especially diabetics or people who suffer from undetected high blood pressure, develop this condition. These patients require a process called hemodialysis to live. In hemodialysis, the patient's blood is circulated through a dialysis machine, which filters out impurities, wastes, and excess fluids from the blood. The cleaned blood is then returned to the body.

The National Association of Nephrology Technicians and Technologists recognizes three types of dialysis technicians: the patient-care technician, the biomedical equipment technician, and the dialyzer reprocessing (reuse) technician. *Dialysis patient-care technicians* are responsible for preparing the patient for dialysis, monitoring the procedure, and responding to any emergencies that occur during the treatment. *Biomedical equipment technicians* maintain and repair the dialysis machines. *Dialyzer reprocessing technicians* care for the dialyzers, which are the machines through which the blood is filtered. In many dialysis facilities, the technicians' duties as described above may overlap. This depends on the size, staff, and structure of each facility.

PROFESSIONAL AND PERSONAL REQUIREMENTS

In most states, dialysis technicians are not required to be registered, certified, or licensed. However, California and New Mexico do require practicing dialysis technicians to have certification. A growing number of states are considering legislation to make certification mandatory. In some states, technicians are required to pass a test before they can work with patients. You will need to check with your state's department of health or licensing board to determine specific requirements for your area.

The Board of Nephrology Examiners, Nursing and Technology and the National Nephrology Technology Certification Board offer a voluntary program of certification for technicians. These organizations hope that eventually all dialysis technicians will be certified.

Because the slightest mistake can have deadly consequences, dialysis technicians must be thorough and detail oriented, able to respond to stressful situations calmly, and capable of quick thinking in an emergency. If you are interested in this work, you will also need to have compassion and sensitivity in order to help patients deal with both the physical and the emotional effects of their condition.

STARTING OUT

The best way to enter this field is through a formal training program in a hospital or other training facility. You may also contact your local hospital and dialysis center to determine the possibility of on-the-job training. Some hospitals pay trainees as they learn.

Other ways to enter this field are through schools of nursing. If you attend a formal training program, you have a better chance of advancing into jobs with higher pay and responsibility. Most dialysis centers offer additional in-service training for their employees.

EARNINGS

Earnings for dialysis technicians are dependent on such factors as their job performance, responsibilities, locality, and length of service. Many employers pay higher wages to certified technicians than to those who are not certified. Dialysis technicians earn from $10 to $18 an hour, or $20,800 to $37,400 a year, for full-time work. According to the U.S. Bureau of Labor Statistics, the average salary in 2000 for employees in private dialysis centers was $33,398. Employees of local government dialysis centers earned an average of $28,580. Technicians who rise to management positions can earn from $35,000 to $40,000.

Technicians receive the customary benefits of vacation, sick leave or personal time, and health insurance. Many hospitals or health care centers not only offer in-service training but pay tuition and other education costs as an incentive to further self-development and career advancement.

OUTLOOK

There should continue to be a need for dialysis technicians in the future as the number of people with kidney disease and failure increases. According to the National Kidney Foundation (NKF), the principal cause of kidney failure is diabetes. In 2001, approximately 16 million Americans had diabetes, and the NKF projects this number to increase to 22 million by 2025. Aside from those who have a successful kidney transplant, those with kidney failure or disease must have dialysis in order to live, requiring technicians to administer treatment.

FOR MORE INFORMATION

For more information about certification, contact:

Board of Nephrology Examiners, Nursing and Technology
PO Box 15945-282
Lenexa, KS 66285
Tel: 913-541-9077
Web: http://www.goamp.com/bonent

Contact this association for information on scholarships, certification, and the career.

National Association of Nephrology Technicians and Technologists
PO Box 2307
Dayton, OH 45401-2307
Tel: 877-607-6268
Email: nant@nant.meinet.com
Web: http://www.dialysistech.org

DIETETIC TECHNICIANS

School Subjects **Biology** **Chemistry**	*Salary Range* **$13,000 to $21,000** **to $34,000+**
Personal Skills **Helping/teaching** **Technical/scientific**	*Certification or Licensing* **Recommended**
Work Environment **Primarily indoors** **Primarily one location**	*Outlook* **Faster than the average**

THE JOB

Dietetic technicians usually work under the direction of a dietitian. They serve in two basic areas: as service personnel in food-service administration and as assistants in the nutrition care of individuals. In food-service management, dietetic technicians often supervise other food-service employees and oversee the production operation on a day-to-day basis. They are responsible for planning menus and modifying existing recipes to meet specific requirements.

Dietetic technicians who specialize in nutrition care and counseling work under the direction of a clinical or community dietitian. They often work in a health care facility, where they may observe and interview patients about their eating habits and food preferences. Dietetic technicians then report diet histories to the dietitians along with the patients' progress reports. They may also supervise the serving of food to ensure that meals are nutritionally adequate and in conformance with the physicians' prescriptions.

PROFESSIONAL AND PERSONAL REQUIREMENTS

Although dietetic technicians are not required to be licensed or certified, those who have completed an approved education program are eligible to take a certifying examination from the American Dietetic Association. Those who successfully complete the certification exam are designated Dietetic Technicians, Registered.

You should have an interest in nutrition and a desire to serve people if you want to work in this field. You should be patient and understanding, since you may have to deal with people who are ill or uncooperative. Communication skills also are vital, since the job often involves working closely with patients and co-workers.

STARTING OUT

Contacts gained during the clinical experience segment of a training program are often good sources of first jobs for dietetic technicians. Applying to the personnel offices of potential employers is another productive approach. Other good places to check are school placement offices, job listings in health care journals, newspaper classified ads, and private and public employment agencies.

EARNINGS

Earnings vary widely depending on the employer, the education, the experience of the dietetic technician, and the nature of his or her responsibilities. Technicians working in clinical nutrition, involving client assessment and counseling, generally earn less than those working in food and nutrition administration. Generally, however, salaries in this field have been increasing for the past few years, and this trend is expected to continue.

According to The U.S. Department of Labor, dietetic technicians had median annual earnings of $21,340 in 2000. Salaries ranged from less than $13,200 to more than $34,170.

Fringe benefits will depend on the employer, but they usually include paid vacations and holidays, health insurance plans, and meals during working hours.

OUTLOOK

Although the demand for dietetic technicians has been uneven for the past several years, the current outlook is good for the near future. The *Occupational Outlook Handbook* reports that employment for dietetic technicians should grow faster than the average through 2010. This growth is due in part to the strong emphasis placed on nutrition and health in this country. The population is growing, and the percentage of older people, who need the most health services, is increasing even faster.

Another reason for the positive employment outlook is that technicians are marketable. Many of the tasks dietitians used to perform can be done well by dietetic technicians, who are less expensive to hire and are therefore more cost efficient for the employer. Job opportunities will most likely be best for those technicians who have received their certification.

FOR MORE INFORMATION

For information on career development, continuing education, and scholarships, contact:

American Dietetic Association
216 West Jackson Boulevard, Suite 800
Chicago, IL 60606-6995
Tel: 312-899-0040
Email: education@eatright.org
Web: http://www.eatright.org

To learn more about nutrition, visit the U.S. Department of Agriculture Web site:

Center for Nutrition Policy and Promotion
Web: http://www.usda.gov/cnpp

DISPENSING OPTICIANS

School Subjects **Biology** **Mathematics** *Personal Skills* **Helping/teaching** **Technical/scientific** *Work Environment* **Primarily indoors** **Primarily one location**	*Salary Range* **$16,000 to $24,000** **to $40,000+** *Certification or Licensing* **Required by certain states** *Outlook* **About as fast as the average**

THE JOB

Dispensing opticians measure and fit clients with prescription eyeglasses, contact lenses, other low-vision aids, and even artificial eyes. Their tasks include ensuring that eyeglasses are made according to the optometrist's prescription, determining exactly where the lenses should be placed in relation to the pupils of the eyes, assisting the customer in selecting appropriate frames, preparing work orders for the optical laboratory mechanic, and sometimes selling optical goods.

Opticians record lens prescriptions, lens size, and the style and color of the frames to submit to the ophthalmic laboratory. After the glasses return from the lab, the optician makes sure the lenses are made according to the prescription and that they fit the customer correctly. Opticians use small hand tools and precision instruments to make minor adjustments to the frames. Most dispensing opticians work with prescription eyeglasses, but some work with contact lenses. With contacts, technicians measure the curvature of the cornea, and, following the prescription, they prepare specifications for the optical mechanic who manufactures the lens. They must teach the customer how to remove, adjust to, and care for the contacts, a process that can take several weeks.

PROFESSIONAL AND PERSONAL REQUIREMENTS

Voluntary certification is offered by the American Board of Opticianry and the National Contact Lens Examiners. More than 20 states currently require dispensing opticians to be licensed to practice. To become licensed, technicians must meet certain educational standards and pass a written examination. Some states require a practical, hands-on examination as well. To find out more about licensing procedures, contact the licensing board of the state or states in which you plan to work.

To work as a dispensing technician, you should be good at dealing with people and handling administrative tasks. You must exercise great precision, skill, and patience to properly fit patients in contact lenses.

STARTING OUT

Since the usual ways of entering the field are either through completion of a two-year associate degree or through completion of an apprenticeship program, you can use the services of your school's placement office for job leads. Another option is applying directly to optical stores.

EARNINGS

The U.S. Department of Labor reported that in 2000, the median annual income for dispensing opticians was $24,430. The lowest-paid 10 percent, which typically included those beginning in the field, earned less than $15,900 a year. The highest-paid 10 percent earned more than $39,660. Supervisors and those with managerial duties typically earn more than skilled workers, depending on their experience, skills, and responsibilities. Dispensing opticians who own their own stores can earn much more.

OUTLOOK

The U.S. Department of Labor predicts that employment of dispensing opticians will grow as fast as the average through 2010. One reason for this steady growth is an increase in the number of people who need corrective eyeglasses. Educational programs such as vision screening have made the public more aware of eye problems, therefore increasing the need for dispensing opticians. Insurance programs cover more optical needs, which means more clients can afford optical care. The wide variety of fashionable frames also has increased demand for eyeglasses.

Employment opportunities should be especially good in larger urban areas because of the greater number of retail optical stores. Those with an associate's degree in opticianry should be most successful in their job search.

FOR MORE INFORMATION

For information on certification, contact:

American Board of Opticianry/National Contact Lens Examiners
6506 Loisdale Road, Suite 209
Springfield, VA 22150
Tel: 703-719-5800
Web: http://www.ncleabo.org

For information on education and training programs, contact the following organizations:

Commission on Opticianry Accreditation
PO Box 3073
Merrifield, VA 22116-3073
Tel: 703-766-1600
Email: coa@erols.com
Web: http://www.coaccreditation.com

National Academy of Opticianry
8401 Corporate Drive, Suite 605
Landover, MD 20785
Tel: 800-229-4828
Web: http://www.nao.org

Opticians Association of America
7023 Little River Turnpike, Suite 207
Annandale, VA 22003
Tel: 703-916-8856
Email: oaa@oaa.org
Web: http://www.oaa.org

DRAFTERS

School Subjects **Art** **Mathematics** *Personal Skills* **Artistic** **Technical/scientific** *Work Environment* **Primarily indoors** **Primarily one location**	*Salary Range* **$23,000 to $35,000** **to $61,000** *Certification or Licensing* **Recommended** *Outlook* **About as fast as the average**

THE JOB

Drafters prepare working plans and detailed drawings of products or structures from the rough sketches and calculations of engineers, architects, and designers. These drawings are used in engineering or manufacturing processes to reproduce exactly the product or structure desired, according to the specified dimensions. The drafter uses knowledge of various machines, engineering practices, mathematics, and building materials, along with other physical sciences and fairly extensive computer skills, to complete the drawings. Drafters often are classified according to the type of work they do, such as chief drafters, detailers, checkers, and tracers. Drafters also may specialize in a particular field of work, such as mechanical, electrical, plumbing, landscaping, automotive, aeronautical, or architectural drafting.

PROFESSIONAL AND PERSONAL REQUIREMENTS

Certification is not presently required but is recommended in this field. More and more, employers are looking for graduates whose skills have been approved by a reliable industry source. The American Design Drafting Association offers student certification. Graduates who take advantage of these services will not only enhance their professional credibility but also gain an edge in the job market. Currently, there are no licensing requirements.

If you are interested in drafting, you should have a good sense of both spatial and formal perception. Good hand-eye coordination is also necessary for the fine detail work involved in drafting.

STARTING OUT

After graduating from a postsecondary program at a technical institute or junior college, you can look for jobs through traditional methods, such as using classified ads and the Internet and through professional associations. If you are interested in a government position, you may need to take a civil service examination.

Beginning or inexperienced drafters often start as tracers, working as an assistant to a drafter. *Tracers* make corrections and prepare drawings for reproduction by tracing them on transparent cloth, paper, or plastic film. If you have some formal postsecondary technical training, you may be able to qualify for a position as a junior drafter, revising detailed drawings and assuming some drawing assignments of a more complex nature.

EARNINGS

Students with more extensive advanced training tend to earn higher beginning salaries. Salaries also are affected by regional demands in specific specialties, so where a drafter chooses to live and work will play a part in his or her salary. According to the U.S. Department of Labor, median hourly earnings of architectural and civil drafters were $16.93 in 2000, although earnings ranged from $11.18 to $26.13 an hour. Median hourly earnings of electrical and electronics drafters were $18.37 and mechanical drafters earned $18.19. In general, full-time drafters earned from less than $23,254 to more than $61,276 a year.

Employers generally offer drafters a range of benefit options, including health and life insurance, retirement plans, and paid vacation.

OUTLOOK

The U.S. Department of Labor predicts employment for drafters to increase about as fast as the average through 2010. Increasing use of computer-aided design (CAD) technology will limit the demand for less skilled drafters, but industrial growth and more complex designs of new products and manufacturing processes will increase the demand for all drafting services. In addition, drafters are beginning to break out of the traditional drafting role and increasingly do work traditionally performed by engineers and architects. Employment trends for drafters do fluctuate with the economy, however. During recessions, fewer buildings and manufactured products are designed, which could reduce the need for drafters in architectural, engineering, and manufacturing firms.

FOR MORE INFORMATION

For information on careers in drafting and certification, contact:

American Design Drafting Association
PO Box 11937
Columbia, SC 29211
Tel: 803-771-0008
Email: national@adda.org
Web: http://www.adda.org

For news on laws affecting the field and other current topics, contact this union for the drafting community:

International Federation of Professional and Technical Engineers
8630 Fenton Street, Suite 400
Silver Spring, MD 20910
Tel: 301-565-9016
Web: http://www.ifpte.org

ELECTRICIANS

School Subjects	Salary Range
Mathematics	**$24,000 to $41,000**
Technical/shop	**to $66,000+**
Personal Skills	*Certification or Licensing*
Mechanical/manipulative	**Required by certain states**
Technical/scientific	*Outlook*
Work Environment	**About as fast as the average**
Primarily indoors	
Primarily multiple locations	

THE JOB

Electricians design, assemble, install, test, and repair electrical fixtures and wiring. They work on a wide range of electrical and data communications systems that provide light, heat, refrigeration, air conditioning, power, and the ability to communicate.

Many electricians specialize in either construction or maintenance work, although some work in both areas. *Construction electricians* are usually employed by electrical contractors. Other construction electricians work for building contractors or industrial plants, public utilities, state highway departments, or other large organizations that employ workers to build or remodel their properties. Some electricians are self-employed.

Maintenance electricians, also known as *electrical repairers*, do similar tasks, but their activities are usually aimed at preventing trouble before it occurs.

PROFESSIONAL AND PERSONAL REQUIREMENTS

Electronics specialists can choose to receive certification training and testing through the International Society of Certified Electronic Technicians. Some states require that electricians be licensed. To obtain a license, electricians usually must pass a written examination on electrical theory, National Electrical Code requirements, and local building and electrical codes.

Working as an electrician, you will need agility and manual dexterity to do sometimes physically taxing work. You should also enjoy working as part of a team, both indoors and outside, and be good at working with your hands.

STARTING OUT

You can enter this field by working as a helper or through an apprenticeship program. To find a helper job, check newspaper classified ads, contact electrical contractors directly, or consult the local office of your state's employment service. If you choose to attend a trade or vocational program, you may be able to find job openings through your school's placement office.

To work as an apprentice, you should contact a local chapter of the International Brotherhood of Electrical Workers or the Independent Electrical Contractors. Information on apprenticeships is also available through your state's employment service.

EARNINGS

Most full-time electricians working for contractors average about $21 per hour, or $41,000 per year, according to the National Joint Apprenticeship Training Committee, though it is possible to make much more. According to the U.S. Department of Labor, median hourly earnings of electricians were $19.29 in 2000. Wages ranged from less than $11.31 to more than $31.71 an hour, or from $23,524 to $65,956 yearly for full-time work. Beginning apprentices earn 40 percent of the base electrician's wage and receive pay increases each year of their apprenticeship.

Overall, it's important to realize that wages can vary widely, depending on a number of factors, including geographic location, the industry in which an electrician works, prevailing economic conditions, and union membership.

Electricians who are members of the International Brotherhood of Electrical Workers, the industry's main labor union, are entitled to benefits including paid vacation days, health insurance, retirement pensions, and unemployment compensation plans.

OUTLOOK

The U.S. Department of Labor predicts that employment of electricians will grow about as fast as the average through 2010. This growth will result from an overall increase in both residential and commercial construction. In addition, growth will be driven by the expanding use of electrical and electronic devices and equipment. In particular, the use of sophisticated computer, telecommunications, and data-processing equipment is expected to provide electricians with many job opportunities.

While the overall outlook for this occupational field is good, the availability of jobs will vary over time. The employment of electricians in construction fluctuates depending on the state of the local and national economy. Maintenance electricians are usually less vulnerable to periodic unemployment because they are more likely to work for one employer that needs steady electrical services.

FOR MORE INFORMATION

For information about the benefits of joining a labor union, contact:

International Brotherhood of Electrical Workers
1125 15th Street, NW
Washington, DC 20005
Tel: 202-833-7000
Web: http://www.ibew.org

For information on certification, contact:

International Society of Certified Electronic Technicians
3608 Pershing Avenue
Fort Worth, TX 76107-4527
Tel: 817-921-9101
Web: http://www.iscet.org

For industry information, contact:

National Electrical Contractors Association
3 Bethesda Metro Center, Suite 1100
Bethesda, MD 20814
Tel: 301-657-3110
Web: http://www.necanet.org

For background information on apprenticeship and training programs aimed at union workers, contact:

National Joint Apprenticeship Training Committee
301 Prince George's Boulevard, Suite D
Upper Marlboro, MD 20774
Email: office@njatc.org
Web: http://www.njatc.org

ELECTRONEURO-DIAGNOSTIC TECHNOLOGISTS

School Subjects **Biology** **Physics** *Personal Skills* **Mechanical/manipulative** **Technical/scientific** *Work Environment* **Primarily indoors** **Primarily one location**	*Salary Range* **$25,000 to $38,000** **to $70,000** *Certification or Licensing* **Recommended** *Outlook* **Little change or more slowly** **than the average**

THE JOB

Electroneurodiagnostic technologists, sometimes called *EEG technologists* or *END technologists,* operate electronic instruments called electroencephalographs. These instruments measure and record the brain's electrical activity. The information gathered is used by physicians (usually neurologists) to diagnose and determine the effects of certain diseases and injuries, including brain tumors, cerebral vascular strokes, Alzheimer's disease, epilepsy, some metabolic disorders, and brain injuries caused by accidents or infectious diseases.

The EEG technologist's first task with a new patient is to take a simplified medical history. This entails asking questions and recording answers about his or her past health problems.

The technologist then applies electrodes to the patient's head, which are connected to the recording equipment. The equipment has several sensitive electronic amplifiers that transmit information to writing instruments. Tracings from each electrode can be seen on a moving strip of paper in response to the amplified impulses coming from the brain. The resulting graph is a recording of the patient's brain waves.

EEG technologists are not responsible for interpreting the tracings (that is the job of neurologists); however, they must be able to recognize abnormal brain activity and any readings on the tracing that are coming from somewhere other than the brain, such as readings of eye movement or nearby electrical equipment.

PROFESSIONAL AND PERSONAL REQUIREMENTS

The American Board of Registration of Electroencephalographic and Evoked Potential Technologists offers certification as a registered electroencephalographic technologist. Although not required, registration shows the technologist's training and can make advancement easier. Registration may also provide a salary increase. There are no licensing requirements.

Good vision and manual dexterity are necessary to work as an EEG technologist. You also must be able to get along well with patients, their families, and members of the hospital staff.

STARTING OUT

Technologists often obtain permanent employment in the hospital where they received their on-the-job or work-study training. You can also find employment through classified ads in newspapers and by contacting the personnel offices of hospitals, medical centers, clinics, and government agencies that employ EEG technologists.

EARNINGS

According to the American Society of Electroneurodiagnostic Technologists, salaries range from $25,000 for new graduates of electroneurodiagnostic programs to more than $70,000 for lab managers of independent contractors. The average salary for all EEG technologists was $37,853 in 2000. Earnings depend on education, experience, level of responsibility, type of employment, and geographic region. Salaries for registered EEG technologists tended to be higher than for nonregistered technologists with equivalent experience.

Technologists working in hospitals receive the same fringe benefits as other hospital workers, usually including health insurance, paid vacations, and sick leave. In some cases, the benefits may also include educational assistance, pension plans, and uniform allowances.

OUTLOOK

Employment of electroneurodiagnostic technologists is expected to grow more slowly than the average, primarily because of new procedures and technologies that require fewer workers or even lesser trained workers to do the work of EEG technologists. The slow growth should be offset somewhat by population growth and an increase in the use of electroencephalographs in surgery, diagnosis, monitoring, and research. There is some promise of employment for EEG technologists in the area of polysomnography and long-term monitoring for epilepsy and intraoperative monitoring.

FOR MORE INFORMATION

For information and an application to start the EEG or Evoked Potential examination process, contact:

American Board of Registration of Electroencephalographic and Evoked Potential Technologists
1904 Croydon Drive
Springfield, IL 62703
Tel: 217-553-3758
Email: abreteo@aol.com
Web: http://www.abret.org

For a career brochure and information about scholarship, contact:

American Society of Electroneurodiagnostic Technologists
204 West 7th Street
Carroll, IA 51401-2317
Tel: 712-792-2978
Email: info@aset.org
Web: http://www.aset.org

For information on polysomnograms and sleep disorders, contact:

Association of Polysomnographic Technology
PO Box 14861
Lenexa, KS 66285-4861
Tel: 913-541-1991
Web: http://www.aptweb.org

ELECTRONICS ENGINEERING TECHNICIANS

School Subjects	Salary Range
Computer science **Mathematics**	**$25,000 to $40,000** **to $58,000+**
Personal Skills **Mechanical/manipulative** **Technical/scientific**	*Certification or Licensing* **Voluntary**
Work Environment **Primarily indoors** **Primarily one location**	*Outlook* **About as fast as the average**

THE JOB

Electronics engineering technicians work with electronics engineers to design, develop, and manufacture industrial and consumer electronic equipment, including sonar, radar, and navigational equipment and computers, radios, televisions, stereos, and calculators. They are involved in operating, testing, troubleshooting, repairing, and maintaining equipment. Those involved in the development of new electronics help make changes or modifications in circuitry or other design elements. Other electronics technicians inspect newly installed equipment or instruct and supervise less-experienced technicians.

As part of their normal duties, all electronics engineering technicians set up testing equipment, conduct tests, and analyze results. They also prepare reports, sketches, graphs, and schematic drawings to describe electronics systems and their characteristics. Their work involves the use of a variety of hand and machine tools, including such equipment as bench lathes and drills.

PROFESSIONAL AND PERSONAL REQUIREMENTS

Certification, which is voluntary, is offered by the International Society of Certified Electronics Technicians, the Electronics

Technicians Association, and the American Society of Certified Engineering Technicians.

If you are interested in this work, you should have an interest in and an aptitude for mathematics and science and should enjoy using tools and scientific equipment. On the personal side, you should be patient, methodical, persistent, and able to get along with different kinds of people. You need to be a quick learner and willing to stay informed about new developments in the industry.

STARTING OUT

You may be able to find your first full-time position through your school's job placement office. These offices tend to develop very good working relationships with area employers and can offer you excellent interviewing opportunities.

Another way to find a job is by directly contacting a particular company. It is best to write to the personnel department and include a resume summarizing your education and experience. There are also many excellent public and commercial employment organizations that can help graduates obtain jobs appropriate to their training and experience. In addition, the classified ads in most metropolitan Sunday newspapers list a number of job openings with companies in the area.

EARNINGS

According to the Economic Research Institute, earnings for electronics technicians ranged from $27,000 for beginning technicians to $40,000 for those with 10 years of experience. The Bureau of Labor Statistics reports that in 2000, median annual earnings were $40,020, and salaries ranged from less than $25,210 to more than $58,320.

Electronics engineering technicians generally receive premium pay for overtime work on Sundays, holidays, evenings, and night-shift work. Most employers offer benefits packages that include paid holidays, paid vacations, sick days, and health insurance. Companies may also offer pension and retirement plans, profit sharing, 401-K plans, tuition assistance programs, and release time for additional education.

OUTLOOK

The U.S. Department of Labor estimates that opportunities for electronics engineering technicians will increase as fast as the average through 2010. Foreign competition, general economic conditions, and levels of government spending may affect certain areas of the field to some degree. However, this is an industry that is becoming so central to our lives and for which there is still such growth potential that it seems unlikely that any single factor could substantially curb its growth and its need for specially trained personnel.

Although there will be fluctuations in growth for certain subfields, there will be a need for qualified personnel in others. The key to success for an electronics technician is to stay up to date with technology and to be professionally versatile. Building a career on a solid academic and hands-on foundation in basic electronics enables an electronics technician to remain competitive in the job market.

FOR MORE INFORMATION

For information on careers, educational programs, student chapters, and certification, contact the following organizations:

American Society of Certified Engineering Technicians
PO Box 1348
Flowery Branch, GA 30542
Tel: 770-967-9173
Web: http://www.ascet.org

Institute of Electrical and Electronics Engineers, Inc.
1828 L Street, NW, Suite 1202
Washington, DC 20036-5104
Tel: 202-785-0017
Email: ieeeusa@ieee.org
Web: http://www.ieee.org

International Society of Certified Electronics Technicians
3608 Pershing Avenue
Fort Worth, TX 76107-4527
Tel: 817-921-9101
Email: info@iscet.org
Web: http://www.iscet.org

EMERGENCY MEDICAL TECHNICIANS

School Subjects **Biology** **Health**	*Salary Range* **$15,000 to $22,000** **to $38,000+**
Personal Skills **Helping/teaching** **Technical/scientific**	*Certification or Licensing* **Required**
Work Environment **Indoors and outdoors** **Primarily multiple locations**	*Outlook* **Much faster than the average**

THE JOB

Emergency medical technicians (EMTs) provide on-site emergency care. Their goal is to rapidly identify the nature of the emergency, stabilize the patient's condition, and initiate proper medical procedures at the scene and en route to a hospital. Once at the scene, EMTs may find victims who are burned, trapped under fallen objects, lacerated, in childbirth, poisoned, emotionally disturbed, or unconscious. After evaluating the situation and the victim's condition, EMTs must establish the priorities of required care. They administer emergency treatment, monitor patients, and provide care while transporting victims to the hospital. Once at the hospital, EMTs help the staff bring victims to the emergency area and may assist with the initial steps of in-hospital care. EMTs then check in with their dispatchers and prepare the vehicle for another emergency call.

PROFESSIONAL AND PERSONAL REQUIREMENTS

All 50 states have certification requirements. Some states offer new EMTs the choice of the National Registry examination or the state's own certification examination.

At present, the National Registry of Emergency Medical Technicians recognizes three levels of competency: EMT-basic, EMT-intermediate, and EMT-paramedics. Although it is not always essential for EMTs to become registered with one of these three ratings, you can expect better job prospects as you attain higher levels of registration.

If you want to work as an EMT, you should enjoy helping people and be emotionally stable, clearheaded, and in good physical condition. You will need good manual dexterity and motor coordination, the ability to lift and carry up to 125 pounds, good vision and judgment, and competence in giving and receiving verbal and written communication.

STARTING OUT

After your basic EMT program, a good place to start looking for a job is through the school or agency that provided the training. You can also apply directly to local ambulance services, fire departments, and employment agencies.

In some areas, you may face stiff competition if you are seeking full-time paid employment immediately upon graduation. Volunteer work is an option for EMTs. Volunteers are likely to average eight to 12 hours of work per week. If you are a beginning EMT without prior work experience in the health field, you may find it advantageous to start your career as a part-time volunteer to gain experience.

Flexibility about the location of a job may help you gain a foothold on the career ladder. If you are willing to relocate to where demand for EMTs is higher, you should have a better chance of finding employment.

EARNINGS

Earnings of EMTs depend on the type of employer and individual level of training and experience. Those working in the public sector, employed by police and fire departments, usually receive a higher wage than those in the private sector, employed by ambulance companies and hospitals. Salary levels typically rise with increasing levels of skill, training, and certification.

According to the U.S. Department of Labor, median annual earnings of EMTs and paramedics were $22,460 in 2000. Salaries ranged from less than $14,660 to more than $37,760. For those who worked in local government, the median salary was $24,800; in hospitals, $23,590; and in local and suburban transportation, $20,950.

Benefits vary widely depending on the employer but generally include paid holidays and vacations, health insurance, and pension plans.

OUTLOOK

Overall, this industry is expected to grow much faster than the average for all occupations through 2010. The proportion of older people, who most use emergency medical services, is growing in many communities, placing more demands on the emergency medical services delivery system and increasing the need for EMTs.

However, the employment outlook for paid EMTs depends partly on the community in which they are seeking employment. Many communities perceive the advantages of high-quality emergency medical services and are willing and able to raise tax dollars to support them. In these communities, the employment outlook should remain favorable. In other communities, particularly smaller ones, the employment outlook is not so favorable. Maintaining a high-quality emergency medical services delivery system can be expensive, and financial strains on some local governments could limit the employment of EMTs.

FOR MORE INFORMATION

For educational programs and scholarship information, contact:

National Association of Emergency Medical Technicians
408 Monroe Street
Clinton, MS 39056-4210
Tel: 800-346-2368
Email: info@naemt.org
Web: http://www.naemt.org

For information on testing for EMT certification, contact:

National Registry of Emergency Medical Technicians
Rocco V. Morando Building
PO Box 29233
6610 Busch Boulevard
Columbus, OH 43229
Tel: 614-888-4484
Web: http://www.nremt.org

ENVIRONMENTAL TECHNICIANS

School Subjects **Biology** **Chemistry**	*Salary Range* **$17,000 to $34,000** **to $50,000+**
Personal Skills **Mechanical/manipulative** **Technical/scientific**	*Certification or Licensing* **Required for certain** **positions**
Work Environment **Indoors and outdoors** **One location with travel**	*Outlook* **About as fast as the average**

THE JOB

Environmental technicians, also known as *pollution control technicians,* conduct tests and field investigations to obtain soil samples and other data. Their research is used by engineers, scientists, and others who help clean up, monitor, control, or prevent pollution. They apply engineering, chemistry, meteorology, agriculture, and other disciplines in their work, generally specializing in air, water, or soil pollution.

Although work differs by employer and specialty, environmental technicians collect samples for laboratory analysis, using specialized instruments and equipment. They also monitor pollution control devices and systems and perform various other investigations to evaluate pollution problems. They follow strict procedures in collecting and recording data in order to meet the requirements of environmental laws.

PROFESSIONAL AND PERSONAL REQUIREMENTS

Certification is required for some positions in pollution control, especially those in which sanitation, public health, a public water supply, or a sewage treatment system is involved. The Institute of Professional Environmental Practice offers the Qualified Environmental Professional (QEP) and the Environmental Professional Intern (EPI) certifications. See the end of this article for contact information.

To work as an environmental technician, you should be patient, detail oriented, and capable of following instructions. You need to be able to read and understand technical materials, charts, maps, and diagrams. Computer skills are also helpful. Finally, you should be in good physical condition to be able to conduct your field work, such as climbing up smokestacks to take emission samples.

STARTING OUT

Specific job opportunities will vary depending on the geographic area that you live in, your chosen specialization within the environmental industry (air, water, or land), the economy, and other factors. Many beginning technicians find the greatest number of positions available in state or local government agencies.

Most schools provide job-hunting advice and assistance. If you hope to find a job outside your current geographic area, you may find contacting national professional organizations a useful way to start networking.

EARNINGS

Pay for environmental technicians varies widely. Public-sector positions tend to pay less than private-sector positions. According to the U.S. Department of Labor, median hourly earnings of environmental science and protection technicians, including health technicians, were $16.26 (roughly $33,820 a year) in 2000. Government entry-level salaries for environmental technicians ranged from $17,483 to $22,251 per year, depending on education and experience. Those who become managers or supervisors can earn up to $50,000 per year or more.

Environmental technicians generally enjoy benefits such as paid vacation, sick time, and employer-paid training. Technicians who work full-time (and some who work part-time) often have health insurance benefits. Those who are employed by the federal government may get additional benefits, such as pension and retirement benefits.

OUTLOOK

Demand for environmental technicians is expected to increase about as fast as the average through 2010. Those trained to handle increasingly complex technical demands will have the upper hand. Environmental technicians will be needed to regulate waste products; to collect air, water, and soil samples for measuring levels of pollutants; to check for compliance with environmental regulations; and to clean up contaminated sites.

Demand will be higher in some areas of the country than in others depending on specialty. For example, air pollution technicians will be especially in demand in large cities, such as Los Angeles and New York, which face pressure to comply with national air quality standards.

Perhaps one of the greatest factors affecting environmental work is continued mandates for pollution control by the federal government. As long as the federal government is supporting pollution control, the environmental technician will be needed.

FOR MORE INFORMATION

The following organization is an environmental careers resource for high school and college students.

Environmental Careers Organization
179 South Street
Boston, MA 02111
Tel: 617-426-4375
Web: http://www.eco.org

For information on environmental careers and student employment opportunities, contact:

Environmental Protection Agency
Ariel Rios Building
1200 Pennsylvania Avenue, NW
Washington, DC 20460
Tel: 202-260-2090
Web: http://www.epa.gov

For information on certification, contact:

Institute of Professional Environmental Practice
600 Forbes Avenue
333 Fisher Hall
Pittsburgh, PA 15282
Tel: 412-396-1703
Email: ipep@duq.edu
Web: http://www.ipep.org

FASHION DESIGNERS

School Subjects **Art** **Family and consumer science**	*Salary Range* **$25,000 to $49,000** **to $150,000+**
Personal Skills **Artistic** **Communication/ideas**	*Certification or Licensing* **None available**
Work Environment **Primarily indoors** **One location with travel**	*Outlook* **Faster than the average**

THE JOB

Fashion designers create or adapt original designs for clothing for men, women, and children. Some designers specialize in one particular type of clothing, such as women's dresses or men's suits. Most work for textile, apparel, and pattern manufacturers. Other designers are self-employed and develop a clientele of individual customers or manufacturers. Designers also work for fashion salons, high-fashion department stores, and specialty shops. A small percentage of designers work in the entertainment industry, designing costumes.

An interesting specialty within fashion design is theatrical design, a relatively limited field but challenging to those who are interested in combining an interest in theater with a talent for clothing design.

PROFESSIONAL AND PERSONAL REQUIREMENTS

There is no certification or licensing available in this field.

If you are interested in working in fashion design, you must be artistic and imaginative with a flair for color and clothing coordination. You need a working knowledge of clothing construction and an eye for trends. You also must possess a technical aptitude, problem-solving skills, and the ability to conceptualize in two and three dimensions. Personal qualifications include self-motivation, team spirit, and the ability to handle pressure, deadlines, and long hours. This career also demands energy and a good head for business.

STARTING OUT

Few people begin their careers as fashion designers. If you have been well trained, you may be able to get a job as an assistant designer. However, these jobs can be hard to locate, so you may have to accept beginning jobs in apparel manufacturing, spending time cutting or constructing garments.

If you have attended a fashion design school, you may receive placement information from your school's placement office. Approaching stores and manufacturers directly is another way to secure a beginning position. This will be easier for you if you are known in the industry through summer or part-time work.

EARNINGS

Fashion designers earned an average annual salary of $48,530 in 2000, according to the *Occupational Outlook Handbook.* The lowest-paid 10 percent earned less than $24,710; the highest 10 percent earned more than $103,970. A few highly skilled and well-known designers in top firms have annual incomes of over $150,000. Top fashion designers who have successful lines of clothing can earn bonuses that bring their annual incomes into the millions of dollars.

Theatrical designers usually work on a contract basis. Although the compensation for the total contract is usually good, there may be long periods of idleness between contracts. The annual incomes for theatrical designers usually are not as great as those of fashion designers, although while they are working they may be making more than $1,000 per week.

OUTLOOK

According to the *Occupational Outlook Handbook,* employment of designers is expected to grow faster than the average for all occupations through 2010. Increasing populations and growing personal incomes are expected to spur the demand for fashion designers. However, relatively few designers are needed to make employment possible for thousands of people in other apparel occupations. There are approximately 16,000 fashion designers in the United States, which represents less than 1 percent of the garment industry.

Fashion designers at the top of their profession rarely leave their positions. Therefore, opportunities for newcomers are limited. There always will be more people hoping to break into the field than there are available jobs. Experience working with computer-aided design programs is increasingly important to employers and can help to distinguish a qualified job candidate from the rest of his or her competition. Employment prospects may be better in specialized areas, such as children's clothing. Additionally, openings are more readily available for assistant designers.

FOR MORE INFORMATION

Those interested in creating men's fashions should check out the CTDA's Web site for business and training information.

Custom Tailors and Designers Association of America (CTDA)
PO Box 53052
Washington, DC 20009
Tel: 202-387-7220
Web: http://www.ctda.com

For information about programs and an application, contact the FIT:

Fashion Institute of Technology (FIT)
Admissions Office
Seventh Avenue at 27th Street
New York, NY 10001-5992
Tel: 212-217-7999
Email: FITinfo@fitsuny.edu
Web: http://www.fitnyc.suny.edu

For a list of accredited schools, contact:

National Association of Schools of Art and Design
11250 Roger Bacon Drive, Suite 21
Reston, VA 20190
Tel: 703-437-0700
Email: info@arts-accredit.org
Web: http://www.arts-accredit.org/nasad

For information on the fashion industry, check out the following magazine's Web site:

Women's Wear Daily
Web: http://www.wwd.com

FIBER OPTICS TECHNICIANS

School Subjects **Mathematics** **Technical/shop**	*Salary Range* **$20,000 to $38,000** **to $55,000+**
Personal Skills **Mechanical/manipulative** **Technical/scientific**	*Certification or Licensing* **Voluntary**
Work Environment **Indoors and outdoors** **Primarily multiple locations**	*Outlook* **Faster than the average**

THE JOB

Fiber optics technicians prepare, install, and test fiber optics transmission systems. These systems are composed of fiber optic cables that allow for data communication between computers, phones, and faxes. When working for a telecommunications company, these technicians are often required to install lines for local area networks (LANs), which serve small areas of linked computers, such as in an office.

The telecommunications company for which a technician works will contract with a company to create a communications system. A salesman will evaluate the customer's need and then order the materials for the installation. Fiber optics technicians take these materials to the job site. Because each job site is different, technicians first need to get a sense of the area. They walk through with the client, evaluating the areas where they'll be installing fiber optic cable. Newer buildings should be readily equipped for installation. However, in some older buildings, it may be more difficult to get behind ceiling tiles and in the walls.

After they've readied the area for cable, fiber optics technicians run the cable from the computer's mainframe to individual workstations. They test the connection, using power meters and other devices, to measure the amount of time it takes for signals to be transmitted. If there are any faults in the fiber link, or if there is signal loss, technicians must correct it until the LAN is running smoothly.

PROFESSIONAL AND PERSONAL REQUIREMENTS

There are no licensing requirements to work as a fiber optics technician. The Fiber Optic Association offers voluntary certification to qualified applicants. See the contact information listed at the end of the article.

Because of the fine nature of the fibers, you will need a steady hand and good eyesight if you are interested in assembling fiber optic cables. You also need good math skills to work with detailed plans and designs. Some companies may require technicians to have their own special fiber optic tools.

STARTING OUT

There are many sources of information about developments and employment opportunities in fiber optics and the telecommunications industry, including FiberOptic Product News Online (http://www.fpnmag.com). When you complete a fiber optics technology program, your school should be able to direct you to local job opportunities. Another good source is Information Gatekeepers, which publishes a fiber optics career directory listing over 1,000 companies. Visit the Web site, http://www.igigroup.com, for more information.

EARNINGS

Telecommunications line installers and repairers had median hourly earnings of $18.32 in 2000, or roughly $38,106 a year, according to the U.S. Department of Labor. Ten percent earned less than $9.79 an hour ($20,363 a year), and 10 percent earned more than $26.68 an hour ($55,494 a year).

Companies offer a variety of benefit packages, which can include any of the following: paid holidays, vacations, and sick days; personal days; medical, dental, and life insurance; profit-sharing plans; 401-K plans; retirement and pension plans; and educational assistance programs.

OUTLOOK

Digital transmissions will soon be the standard in telecommunications. Not only do modern offices require data communications systems, but cable companies are also investing in fiber optics to offer digital TV and cable as well as quality phone service. Also, the cost of fiber optics is dropping, which means more companies can and will invest in it. As a result, experienced fiber optics assemblers and installers should find plenty of job opportunities.

FOR MORE INFORMATION

To learn about certification and training opportunities, contact:

The Fiber Optic Association
2 Florence Street, Third Floor
Malden, MA 02148
Tel: 781-397-2400
Email: info@thefoa.org
Web: http://www.thefoa.org

To learn about telecommunications technology and the number of uses for fiber optics, visit the OSA Web site:

Optical Society of America (OSA)
2010 Massachusetts Avenue, NW
Washington, DC 20036
Tel: 202-223-8130
Web: http://www.osa.org

To learn about opportunities for women in the fiber optics industry, contact:

Women in Cable and Telecommunications
230 West Monroe, Suite 2630
Chicago, IL 60606
Tel: 312-634-2330
Web: http://www.wict.org

FIRE SAFETY TECHNICIANS

School Subjects **Chemistry** **Mathematics** *Personal Skills* **Following instructions** **Technical/scientific** *Work Environment* **Indoors and outdoors** **One location with travel**	*Salary Range* **$21,000 to $33,000** **to $60,000+** *Certification or Licensing* **Recommended** *Outlook* **Faster than the average**

THE JOB

Fire safety technicians work to prevent fires. Typical duties include conducting safety inspections and planning fire protection systems. In the course of their job, fire safety technicians recognize fire hazards and control and prevent fires. Fire safety technicians are employed by local fire departments, fire insurance companies, industrial organizations, government agencies, and businesses dealing with fire protection equipment and consulting services.

Public education is an important job of fire control and safety technicians. By working with the public through schools, businesses, and service organizations, technicians can spread understanding of the dangers of fires and teach people about fire protection and fire prevention.

Specific positions in this field include fire science specialists, fire extinguisher servicers, fire insurance inspectors, fire insurance underwriters, fire inspectors, plant protection inspectors, fire alarm superintendents, and fire service field instructors.

PROFESSIONAL AND PERSONAL REQUIREMENTS

Certification is required for some fire safety professions. The Board of Certified Safety Professionals offers the designations Associate Safety Professional (ASP) and Certified Safety Professional (CSP). Although there is no specific certification unique to fire safety technicians, anyone wishing to advance in the field of fire safety should get the ASP and CSP designations. These credentials demonstrate that the technician has completed a high level of education, has passed written examinations, and has acquired a certain amount of professional experience. There is no separate licensing requirement for this work.

To be successful as a fire science technician, you must have excellent oral and written communication skills. You must be willing to study to keep abreast of new developments in the field, including improvements in fire detection instruments, equipment, and methods for fireproofing materials.

STARTING OUT

After graduating from your two-year program in a technical college, community college, or technical institute, you should be able to secure a job before you graduate. Company recruiters are sent to school placement offices, which arrange interviews for graduating students. Your placement officers or fire science instructors usually keep contacts open to help place graduates.

If available, take advantage of cooperative work-study programs where you can study part-time and work part-time for pay. Employers who participate in cooperative programs will provide you with experience in different tasks so you can learn about various aspects in fire safety. Many times, students in such programs are hired permanently by the cooperating employer.

You can also find a job with a fire department that is large enough to need special technicians outside the ranks of regular firefighters. You may also choose to become a firefighter and eventually advance to technical positions.

EARNINGS

Beginning salaries for fire safety technicians tend to be higher than those of other technicians. This is partly due to the shortage of qualified personnel in the field. Starting salaries are approximately $20,500 to $22,000. Experienced technicians earn salaries that average between $33,000 to $44,000 per year. Those who advance to positions of great responsibility may earn $60,000 per year or more.

Benefits for these employees usually include time off or overtime pay for hours worked beyond the regular work schedule.

Other benefits include pension plans, disability benefits, early retirement options, paid vacations, paid sick leave, and in some cases, paid holidays or time off for holidays worked.

OUTLOOK

Technical careers in fire prevention and control are predicted to grow more rapidly than the average for all other occupations. In the future, fire safety technicians will probably be needed in more places than ever before. The greatest increase in employment will be in industry. More industries are finding that the cost of replacing buildings and property destroyed by fire is greater than the yearly cost of fire protection and the expertise and equipment of these specialists.

New fire prevention and control techniques must be developed as technology continues to change. Skilled and ambitious fire safety technicians will be needed to address and monitor this changing technology.

FOR MORE INFORMATION

For information on ASP and CSP certifications, contact:

Board of Certified Safety Professionals
208 Burwash Avenue
Savoy, IL 61874
Tel: 217-359-9263
Web: http://www.bcsp.com

For information on fire prevention careers, contact:

National Fire Protection Association
One Batterymarch Park
Quincy, MA 02269-9101
Tel: 617-770-3000
Web: http://www.nfpa.org

For information on student chapters and a list of universities that offer programs in fire protection engineering, contact:

Society of Fire Protection Engineers
7315 Wisconsin Avenue, Suite 1225W
Bethesda, MD 20814
Tel: 301-718-2910
Web: http://www.sfpe.org

FIREFIGHTERS

School Subjects	*Salary Range*
Biology	**$21,000 to $43,000**
Chemistry	**to $78,000**
Personal Skills	*Certification or Licensing*
Leadership/management	**Recommended**
Mechanical/manipulative	*Outlook*
Work Environment	**Little change or more slowly**
Indoors and outdoors	**than the average**
Primarily multiple locations	

THE JOB

Firefighters are responsible for protecting people's lives and property from the hazards of fire and other emergencies. They provide this protection by fighting fires to prevent property damage and by rescuing people trapped or injured by fires or other accidents. Through inspections and safety education, firefighters also work to prevent fires and unsafe conditions that could result in dangerous, life-threatening situations. They assist in many types of emergencies and disasters in everyday life. Firefighters often answer calls requesting emergency medical care, such as help in giving artificial respiration to drowning victims or emergency aid for heart attack victims. They may also administer emergency medical care. Many fire departments operate emergency medical services. Most firefighters are cross-trained to participate in both fire and emergency activities.

PROFESSIONAL AND PERSONAL REQUIREMENTS

Regulations vary by state, but generally firefighters do not need certification before they are hired, and certification is voluntary but recommended. Certification is typically offered through a state's fire academy, fire-service certification board, fire-service training board, or other agency regulating fire and public safety personnel. Certification programs are accredited by the International Fire Service Accreditation Congress (IFSAC), which provides a listing of states offering the Firefighter I and Firefighter II designations. To become certified, candidates must pass written and practical tests. (Contact information for the IFSAC is at the end of this article.)

Firefighters must meet a wide array of criteria in such areas as age, size, vision, physical fitness, stamina, and intelligence. Mechanical aptitude is an asset to a person in this career. Firefighters need sound judgment, mental alertness, and the ability to reason and think logically in situations demanding courage and bravery. The ability to remain calm in high-pressure situations is a valuable asset.

STARTING OUT

After completing an associate degree, many people enter this occupation by applying to take the local civil service examinations. If they successfully pass all of the required tests and receive a job appointment, new firefighters may serve a probationary period during which they receive intensive training. After the completion of this training, they may be assigned to a fire department or engine company for specific duties.

In some small towns and communities, applicants may enter this occupation through on-the-job training as volunteer firefighters or by applying directly to the local government for the position.

EARNINGS

The median hourly pay for firefighters was $16.43 in 2000 (or $42,718 annually based on a 50-hour workweek), according to the U.S. Department of Labor. Ten percent of all firefighters earned less than $8.03 (or $20,878 annually), while the top 10 percent earned more than $26.58 (or $69,108 annually). The department also reports that firefighters employed by local government earned a median hourly salary of $16.71 (or $43,446 annually) in 2000; those employed by the federal government earned a median hourly salary of $15.00 (or $39,000 annually) in 2000. Many firefighters receive longevity pay for each year they remain in service, which may add as much as $1,000 per year to their salaries. Firefighters also earn overtime pay and are usually given shift, weekend, and holiday pay differentials. In addition, firefighters generally receive a uniform allowance and are eligible to retire at the age of 50 or after 20 years of service. Benefits, including health, life, and disability insurance, vary widely according to the community.

OUTLOOK

Fire fighting is forecasted to remain a very competitive field, and the number of people interested in becoming firefighters will outweigh the number of available positions in most areas. Employment of firefighters is expected to grow more slowly than the average through 2010, according to the U.S. Department of Labor.

Most new jobs will be created as small communities grow and augment their volunteer staffs with career firefighters. There are also growing numbers of "call" firefighters, who are paid only when responding to fires. Little growth is expected in large, urban fire departments. Some local governments are expected to contract for fire-fighting services with private companies.

FOR MORE INFORMATION

For news in the fire-fighting field, visit the IAFC Web site.

International Association of Fire Chiefs (IAFC)
4025 Fair Ridge Drive, Suite 300
Fairfax, VA 22033-2868
Tel: 703-273-0911
Web: http://www.iafc.org

The IAFF Web site has a Virtual Academy with information on scholarships for postsecondary education.

International Association of Fire Fighters (IAFF)
1750 New York Avenue, NW
Washington, DC 20006
Tel: 202-737-8484
Web: http://www.iaff.org

For more information on certification, contact:

International Fire Service Accreditation Congress
1700 West Tyler
Oklahoma State University
Stillwater, OK 74078-8075
Tel: 405-744-8303
Web: http://www.ifsac.org

FLUID POWER TECHNICIANS

School Subjects	*Salary Range*
Mathematics	**$35,000 to $40,000**
Technical/shop	**to $50,000+**
Personal Skills	*Certification or Licensing*
Mechanical/manipulative	**Voluntary**
Technical/scientific	*Outlook*
Work Environment	**About as fast as the average**
Primarily indoors	
Primarily multiple locations	

THE JOB

Fluid power technicians deal with equipment that uses the pressure of a liquid or gas in a closed container to transmit, multiply, or control power. Working under the supervision of an engineer or engineering staff, they assemble, install, maintain, and test fluid power equipment, which is found in almost every facet of American daily life. Many different machines use some kind of fluid power system, including equipment used in industries such as agriculture, manufacturing, defense, and mining. Fluid power machines can be either hydraulic (activated by liquid) or pneumatic (activated by gas).

Fluid power technicians analyze blueprints, drawings, and specifications; set up various milling, shaping, grinding, and drilling machines and make precision parts; use sensitive measuring instruments to make sure the parts are exactly the required size; and use hand and power tools to put together components of the fluid power system they are assembling or repairing.

Some technicians work on research and development teams; others work as sales and service representatives for companies that make and sell fluid power equipment to industrial plants. Some technicians repair and maintain fluid power components of heavy equipment used in construction, on farms, or in mining. Many technicians are also employed in the aircraft industry.

PROFESSIONAL AND PERSONAL REQUIREMENTS

Certification for fluid power technicians, which is voluntary, is offered through the Fluid Power Certification Board. This certification may be beneficial to technicians in finding jobs, obtaining more advanced positions, or receiving higher pay.

To succeed as a fluid power technician, you must be able to understand and analyze mechanical systems. You should have both mechanical aptitude and an analytical mindset, as well as the ability to communicate easily with others. Finally, you should enjoy challenges and troubleshooting problems.

STARTING OUT

Most fluid power technicians obtain their jobs through their community and technical college placement offices. In addition, organizations such as the Fluid Power Society and the Fluid Power Educational Foundation have lists of their corporate members that can be used to start a job search. Some openings might be listed in the employment sections of newspapers.

EARNINGS

Salaries for fluid power technicians vary according to geographic location and industry. A Fluid Power Educational Foundation survey reports that college graduates (of both two- and four-year programs) earned starting salaries that ranged from $35,000 to $39,000 in 1999. An estimated national average wage for technicians might be in the low to mid-$40,000s. Those who move into consulting or other advanced positions can earn even more. Most workers in this field receive a full benefits package, often including vacation days, sick leave, medical and life insurance, and a retirement plan.

OUTLOOK

Because fluid power is used in so many different industries, the need for technicians is growing rapidly. Currently, the demand for these workers exceeds the supply. In the 1990s, electrohydraulic and electropneumatic technologies opened up new markets, such as active suspensions on automobiles, and reestablished older markets, such as robotics. Therefore, the fluid power industry is expected to continue growing and the outlook for technicians should remain strong through the next decade.

FOR MORE INFORMATION

For a list of schools offering courses in fluid power technology and information about available scholarships, contact:

Fluid Power Educational Foundation
3333 North Mayfair Road, Suite 101
Milwaukee, WI 53222
Tel: 414-778-3364
Web: http://www.fpef.org

For information on certification, contact:

Fluid Power Society
3245 Freemansburg Avenue
Palmer, PA 18045-7118
Tel: 800-303-8520
Email: info@ifps.org
Web: http://www.ifps.org

For career information and job listings, contact:

National Fluid Power Association
3333 North Mayfair Road
Milwaukee, WI 53222-3219
Tel: 414-778-3344
Email: nfpa@nfpa.com
Web: http://www.nfpa.com

FUNERAL HOME WORKERS

School Subjects	Salary Range
Biology	$19,000 to $41,000
Psychology	to $86,000+
Personal Skills	Certification or Licensing
Helping/teaching	Required by certain states
Leadership/management	Outlook
Work Environment	Little change or more slowly
Primarily indoors	than the average
One location with travel	

THE JOB

Funeral directors, also called *morticians* or *undertakers*, make arrangements with the families of the deceased for removal of the body to the funeral home, secure information for and file the death certificate, and make complete arrangements for the burial plans and funeral service, in accordance with the family's wishes. The director also supervises the personnel who prepare bodies for burial. Most directors are also trained, licensed, and practicing embalmers. An *embalmer* uses chemical solutions to disinfect, preserve, and restore the body and employs cosmetic aids to simulate a lifelike appearance. A *mortuary science technician* works under the direction of a mortician or funeral director to perform embalming and related funeral service tasks. Most are trainees working to become licensed embalmers and funeral directors.

Funeral home workers are employed throughout the world in small communities as well as large metropolitan areas. Because societies vary worldwide regarding the rites of passage, some areas of the world may have different legal and traditional requirements regarding death and burial procedures.

PROFESSIONAL AND PERSONAL REQUIREMENTS

All states require embalmers to be licensed, and every state except for Colorado require funeral directors to be licensed. Some states grant a combination single license covering the activity of both the embalmer and the funeral director. In order to maintain licensure, a growing number of states require continuing education classes. There is no certification available for funeral home workers.

Working as a funeral service worker, you must be compassionate, courteous, and sympathetic as well as confident, knowledgeable, and stable. The work sometimes requires lifting the deceased or their caskets, which can require strength. Good coordination is also needed to perform the precise procedures used in embalming, restoration, and cosmetology.

STARTING OUT

After attending an accredited school of mortuary science for two to four years, you can start out as a mortuary science technician, working under the supervision of a licensed director or embalmer.

Most mortuary science schools provide placement assistance for graduates. Additionally, since many schools require internship programs, students are often able to obtain permanent jobs where they have trained.

EARNINGS

Salaries of funeral home workers vary depending on experience, services performed, level of formal education, and location. According to the U.S. Department of Labor, the median annual salary for funeral directors was $41,110 in 2000. The lowest 10 percent earned less than $22,140, and the highest 10 percent earned more than $85,780 a year. The department also reports that embalmers earned a median annual salary of $32,870 in 2000. Salaries ranged from a low of $18,840 to a high of $52,130 or more per year.

In some metropolitan areas, many funeral-home employees are unionized; in these cases, salaries are determined by union contracts and are generally higher. Benefits may vary depending on the position and the employer.

OUTLOOK

The U.S. Department of Labor predicts little or no change in employment for funeral home workers through 2010. Demand will vary by industry occupation. Employment for funeral directors should grow 3 percent through 2010 as the population expands and grows older. In addition, the need to replace those retiring (more directors are 55 or older than in other occupations) or leaving the profession will spur a demand for newly trained directors. Embalmers, on the other hand, will experience an employment decline because their duties can often be handled by funeral directors who are trained and licensed as embalmers.

Job security in the funeral service industry is relatively unaffected by economic downturns. Despite the flux and movement in the population, funeral homes are a stable institution. The average firm has been in its community for more than 40 years, and funeral homes with a history of over 100 years are not uncommon.

FOR MORE INFORMATION

For information on careers in the funeral service industry, colleges that offer programs in mortuary science, and scholarships, contact:

American Board of Funeral Service Education
38 Florida Avenue
Portland, ME 04103
Tel: 207-878-6530
Web: http://www.abfse.org

Visit the NFDA Web site to read a career brochure and browse other helpful resources.

National Funeral Directors Association (NFDA)
13625 Bishop's Drive
Brookfield, WI 53005-6607
Tel: 800-228-6332
Email: nfda@nfda.org
Web: http://www.nfda.org

GRAPHIC DESIGNERS

School Subjects	Salary Range
Art	**$20,000 to $40,000**
Computer science	**to $100,000+**
Personal Skills	*Certification or Licensing*
Artistic	**None available**
Communication/ideas	*Outlook*
Work Environment	**Faster than the average**
Primarily indoors	
Primarily one location	

THE JOB

Graphic designers are practical artists whose creations are intended to express ideas, convey information, or draw attention to a product. They design a wide variety of materials including advertisements; displays; packaging; signs; computer graphics and games; book and magazine covers and interiors; animated characters; and company logos to fit the needs and preferences of their various clients.

Most designs commissioned to graphic designers involve both artwork and copy (that is, words). Thus, designers must not only be familiar with the wide range of art media (photography, drawing, painting, collage, etc.) and styles, but they must also be familiar with a wide range of typefaces and know how to manipulate them for the right effect. When a design has been approved by the client, the designer prepares the design for printing, which requires a good understanding of the printing process, including color separation, paper properties, and halftone (i.e., photograph) reproduction.

PROFESSIONAL AND PERSONAL REQUIREMENTS

There is no certification or licensing available in this field.

As with all artists, you need a degree of artistic talent, creativity, and imagination to work as a graphic designer. You must be sensitive to beauty and have an eye for detail and a strong sense of color, balance, and proportion. You also need solid computer skills and working knowledge of several of the common drawing, image editing, and page layout programs.

STARTING OUT

The best way to enter the field of graphic design is to have a strong portfolio. Potential employers rely on portfolios to evaluate talent and how that talent might be used to fit the company's special needs. You can assemble a portfolio from work completed at school, in art classes, and in part-time or freelance jobs.

Job interviews may be obtained by applying directly to companies that employ designers. Many colleges and professional schools have placement services to help graduates find positions, and sometimes it is possible to get a referral from a previous part-time employer.

EARNINGS

The range of salaries for graphic designers is quite broad. Many earn as little as $20,000, while others receive more than $100,000. Salaries depend primarily on the nature and scope of the employer, with computer graphic designers earning wages on the high end of the range.

The American Institute of Graphic Arts/Aquent Survey of Design Salaries reports that designers earned a median salary of $40,000 in 2001, while senior designers earned a median of $50,000 annually. Salaried designers who advance to the position of creative/design director earned a median of $77,500 a year. The owner of a consulting firm can make $80,000 or more.

Graphic designers who work for large corporations receive full benefits, including health insurance, paid vacation, and sick leave. Self-employed designers should expect inconsistency in their earnings, and they also must provide their own insurance and benefits.

OUTLOOK

The U.S. Department of Labor predicts that employment for qualified graphic designers will be very good through 2010, especially for those involved with computer graphics. The design field in general is expected to grow at a faster-than-average rate, according to the U.S. Department of Labor. As computer graphic technology continues to advance, there will be a need for well-trained computer graphic designers. Companies that have always used graphics will expect their designers to perform work on computers. Companies for which graphic design was once too time consuming or costly are now sprucing up company newsletters and magazines, among other things, and they need graphic designers to do it.

Because the design field is a popular one, appealing to many talented individuals, competition is expected to be strong in all areas. Beginners and designers with only average talent or without formal education and technical skills may encounter some difficulty in securing employment.

FOR MORE INFORMATION

For more information about careers in graphic design, contact the following organizations:

American Institute of Graphic Arts
National Design Center
164 Fifth Avenue
New York, NY 10010
Tel: 212-807-1990
Email: comments@aiga.org
Web: http://www.aiga.org

Society of Publication Designers
60 East 42nd Street, Suite 721
New York, NY 10165
Tel: 212-983-8585
Email: spdnyc@aol.com
Web: http://www.spd.org

For information on accredited schools, contact:

National Association of Schools of Art and Design
11250 Roger Bacon Drive, Suite 21
Reston, VA 20190
Tel: 703-437-0700
Email: info@arts-accredit.org
Web: http://www.arts-accredit.org/nasad

HEATING AND COOLING TECHNICIANS

School Subjects **Mathematics** **Technical/shop**	*Salary Range* **$20,000 to $33,000** **to $51,000+**
Personal Skills **Following instructions** **Mechanical/manipulative**	*Certification or Licensing* **Required for certain** **positions**
Work Environment **Indoors and outdoors** **Primarily multiple locations**	*Outlook* **About as fast as the average**

THE JOB

Heating and cooling technicians work on systems that control the temperature, humidity, and air quality of enclosed environments. They help design, manufacture, install, and maintain climate-control equipment. They provide people with heating and air conditioning in such structures as shops, hospitals, malls, theaters, factories, restaurants, offices, apartment buildings, and private homes. They may work to provide climate-controlled environments for temperature-sensitive products such as computers, foods, medicines, and precision instruments. They may also provide comfortable environments or refrigeration in such modes of transportation as ships, trucks, planes, and trains.

PROFESSIONAL AND PERSONAL REQUIREMENTS

Technicians who handle refrigerants must receive approved refrigerant recovery certification, which is a requirement of the Environmental Protection Agency and requires passing a special examination.

Voluntary certification for various specialties is available through professional associations. The heating and cooling industry recently adopted a standard certification program for experienced technicians. The Air Conditioning Excellence program is available to both installation and service technicians and is offered by North American Technician Excellence, Inc. Technicians must take and pass a core exam (covering safety, tools, soft skills, principles of heat transfer, and electrical systems) and one specialty exam of their choice (covering installation, service, system components, regulations, codes, and safety). The five specialties available are air conditioning, air distribution, gas heating, heat pumps, and oil heating. Technicians who become certified as a service technician are automatically certified as an installation technician without additional testing.

As a heating and cooling technician, you will need an aptitude for working with tools, manual dexterity and manipulation, and a desire to perform challenging work that requires a high level of competence and quality.

STARTING OUT

Many students in two-year educational programs work at a job related to their area of training during the summer between their first and second years. At some schools, work experience is part of the curriculum, particularly during the latter part of their program. It is not unusual for graduates of two-year programs to receive several offers of employment, either from contacts they have made themselves or from companies that routinely recruit new graduates.

In addition to using your schools' job placement services, you can independently explore other leads by applying directly to local heating and cooling contractors; sales, installation, and service shops; or manufacturers of air-conditioning, refrigeration, and heating equipment.

EARNINGS

The earnings of heating and cooling technicians vary widely according to the level of training and experience, the nature of their work, type of employer, region of the country, and other factors. Heating and cooling technicians had median hourly earnings of $15.76 in 2000, according to the U.S. Department of Labor. The lowest 10 percent earned less than $9.71, while the top 10 percent earned more than $24.58.

Heating and cooling apprentices usually earn about 50 percent of the wage rate paid to experienced workers. This percentage rises as apprentices gain experience and skill training in the field.

Many employers offer medical insurance and paid vacation days, holidays, and sick days, although the actual benefits vary from employer to employer.

OUTLOOK

Employment in the heating and cooling field is expected to increase about as fast as the average for all occupations through 2010, according to the U.S. Department of Labor. Some openings will occur when experienced workers retire or transfer to other work. Other openings will be generated because of a demand for new climate-control systems for residences and industrial and commercial users. In addition, many existing systems are being upgraded to provide more efficient use of energy and to provide benefits not originally built into the system. There is a growing emphasis on improving indoor air. There is an increasing awareness of making equipment more environmentally friendly, and with the implementation of the Clean Air Act Amendment of 1990, systems that use chlorofluorocarbons (CFCs) need to be retrofitted or replaced with new equipment.

FOR MORE INFORMATION

For information on careers, educational programs, and certification, contact the following organizations:

American Society of Heating, Refrigerating and Air-Conditioning Engineers, Inc.
1791 Tullie Circle, NE
Atlanta, GA 30329
Tel: 404-636-8400
Web: http://www.ashrae.org

North American Technician Excellence, Inc.
4100 North Fairfax Drive, Suite 210
Arlington, VA 22203
Tel: 703-276-7247
Web: http://www.natex.org

Check out the following Web site for information on the industry:

Cool Careers
Web: http://www.coolcareers.org

HORTICULTURAL TECHNICIANS

School Subjects **Agriculture** **Earth science** *Personal Skills* **Artistic** **Technical/scientific** *Work Environment* **Indoors and outdoors** **Primarily multiple locations**	*Salary Range* **$11,000 to $25,000** **to $42,000** *Certification or Licensing* **Required by certain states** *Outlook* **About as fast as the average**

THE JOB

Horticultural technicians cultivate and market plants and flowers that make human surroundings more beautiful. They work with flowers, shrubs, trees, and grass. Horticulturists research and develop methods to improve the quality, yield, and disease resistance of fruits, vegetables, and plants. Horticultural technicians are engaged in the practical application of the horticulturist's research. They plant and care for ground cover and trees in parks and playgrounds, along public highways, and in other areas. They also landscape public and private lands. There are over 1.1 million people employed in landscape and horticultural services.

Horticultural technicians usually specialize in one or more of the following areas: floriculture (flowers), nursery operation (shrubs, hedges, and trees), turfgrass (grass), and arboriculture (trees). Most entry-level technicians work as growers, propagators, or salespeople.

PROFESSIONAL AND PERSONAL REQUIREMENTS

Though there are no national certification standards, many states require certification for workers who apply pesticides. Other states require landscape contractors to obtain a license.

Voluntary certification is available to those who want increased opportunities or to advance their career. The Professional Lawn Care Association offers the Certified

Turfgrass Professional (CTP) designation through its "Principles of Turfgrass Management" national home-study course. Other organizations, such as the Associated Landscape Contractors of America (http://www.alca.org) and the Professional Grounds Management Society (http://www.pgms.org), offer additional levels of certification based on education and experience levels.

You should have an eye for detail and aesthetic beauty and a love of nature. Creative and artistic talents are helpful for arranging flowers in a retail setting or organizing plants in a garden or greenhouse, and people skills are important for working with clients as well as other horticulturists.

STARTING OUT

If you're enrolled in a horticulture technology program, you'll be able to take advantage of its job placement or internship services. Often, internships and part-time jobs lead to full-time positions with the same employer. In addition to checking the classifieds of your newspaper, apply to the many different businesses and services in your area that need technicians; keep in mind that many chain grocery, hardware, and drug stores have greenhouses and plant departments and often need knowledgeable technicians in the spring and summer months. Approximately half of all landscape and horticultural technicians work for public facilities such as parks, schools, and hospitals.

EARNINGS

Because of the wide range of jobs available to horticultural technicians, average hourly salaries vary from minimum wage to more than $20 an hour (which translates into approximately $11,000 to $41,600 per year). According to U.S. Department of Labor data, in 2000 landscaping and groundskeeping laborers earned an average of $8.80 an hour (approximately $18,304 annually for full-time work). With more experience, workers in management positions in nurseries, greenhouses, and lawn service companies earned an average of $14.70 an hour (approximately $30,576 annually).

Fringe benefits vary from employer to employer but generally include hospitalization and other insurance coverage, retirement benefits, and educational assistance.

OUTLOOK

According to the U.S. Department of Labor, employment for horticultural technicians is expected to grow about as fast as the average for all occupations through 2010. High turnover in the business continually provides openings. Many horticultural technicians work only part-time, so employers are often looking to fill vacant positions. Because wages for beginning workers are low, employers have difficulty attracting enough workers.

FOR MORE INFORMATION

To learn more about special gardening programs, and to get other information about public gardens, contact:

American Association of Botanical Gardens and Arboreta
100 West 10th Street, Suite 614
Wilmington, DE 19801
Tel: 302-655-7100
Web: http://www.aabga.org

To learn about certification, careers, and industry facts about landscape and horticultural services, contact:

Professional Lawn Care Association of America
1000 Johnson Ferry Road, NE, Suite C-135
Marietta, GA 30068-2112
Tel: 800-458-3466
Email: plcaa@plcaa.org
Web: http://www.plcaa.org

HOTEL AND MOTEL MANAGERS

School Subjects	*Salary Range*
Business	**$19,000 to $31,000**
Mathematics	**to $55,000**
Personal Skills	*Certification or Licensing*
Helping/teaching	**Voluntary**
Leadership/management	*Outlook*
Work Environment	**Little change or more slowly**
Primarily indoors	**than the average**
Primarily one location	

THE JOB

Hotel and motel managers are responsible for the overall supervision of the hotel, the different departments, and their staff. They follow operating guidelines set by the hotel's owners, or, if part of a chain, by the hotel's main headquarters and executive board. The *general manager,* also known as the *GM,* allocates funds to all departments of the hotel, approves expenditures, sets room rates, and establishes standards for food and beverage service, hotel decor, and all guest services. GMs tour the hotel property every day, usually with the head of the housekeeping department (known as the *executive housekeeper*), to make certain the hotel is kept clean and orderly. GMs are responsible for keeping the hotel's accounting books in order; advertising and marketing the hotel; maintaining and ordering supplies; and interviewing and training new employees. However, in larger hotels, the GM is usually supported by one or more assistants.

Specific positions within this field include resident managers, front office managers, personal managers, restaurant managers, food and beverage managers, and convention services managers.

PROFESSIONAL AND PERSONAL REQUIREMENTS

Certification, though not required, is widely recognized as a measurement of industry knowledge and job experience. Programs are offered by industry trade associations, such as the

Educational Institute of the American Hotel and Motel Association.

As a hotel manager, you need to be a strong leader with a flair for organization and communication. You need outstanding people skills and a calm demeanor when dealing with difficult situations.

STARTING OUT

The position of general manager is among the top rungs of the hotel career ladder. As a result, it is unlikely this would be your first industry job. In today's highly technical age, experience, though still important, is not enough for job advancement. Most candidates have some postsecondary education; many have at least an associate degree in hotel and restaurant management. Graduates entering the hotel industry usually pay their dues by working as assistant hotel managers, assistant departmental managers, or shift managers.

College career centers, the local library, and the Internet can all be helpful when researching college programs or specific businesses.

EARNINGS

According to the U.S. Department of Labor, lodging managers reported a median yearly income of $30,770 in 2000. The lowest-paid 10 percent earned less than $19,080 annually, and the highest-paid 10 percent made more than $55,050 per year. Managers may receive bonuses of 20 to 25 percent of their base salary when conditions are favorable, such as during a strong economy and when managers have increased business. These bonuses can often boost earnings by thousands of dollars.

All managers receive paid holidays and vacations, sick leave, and other benefits, such as medical and life insurance, pension or profit-sharing plans, and educational assistance.

OUTLOOK

Overall, the employment outlook for lodging managers is predicted to grow more slowly than the average through 2010, according to the U.S. Department of Labor. Many factors influence the employment of managers, including hotel consolidations that mean layoffs for excess workers and the increasing number of budget hotels and motels with fewer extras, such as a restaurant or room service. Hotels and motels with fewer offerings need fewer managers.

Candidates with the best opportunities will be college graduates with degrees in hotel or restaurant management or business, managers with excellent work experience, and those who obtain certification.

FOR MORE INFORMATION

For information on careers in hotel management, contact:

American Hotel and Lodging Association
1201 New York Avenue, NW, Suite 600
Washington, DC 20005-3931
Tel: 202-289-3100
Email: ahlamembership@ahla.com
Web: http://www.ahlaonline.org

For information on internships, scholarships, and certification, contact the following organizations:

Educational Institute of the American Hotel & Lodging Association
800 North Magnolia Avenue, Suite 1800
Orlando, FL 32803
Tel: 800-752-4567
Web: http://www.ei-ahla.org

International Council on Hotel, Restaurant, and Institutional Education
2613 North Parham Road, Second Floor
Richmond, VA 23294
Tel: 804-346-4800
Email: info@chrie.org
Web: http://chrie.org

International Executive Housekeepers Association
1001 Eastwind Drive, Suite 301
Westerville, OH 43081-3361
Tel: 800-200-6342
Email: excel@ieha.org
Web: http://www.ieha.org

HUMAN SERVICES WORKERS

School Subjects **Health** **Sociology**	*Salary Range* **$15,000 to $22,000** **to $35,000+**
Personal Skills **Communication/ideas** **Helping/teaching**	*Certification or Licensing* **None available**
Work Environment **Primarily indoors** **Primarily one location**	*Outlook* **Much faster than the average**

THE JOB

Under the supervision of social workers, psychologists, sociologists, and other professionals, *human services workers* offer support to families, the elderly, the poor, and others in need. They teach life and communication skills to people in mental health facilities or substance abuse programs. Employed by agencies, shelters, halfway houses, and hospitals, they work individually with clients or in group counseling. They also direct clients to social services and benefits.

Record keeping is an important part of the duties of human services workers because records may affect a client's eligibility for future benefits, the proper assessment of a program's success, and the prospect of future funding. Workers prepare and maintain records and case files of every person with whom they work. They record clients' responses to the various programs and treatment. They must also track costs in group homes in order to stay within budget.

PROFESSIONAL AND PERSONAL REQUIREMENTS

There is no certification or licensing available in this field.

A genuine interest in the lives and concerns of others and a sensitivity to their situations are important qualities for you to have if this career interests you. Your responsibilities can be difficult, and your work can be very stressful. The workload can also be overwhelming; since staff are often overworked due to funding limitations, employee burnout is a common problem.

STARTING OUT

You may find a job through your high school counselor or local and state human services agency. Sometimes summer jobs and volunteer work can develop into full-time employment upon graduation. Employers try to be selective in their hiring because many human services jobs involve direct contact with people who are impaired and therefore vulnerable to exploitation. Experience with helping others is a definite advantage.

EARNINGS

Salaries of human services workers depend in part on their employer and amount of experience. According to the *Occupational Outlook Handbook,* median annual earnings of social and human service assistants were $22,330 in 2000. Salaries ranged from less than $14,660 to more than $35,220.

OUTLOOK

Employment for human services workers will grow much faster than the average through 2010, according to the U.S. Department of Labor. The best opportunities will be in job-training programs, residential care facilities, and private social service agencies, which include such services as adult day care and meal delivery programs. Correctional facilities are also expected to employ many more human services workers. Because counseling inmates and offenders can be undesirable work, there are a number of high-paying jobs available in that area.

New ideas in treating disabled or mentally ill people also influence employment growth in group homes and residential care facilities. Public concern for the homeless—many of whom are former mental patients who were released under service reductions in the 1980s—as well as for troubled teenagers and those with substance abuse problems is likely to bring about new community-based programs and group residences.

Job prospects in public agencies are not as bright as they once were because of fiscal policies that tighten eligibility requirements for federal welfare and other payments. State and local governments are expected to remain major employers, however, as the burden of providing social services such as welfare, child support, and nutrition programs is shifted from the federal government to the state and local level.

FOR MORE INFORMATION

For more information on careers in counseling, contact:

American Counseling Association
5999 Stevenson Avenue
Alexandria, VA 22304-3300
Tel: 800-347-6647
Web: http://www.counseling.org

For information on employment with government human service agencies, contact:

The U.S. Department of Health and Human Services
200 Independence Avenue, SW
Washington, DC 20201
Tel: 877-696-6775
Web: http://www.hhs.gov

For information on student memberships, scholarships, and the online career pamphlet, The Human Services Worker, *check out the following Web site:*

National Organization for Human Service Education
Web: http://www.nohse.com

INDUSTRIAL ENGINEERING TECHNICIANS

School Subjects **Computer science** **Mathematics** *Personal Skills* **Communication/ideas** **Technical/scientific** *Work Environment* **Primarily indoors** **Primarily one location**	*Salary Range* **$22,000 to $35,000** **to $73,000+** *Certification or Licensing* **Voluntary** *Outlook* **About as fast as the average**

THE JOB

Industrial engineering technicians collect and analyze data and make recommendations for the efficient use of personnel, materials, and machines to produce goods or to provide services. They may study the time, movements, and methods a worker uses to accomplish daily tasks in production, maintenance, or clerical areas.

Industrial engineering technicians prepare charts to illustrate workflow, floor layouts, materials handling, and machine utilization. They make statistical studies, analyze production costs, prepare layouts of machinery and equipment, help plan work flow and work assignments, and recommend revisions to revamp production methods or improve standards.

Specific positions in this field include work measurement technicians; time study technicians; production control technicians; inventory control technicians; quality control technicians; cost control technicians; budget technicians; and plant layout technicians.

PROFESSIONAL AND PERSONAL REQUIREMENTS

The National Institute for Certification in Engineering Technologies has established a certification program that some technicians may wish to participate in. Although certification is not generally required by employers, those with certification often have a competitive advantage when it comes to hiring and promotions.

You should be adept at compiling and organizing data and be able to express yourself clearly and persuasively both orally and in writing. You should also be detail oriented and enjoy solving problems.

STARTING OUT

Many industrial engineering technicians find their first jobs through interviews with company recruiters who visit campuses. In many cases, students are invited to visit the prospective employer's plant for further consultation and to become better acquainted with the area, product, and facilities. For many students, the job placement office of their college or technical school is the best source of possible jobs. Local manufacturers or companies are in constant contact with these facilities, so they have the most current, up-to-date job listings.

EARNINGS

The salary range for entry-level industrial engineering technicians varies according to the product being manufactured, geographic location, and the education and skills of the technician. Industrial engineering technicians earn salaries that range from $22,000 to $68,000, with a median salary of about $35,000. The U.S. Department of Labor reports that industrial engineering technicians who work in computer and data processing services earned an average salary of $73,320 in 2000. Technicians employed in the electric components and accessories industry earned a median salary of $36,300 in 2000. In addition to salary, most employers offer paid vacation time, holidays, insurance and retirement plans, and tuition assistance for work-related courses.

OUTLOOK

As products become more technically demanding to produce, competitive pressures will force companies to improve and update manufacturing facilities and product designs. Thus, the demand for well-trained industrial engineering technicians will stay about average through 2010, according to the U.S. Department of Labor. Opportunities will be best for individuals who have up-to-date skills. As technology becomes more sophisticated, employers will continue to seek technicians who require the least amount of additional job training.

Prospective technicians should keep in mind that advances in technology and management techniques make industrial engineering a constantly changing field. Technicians will be able to take advantage of new opportunities only if they are willing to continue their training and education throughout their careers.

FOR MORE INFORMATION

For information about membership, contact:

American Society of Certified Engineering Technicians
PO Box 1348
Flowery Branch, GA 30542
Tel: 770-967-9173
Web: http://www.ascet.org

For information on careers and training, contact:

Institute of Electrical and Electronics Engineers
3 Park Avenue, 17th Floor
New York, NY 10016-5997
Tel: 212-419-7900
Web: http://www.ieee.org

For more information on careers as an engineering technician, contact JETS:

Junior Engineering Technical Society (JETS)
1420 King Street, Suite 405
Alexandria, VA 22314-2794
Tel: 703-548-5387
Web: http://www.jets.org

For information about obtaining certification, contact:

National Institute for Certification in Engineering Technologies
1420 King Street
Alexandria, VA 22314-2794
Tel: 888-476-4238
Web: http://www.nicet.org

LABORATORY TESTING TECHNICIANS

School Subjects **Chemistry** **Physics** *Personal Skills* **Following instructions** **Technical/scientific** *Work Environment* **Primarily indoors** **Primarily one location**	*Salary Range* **$19,000 to $28,000** **to $42,000+** *Certification or Licensing* **Voluntary (certification)** **Required by certain states** **(licensing)** *Outlook* **About as fast as the average**

THE JOB

Laboratory testing technicians conduct tests on countless substances and products. Their laboratory duties include measuring and evaluating materials and running quality control tests. They work in a variety of unrelated fields such as medicine, metallurgy, manufacturing, geology, and meteorology. Specific positions in this field include quality control technicians; assayers; medical technicians; geological technicians; and pharmaceutical technicians.

Regardless of the specific nature of the tests conducted by technicians, they must always keep detailed records of every step. Laboratory technicians often do a great deal of writing and must make charts, graphs, and other displays to illustrate results. They may be called on to interpret test results, to draw overall conclusions, and to make recommendations. Occasionally, laboratory testing technicians are asked to appear as witnesses in court to explain why a product failed and who may be at fault.

PROFESSIONAL AND PERSONAL REQUIREMENTS

Depending on what type of laboratory technician you want to be, you may need certification or licensing. For example, certification for those who work as medical technicians is voluntary. However, it is highly recommended, and some employers may even require it. Organizations offering certification include the

American Medical Technologists and the American Association of Bioanalysts. In addition, a number of states require that laboratory workers be licensed. Check with your state's occupational licensing board to find out specific requirements.

You should be detail oriented and enjoy figuring out how things work. You also must have the patience to repeat a test many times, perhaps even on the same material. Finally, you need to be independent and motivated to work on your own until assigned tasks are completed.

STARTING OUT

Technical schools often help place graduating technicians. Many laboratories contact these schools directly looking for student employees or interns. Students can also contact local manufacturing companies and laboratories to find out about job openings in their area.

EARNINGS

Earnings for laboratory testing technicians vary based on the type of work they do, their education and experience, and even the size of the laboratory and its location. For example, the U.S. Department of Labor reported that in 2000 the lowest-paid 10 percent of medical technicians earned less than $18,550 annually. This 10 percent typically includes those workers who are just starting out in the field. The department also reported a median yearly income of $27,540. The highest-paid medical technicians earned $42,370 or more annually. Geological technicians had median hourly earnings of $17.55 in 2000.

Salaries increase as technicians gain experience and as they take on supervisory responsibility. Most companies that employ laboratory testing technicians offer medical benefits, sick leave, and vacation time. However, these benefits will depend on the individual employer.

OUTLOOK

Overall, job opportunities for laboratory testing technicians are expected to grow about as fast as the average through 2010. However, those in some specialties may face growth that is slightly slower than the average; for example, testing technicians who work with stone, clay, glass, fabricated metal products, and transportation equipment may experience this slow growth. In addition, employment possibilities at testing laboratories will be affected by advances in technology. New testing procedures that are developed will lead to an increase in the testing that is done. However, increased automation will mean each technician can complete more work, leading to moderate employment growth.

On the bright side, environmental concerns and dwindling natural resources are causing many manufacturers to look for better ways to develop ores, minerals, and other substances from the earth. Laboratory technicians will be needed to test new production procedures as well as prototypes of new products. Technicians in any specialty who have strong educational backgrounds, keep up with developing technologies, and demonstrate knowledge of testing equipment will have the best employment opportunities.

FOR MORE INFORMATION

This organization has information on certification for medical laboratory technicians.

American Association of Bioanalysts
917 Locust Street, Suite 1100
St. Louis, MO 63101-1419
Tel: 314-241-1445
Email: aab@aab.org
Web: http://www.aab.org

Contact this organization for certification information:

American Medical Technologists
710 Higgins Road
Park Ridge, IL 60068-5765
Tel: 847-823-5169
Email: mail@amt1.com
Web: http://www.amt1.com

This society offers student membership and provides industry news.

The Minerals, Metals, and Materials Society
184 Thorn Hill Road
Warrendale, PA 15086-7514
Tel: 724-776-9000
Web: http://www.tms.org

LANDSCAPERS AND GROUNDS MANAGERS

School Subjects **Biology** **Chemistry**	*Salary Range* **$19,000 to $25,000** **to $50,000+**
Personal Skills **Following instructions** **Mechanical/manipulative**	*Certification or Licensing* **Required for certain** **positions**
Work Environment **Primarily outdoors** **Primarily multiple locations**	*Outlook* **Faster than the average**

THE JOB

Landscapers and *grounds managers* plan, design, and maintain gardens, parks, lawns, and other landscaped areas and supervise the care of the trees, plants, and shrubs that are part of these areas. Specific job responsibilities depend on the type of area involved. Landscapers and grounds managers direct projects at private homes, parks, schools, arboretums, office parks, shopping malls, government offices, and botanical gardens. They are responsible for purchasing material and supplies and for training, directing, and supervising employees. Grounds managers maintain the land after the landscaping designs have been implemented. They may work alone or supervise a grounds staff. They may have their own business or be employed by a landscaping firm.

Specific jobs in this field include greenskeepers, greens superintendents, arboriculture technicians, tree surgeons, tree-trimming supervisors, pest management scouts, lawn-service workers, horticulturists, and turf grass consultants.

PROFESSIONAL AND PERSONAL REQUIREMENTS

Licensing and certification differ by state and vary according to specific job responsibilities. For example, in most states landscapers and grounds managers need a certificate to spray insecticides or other chemicals. The Associated Landscape Contractors of America offers the following certification designations: Certified

Landscape Professional: Exterior and Interior (CLP), Certified Landscape Technician: Interior (CLT-I), and Certified Landscape Technician: Exterior (CLT-E).

If you are interested in a career as a landscaper or grounds manager, you should have a "green thumb" and an interest in preserving and maintaining natural areas. You should be reasonably physically fit, have an aptitude for working with machines, and display good manual dexterity.

STARTING OUT

Summer or part-time jobs often lead to full-time employment with the same employer. If you enroll in a college or other training program, you can receive help in finding work from the school's job placement office. In addition, applying directly to botanical gardens, nurseries, or golf courses is common practice. Jobs may also be listed in newspaper want ads. Most landscaping and related companies provide on-the-job training for entry-level personnel.

EARNINGS

Salaries depend on the experience and education level of the worker, the type of work being done, and geographic location. The *Occupational Outlook Handbook* reports the following median hourly earnings for workers in this industry in 2000: landscaping and groundskeeping workers, $8.80; tree trimmers and pruners, $11.41; first-line supervisors/managers of landscaping, lawn service, and groundskeeping workers, $14.70. Landscape contractors and others who run their own businesses earn between $25,000 and $50,000 per year, with those with a greater ability to locate customers earning even more.

A readership salary survey conducted by *Grounds Maintenance* magazine found the average golf course superintendent earned $38,600 a year; company grounds manager, $38,900; and lawn care contractor, $32,500.

Fringe benefits vary from employer to employer but generally include medical insurance and paid vacation.

OUTLOOK

Job growth for this field is expected to grow faster than the average for all occupations through 2010, according to the U.S.

Department of Labor. Landscapers and their services will be in strong demand due to increased construction of buildings, shopping malls, homes, and other structures. Upkeep and renovation of existing landscapes will create jobs as well. There is also a high degree of turnover in this field as many workers transfer to better-paying occupations, retire, or leave the field for other reasons.

FOR MORE INFORMATION

Visit the ASHS Web site to read the online publication, Careers in Horticulture.

American Society for Horticultural Sciences (ASHS)
113 South West Street, Suite 200
Alexandria, VA 22314-2851
Tel: 703-836-4606
Web: http://www.ashs.org

For information on careers, certification, student chapters, and scholarships, contact:

Associated Landscape Contractors of America
150 Elden Street, Suite 270
Herndon, VA 20170
Tel: 800-395-2522
Web: http://www.alca.org

For information on career opportunities and education, contact the following organizations:

American Nursery and Landscape Association
1000 Vermont Avenue, NW, Suite 300
Washington, DC 20005-4914
Tel: 202-789-2900
Web: http://www.anla.org

Professional Grounds Management Society
720 Light Street
Baltimore, MD 21230-3816
Tel: 800-609-7467
Email: pgms@assnhqtrs.com
Web: http://www.pgms.org

LASER TECHNICIANS

School Subjects **Computer science** **Mathematics** *Personal Skills* **Mechanical/manipulative** **Technical/scientific** *Work Environment* **Primarily indoors** **Primarily one location**	*Salary Range* **$21,000 to $30,000** **to $38,000** *Certification or Licensing* **None available** *Outlook* **Faster than the average**

THE JOB

Laser technicians produce, install, operate, service, and test laser systems and fiber optics equipment in industrial, medical, or research settings. They work under the direction of engineers or physicists who conduct laboratory activities in laser research and development or design. Depending upon the type of laser system—gas or solid state—a technician generally works either with information systems or with robotics, manufacturing, or medical equipment.

Laser technicians working with semiconductor systems are involved mainly with computer and telephone systems. In addition to helping to test, install, and maintain these systems, technicians work with engineers in their design and improvement. Technicians who work with gas-type systems usually assist scientists, engineers, or doctors. These systems are used primarily in the fields of robotics, manufacturing, and medical procedures.

In general, most technicians are employed in one of five areas: materials processing, communications, military, medical, and research. Technicians' duties include taking measurements, cleaning, aligning, inspecting, and operating lasers, and collecting data.

PROFESSIONAL AND PERSONAL REQUIREMENTS

There is no certification or licensing available in this field.

You should have an interest in instruments, laboratory apparatus, and how devices and systems work. Written and spoken communications are very important, since you will often have to work closely with people of varied technological backgrounds.

Good manual dexterity and coordination are important. Because lasers can be extremely dangerous and the work is very detailed, you must be able to work carefully, efficiently, and patiently.

STARTING OUT

Colleges that offer associate's degrees in laser technology usually work closely with industry, providing their graduating students with placement services and lists of potential employers. Most laser technicians graduating from a two-year program, in fact, are interviewed and recruited while still in school by representatives of companies who need laser technicians. If hired, they begin working soon after graduation.

Another way to enter the career is to join a branch of the U.S. Armed Forces under a technical training program for laser technicians. Military laser training is not always compatible to civilian training, however, and further study of theory and applications may be needed to enter the field as a civilian.

EARNINGS

According to a survey done by the Laser Institute of America, the overall average starting salary for laser technicians is between $21,000 and $25,000 per year. Salaries for technicians with at least five years of experience average approximately $30,000 per year, depending on background, experience, and the industry in which they are employed. According to the U.S. Department of Labor, median salaries for laser technicians were $18.25 an hour (or $38,000 annually) in 2000.

In addition to salary, technicians usually receive benefits such as insurance, paid holidays and vacations, and retirement plans.

OUTLOOK

Employment opportunities for laser technicians are expected to be very good through 2010. Rapid changes in technology and continued growth in the industry will almost certainly lead to an increase in the number of technicians employed.

Fiber optics is one of the fastest-growing areas for laser technicians. Optical fiber is replacing wire cables in communication lines and in many electronic products. This trend is expected to continue, so the demand for technicians in the fiber optics field should be especially strong. Growth is also expected to be strong in production, defense, medicine, construction, and entertainment. Technicians interested in research and development, however, should keep in mind that job growth often slows in the face of economic downturns.

FOR MORE INFORMATION

For information on becoming a laser technician, contact:

Laser Institute of America
13501 Ingenuity Drive, Suite 128
Orlando, FL 32826
Tel: 800-345-2737
Email: lia@laserinstitute.org
Web: http://www.laserinstitute.org

For information on laser technology and fellowships, contact:

Lasers and Electro-Optical Society
PO Box 1331
445 Hoes Lane
Piscataway, NJ 08855-1331
Tel: 732-562-3892
Email: soc.leo@ieee.org
Web: http://www.i-leos.org

LEGAL SECRETARIES

School Subjects **English** **Government** *Personal Skills* **Communication/ideas** **Following instructions** *Work Environment* **Primarily indoors** **Primarily one location**	*Salary Range* **$22,000 to $35,000** **to $51,000+** *Certification or Licensing* **Recommended** *Outlook* **About as fast as the average**

THE JOB

Legal secretaries, sometimes called *litigation secretaries* or *trial secretaries,* assist lawyers by performing the administrative and clerical duties in a law office or firm.

They may type letters and legal documents, such as subpoenas, appeals, and motions; handle incoming and outgoing mail; maintain a detailed filing system; and deliver legal documents to the court. Besides these duties, legal secretaries spend much of their time making appointments with clients and dealing with client questions. The legal secretary is a sort of personal assistant to one or more lawyers as well and must maintain the calendars and schedules for the office.

Legal secretaries are often called upon to conduct legal research for the cases that are current within the office. They may research and write legal briefs on a topic or case that is relevant to the lawyer's current cases. They also help lawyers find information such as employment, medical, and criminal records.

PROFESSIONAL AND PERSONAL REQUIREMENTS

Two general legal secretary certifications are offered by the National Association of Legal Secretaries. The Accredited Legal Secretary (ALS) certification is for legal secretaries with education but no experience. The Professional Legal Secretary (PLS) certification designates a legal secretary with exceptional skills and experience. Other specific legal secretary certifications are given by Legal Secretaries International, Inc. You can become board certified in civil trial, probate, real estate, business law, or criminal law. Exams consist of three parts and take four hours to complete. There is no licensing required for legal secretaries.

You must learn a great deal about court structures and practices and legal terminology. You need to be able to grasp the inner workings of the law. You must also be able to quickly learn computer programs, especially word processing and database programs, and be able to use them skillfully.

STARTING OUT

Many legal secretaries get their first jobs through the career placement offices of their colleges or vocational schools. Still other legal secretaries take the part-time job route to get their first full-time position. New graduates should contact the local law offices in their area and let them know they are available; often direct contact now can lead to a job later.

EARNINGS

According to the U.S. Department of Labor, the average salary for legal secretaries was approximately $34,740 in 2000. Starting salaries were $22,440; however, those with experience averaged much higher pay, earning more than $50,970. Certified legal secretaries and those who work for high-ranking attorneys (such as partners in a firm) receive higher pay.

Most law firms provide employees with sick days, vacation days, and holidays. Health insurance, 401-K programs, and profit sharing may be offered as well.

OUTLOOK

According to the U.S. Department of Labor, the legal secretary field will continue to grow about as fast as the average. Because the legal services industry as a whole is growing, legal secretaries will be in high demand. Qualified legal secretaries will have plentiful job opportunities, especially in the larger metropolitan areas.

FOR MORE INFORMATION

For information about certification and an online application form, contact:

Legal Secretaries International, Inc.
15 Greenway Drive
RR 4, Box 4225
Trinity, TX 75862-9324
Tel: 936-594-9234
Web: http://www.legalsecretaries.org

For information on certification, job openings, and more, contact:

National Association of Legal Secretaries
314 East 3rd Street, Suite 210
Tulsa, OK 74120
Tel: 918-582-5188
Email: info@nals.org
Web: http://www.nals.org

LIBRARY TECHNICIANS

School Subjects	Salary Range
Computer science **English**	**$14,000 to $23,000 to $36,000+**
Personal Skills **Helping/teaching** **Technical/scientific**	*Certification or Licensing* **None available**
	Outlook
Work Environment **Primarily indoors** **Primarily one location**	**About as fast as the average**

THE JOB

Library technicians, also called *library technical assistants,* work in all areas of library services, supporting professional librarians or working independently to help people access information. They order and catalog books, help library patrons locate materials, and make the library's services and facilities readily available. Technicians verify bibliographic information on orders and perform basic cataloging of materials received. They answer routine questions about library services and refer questions requiring professional help to librarians. Technicians also help with circulation desk operations and oversee the work of stack workers and catalog-card typists. They circulate audiovisual equipment and materials and inspect items upon return.

Work in libraries falls into three general categories: technical services, user services, and administrative services. In technical services, library technicians are involved with acquiring and organizing resources so that material can be easily accessed. They process order requests, verify bibliographic information, and prepare order forms for new materials, such as books, magazines, journals, videos, and CD-ROMs. Technicians who work in technical services may have the following job titles: acquisitions technician, classifier, cataloger, circulation counter attendant, and media technician.

Under the guidance of librarians in user services, technicians work directly with library patrons and help them to access the information needed for their research. They direct library patrons to the computer or card catalog in response to inquiries and assist with identifying the library's holdings. Library technicians who work in user services may have the following job titles: reference library technician, children's library technician, and young-adult library technician.

Technicians who work in administrative services help with the management of the library. They help prepare budgets, coordinate the efforts of different departments within the library, write policy and procedures, and work to develop the library's collection. If they have more responsibility, they might supervise and coordinate staff members, recruit and supervise volunteers, organize fund-raising efforts, sit on community boards, and develop programs to promote and encourage reading and learning in the community.

PROFESSIONAL AND PERSONAL REQUIREMENTS

There is no certification or licensing available in this field.

As a library technician, you should demonstrate aptitude for careful, detailed, analytical work. You should enjoy problem solving and working with people as well as with books and other library materials. Good interpersonal skills are invaluable, as are patience and flexibility. Good time-management skills and judgment are also important qualities.

STARTING OUT

In most cases, graduates of training programs for library technicians may seek employment through the placement offices of their community colleges. Job applicants may also approach libraries directly, usually by contacting the personnel officer of the library or the human resources administrator of the organization.

Many state library agencies maintain job hotlines listing openings. State departments of education also may keep lists of openings available for library technicians.

EARNINGS

Salaries for library technicians vary depending on such factors as the type of library, geographic location, and specific job responsibilities. According to the U.S. Department of Labor, the median annual salary for all library technicians in 2000 was $23,170. The lowest-paid 10 percent made less than $13,810, while the highest-paid 10 percent earned more than $35,660. The U.S. Department of Labor also reported that library technicians working for the federal government averaged an annual salary of about $33,224 in 2001.

Benefits vary according to employer, but most full-time library technicians receive health insurance, dental insurance, paid vacations, paid holidays, compensated sick time, and retirement savings plans.

OUTLOOK

The U.S. Department of Labor predicts employment for library technicians to grow about as fast as the average through 2010. Job openings will result from technicians leaving the field for other employment or retirement, as well as from libraries looking to stretch their budgets. Since a library technician earns less than a librarian, a library may find it more economical to hire the technician. The continued growth of special libraries in medical, business, and law organizations will lead to growing opportunities for technicians who develop specialized skills. A technician who has excellent computer skills and is able to learn quickly will be highly employable, as will a technician who shows the drive to gain advanced degrees and accept more responsibility.

FOR MORE INFORMATION

For information on library careers, accredited schools, scholarships and grants, and student membership, contact:

American Library Association
50 East Huron Street
Chicago, IL 60611
Tel: 800-545-2433
Email: ala@ala.org
Web: http://www.ala.org

For information on careers in special libraries, contact:

Special Libraries Association
1700 18th Street, NW
Washington, DC 20009-2514
Tel: 202-234-4700
Email: sla@sla.org
Web: http://www.sla.org

LICENSED PRACTICAL NURSES

School Subjects **Biology** **Chemistry** *Personal Skills* **Helping/teaching** **Technical/scientific** *Work Environment* **Primarily indoors** **Primarily multiple locations**	*Salary Range* **$22,000 to $29,000** **to $42,000+** *Certification or Licensing* **Required** *Outlook* **About as fast as the average**

THE JOB

Licensed practical nurses (LPNs), a specialty of the nursing profession, are sometimes called *licensed vocational nurses.* LPNs are trained to assist in the care and treatment of patients. They are responsible for many general duties of nursing such as administering prescribed drugs and medical treatments to patients; taking patients' temperatures and blood pressures; assisting patients with daily hygiene tasks; assisting in the preparation of medical examination and surgery; supervising nurse assistants; and performing routine laboratory tests. LPNs assist with therapeutic and rehabilitation sessions; they may also participate in the planning, practice, and evaluation of a patient's nursing care.

LPNs working in nursing homes have duties similar to those of nurses employed by hospitals. Those working in doctors' offices and clinics are sometimes required to perform clerical duties such as keeping records and maintaining files and paperwork as well as answering phones and tending the appointment book. *Home health LPNs,* in addition to their nursing duties, may sometimes prepare and serve meals to their patients.

PROFESSIONAL AND PERSONAL REQUIREMENTS

LPNs may take the Certification Exam for Practical and Vocational Nurses in Long-Term Care (CEPN-LTC). Contact the National Council of State Boards of Nursing, Inc., for more information. After graduating from a state-approved practical nursing program, a licensing examination is required by all 50 states.

You should be patient, nurturing, and capable of following orders and working under close supervision. Stamina, both physical and mental, is a must for this occupation.

STARTING OUT

After fulfilling licensing requirements, you should check with human resource departments of hospitals, nursing homes, and clinics for openings. Employment agencies that specialize in health professions, and state employment agencies, are other ways to find employment, as are school placement centers. Newspaper classified ads, nursing associations, and professional journals are great sources of job opportunities.

EARNINGS

According to the *Occupational Outlook Handbook*, LPNs earned an average of $29,440 annually in 2000. Ten percent earned less than $21,520, and 10 percent earned over $41,800. Many LPNs are able to supplement their salaries with overtime pay and shift differentials. One-fifth of all LPNs work part-time.

OUTLOOK

Employment for LPNs is expected to grow about as fast as the average for all occupations through 2010, according to the U.S. Department of Labor. A growing elderly population requiring long-term health care is the primary factor in the demand for qualified LPNs. Traditionally, hospitals have provided the most job opportunities for LPNs. However, this source will provide only a moderate number of openings in the future. Faster-than-average employment growth is predicted for LPNs in nursing homes and home health care agencies. Due to advanced medical technology, people are living longer, though many will require medical assistance. Private medical practices will also be excellent job sources because many medical procedures are now being performed on an outpatient basis in doctors' offices.

FOR MORE INFORMATION

For information on education programs and careers, contact the following organizations:

**National Association for Practical Nurse
Education and Services**
8607 2nd Avenue, Suite 404A
Silver Spring, MD 20910
Email: napnes@bellatlantic.net

For information on careers and certification, contact the following organization:

National Council of State Boards of Nursing
676 North St. Clair Street, Suite 550
Chicago, IL 60611-2921
Email: info@ncsbn.org
Web: http://www.ncsbn.org

For career information, contact the following organizations:

National Federation of Licensed Practical Nurses, Inc.
605 Poole Drive
Garner, NC 27529
Web: http://www.nflpn.org

Discover Nursing, sponsored by Johnson & Johnson Health Care Systems, provides information on nursing careers, nursing schools, and scholarships.

Discover Nursing
Web: http://www.discovernursing.com

MARINE SERVICES TECHNICIANS

School Subjects **Mathematics** **Technical/shop**	*Salary Range* **$17,000 to $27,000 to** **$41,000+**
Personal Skills **Following instructions** **Mechanical/manipulative**	*Certification or Licensing* **Required for certain** **positions**
Work Environment **Indoors and outdoors** **One location with travel**	*Outlook* **Little change or more slowly** **than the average**

THE JOB

Marine services technicians work on the more than 16 million boats and other watercraft owned by people in the United States. They test and repair boat engines, transmissions, and propellers; rigging, masts, and sails; and navigational equipment and steering gear. They repair or replace defective parts and sometimes make new parts to meet special needs. They may also inspect and replace internal cabinets, refrigeration systems, electrical systems and equipment, sanitation facilities, hardware, and trim. Marine services technicians may work at boat dealerships, boat repair shops, boat engine manufacturers, or marinas. Naturally, jobs are concentrated near large bodies of water and coastal areas.

Specific positions within this field include motorboat mechanics; marine electronics technicians; field repairers; bench repairers; and fiberglass repairers.

PROFESSIONAL AND PERSONAL REQUIREMENTS

Certification for technicians in the marine electronics industry is voluntary and is administered by the National Marine Electronics Association. There are three grades of Certified Marine Electronic Technicians: basic certification for technicians with one year of experience, advanced grade certification for those with three years of experience, and senior grade certification for those with 10 years of experience. Those who test and repair marine radio transmitting equipment must have a general radio-telephone operator license from the Federal Communications Commission (1919 M Street, NW, Washington, DC 20554, Web: http://www.fcc.gov).

Motorboat technicians' work can sometimes be physically demanding, requiring them to lift heavy outboard motors or other components. Electronics technicians, on the other hand, must be able to work with delicate parts, such as wires and circuit boards. They should have good eyesight, color vision, and good hearing (to listen for malfunctions revealed by sound).

As a marine services technician, you need to be able to adapt to the cyclical nature of this business. You can be very busy in the summer months, then have gaps in your work during the winter. Some workers earn unemployment compensation during this slow period.

STARTING OUT

A large number of technicians get their start by working as general boatyard laborers, cleaning boats, cutting grass, painting, and so on. After showing interest and ability, you can begin to work with experienced technicians and learn skills on the job. You can also attend a vocational school or technical college for training in skills such as engine repair and fiberglass work. Some professional organizations offer scholarships in marine technician training.

EARNINGS

According to the U.S. Department of Labor, the median yearly earnings of motorboat mechanics were $26,660 in 2000. The middle 50 percent earned between $20,760 and $33,680. Salaries ranged from less than $17,320 to more than $41,490 a year. Median annual earnings of boat dealers, the industry employing the largest numbers of motorboat mechanics, were $26,350. The *O*Net Dictionary of Occupational Titles* reported a yearly income of $27,612 specifically for the field of marine services technicians.

Technicians in small shops tend to receive few fringe benefits, but larger employers often offer paid vacations, sick leave, and health insurance.

OUTLOOK

The marine services technician's job can be considered secure for the near future. According to the U.S. Department of Labor, employment opportunities for small-engine mechanics, including marine services technicians, are expected to grow more slowly than the average through 2010. As boat design and construction become more complicated, the outlook will be best for well-trained technicians. Most marine craft purchases are made by the over-40 age group, which is expected to increase over the next decade. The growth of this population segment should help expand the market for motorboats and increase the demand for qualified mechanics.

FOR MORE INFORMATION

To find a marine association in your area, contact:

Marine Retail Association of America
150 East Huron Street, Suite 802
Chicago, IL 60611
Tel: 312-944-5080
Email: mraa@mraa.com
Web: http://www.mraa.com

For information on certification, careers, and membership, contact:

National Marine Electronics Association
7 Riggs Avenue
Severna Park, MD 21146
Tel: 410-975-9425
Email: info@nmea.org
Web: http://www.nmea.org

MASSAGE THERAPISTS

School Subjects **Health** **Physical education**	*Salary Range* **$11,000 to $29,000** **to $40,000+**
Personal Skills **Helping/teaching** **Mechanical/manipulative**	*Certification or Licensing* **Recommended (certification)** **Required by certain states** **(licensing)**
Work Environment **Primarily indoors** **Primarily one location**	*Outlook* **Faster than the average**

THE JOB

Massage therapy is a broad term referring to a number of health-related practices, including Swedish massage, sports massage, Rolfing, Shiatsu and acupressure, trigger point therapy, and reflexology. *Massage therapists* work to produce physical, mental, and emotional benefits through the manipulation of the body's soft tissue. Auxiliary methods, such as the movement of joints and the application of dry and steam heat, are also used. Although their techniques vary, most massage therapists (or *massotherapists*) press and rub the skin and muscles. Relaxed muscles, improved blood circulation and joint mobility, reduced stress and anxiety, and decreased recovery time for sprains and injured muscles are just a few of the potential benefits of massage therapy. Massage therapists are sometimes called *bodyworkers*. The titles *masseur* and *masseuse*, once common, are now rare among those who use massage for therapy and rehabilitation.

PROFESSIONAL AND PERSONAL REQUIREMENTS

Currently more than 25 states and the District of Columbia regulate the practice of massage therapy, requiring licensure, certification, or registration. Because requirements for licensing, certification, registration, and even local ordinances vary, however, you will need to check with your state's department of regulatory agencies to get specifics for your area. Since 1992, the National Certification Board for Therapeutic Massage and Bodywork has offered a certification exam covering massage theory and practice, human anatomy, physiology, kinesiology, business practices, and associated techniques and methods. Those who pass the exam may use the designation Nationally Certified in Therapeutic Massage and Bodywork. Legislation is currently being considered to regulate certification across the country.

If you are interested in becoming a massage therapist, you should be flexible, sensitive, and nurturing. Listening well and responding to the client is vital, as is focusing all attention on the task at hand. Manual dexterity is usually required to administer the treatments, as is the ability to stand for at least an hour at a time.

STARTING OUT

The American Massage Therapy Association offers job placement information to certified massage therapists who belong to the organization. Massage therapy schools have job placement offices, and newspapers often list jobs. Some graduates are able to enter the field as self-employed massage therapists, scheduling their own appointments and managing their own offices.

Networking is a valuable tool in maintaining a successful massage therapy enterprise. Many massage therapists get clients through referrals and often rely on word of mouth to build a solid customer base.

EARNINGS

The earnings of massage therapists vary greatly with the level of experience and location of practice. Some entry-level massage therapists earn as little as minimum wage (ending up with a yearly income of around $11,000), but with experience, a massage therapist can charge from $10 to $70 for a one-hour session.

The *Occupational Outlook Quarterly (OOQ)* reported in 2000 that massage therapists who worked at least six hours a week had median yearly incomes ranging from $20,000 to $29,000. The *OOQ* also reported that massage therapists earned an average of $48 per hour. For massage therapists working full-time, the article estimated yearly earnings of approximately $35,000 to $40,000. Well-established therapists who manage to schedule an average of 20 clients a week for one-hour sessions can earn more than $40,000 annually.

Massage therapists are not, however, paid for the time spent on administrative and other business tasks. Those who are self-employed—more than two-thirds of all massage therapists—must also pay a self-employment tax and provide their own benefits. With membership in some national organizations, self-employed massage therapists may be eligible for group life, health, liability, and renter's insurance through the organization's insurance agency.

OUTLOOK

The employment outlook for massage therapists is good through 2010. The growing acceptance of massage therapy as an important health care discipline has led to the creation of additional jobs for massage therapists in many sectors.

FOR MORE INFORMATION

For information on massage therapy and education, contact:

American Massage Therapy Association
820 Davis Street, Suite 100
Evanston, IL 60201-4444
Tel: 847-864-0123
Web: http://www.amtamassage.org

For information on accreditation and programs, contact:

Commission on Massage Therapy Accreditation
820 Davis Street, Suite 100
Evanston, IL 60201
Tel: 847-869-5039
Web: http://www.comta.org

For information about state certification and education requirements, contact:

National Certification Board for Therapeutic Massage and Bodywork
8201 Greensboro Drive, Suite 300
McLean, VA 22102
Tel: 800-296-0664
Web: http://www.ncbtmb.com

MECHANICAL ENGINEERING TECHNICIANS

School Subjects **Mathematics** **Physics** *Personal Skills* **Mechanical/manipulative** **Technical/scientific** *Work Environment* **Primarily indoors** **Primarily one location**	*Salary Range* **$25,000 to $41,000** **to $65,000+** *Certification or Licensing* **Voluntary** *Outlook* **About as fast as the average**

THE JOB

Mechanical engineering technicians work under the direction of mechanical engineers to design, build, maintain, and modify many kinds of machines, mechanical devices, and tools. They are employed in a broad range of industries. Technicians may specialize in any one of many areas including biomedical equipment, measurement and control, products manufacturing, solar energy, turbo machinery, energy resource technology, and engineering materials and technology.

Within each application, there are various aspects of the work with which the technician may be involved. One phase is research and development. In this area, the mechanical technician may assist an engineer or scientist in the design and development of anything from a ballpoint pen to a sophisticated measuring device. These technicians prepare rough sketches and layouts of the project being developed.

A second common type of work for mechanical engineering technicians is testing. For products such as engines, motors, or other moving devices, technicians may set up prototypes of the equipment to be tested and run performance tests. Technicians collect and compile all necessary data from the testing procedures and prepare reports for the engineer or scientist.

PROFESSIONAL AND PERSONAL REQUIREMENTS

Voluntary certification is offered through the National Institute for Certification in Engineering Technologies. There are no licensing requirements for mechanical engineering technicians.

You will need mathematical and mechanical aptitude and the ability to carry out detailed work. You must understand abstract concepts and apply scientific principles to problems in the shop or laboratory in both the design and the manufacturing process. Finally, you will need the ability to analyze sketches and drawings and must possess patience, perseverance, and resourcefulness.

STARTING OUT

Schools offering associate degrees in mechanical engineering technology and two-year technician programs usually help graduates find employment. At most colleges, in fact, company recruiters interview prospective graduates during their final semester of school. As a result, many students receive job offers before graduation. Other graduates may prefer to apply directly to employers, use newspaper classified ads, or to apply through public or private employment services.

EARNINGS

According to the U.S. Department of Labor, the average annual salary for mechanical engineering technicians was $40,580 in 2000. In general, mechanical engineering technicians who develop and test machinery and equipment under the direction of an engineering staff earn between $30,000 and $50,000 a year. Mechanical engineering technicians at the start of their careers earned approximately $25,000 a year or less, while senior technicians with specialized skills and experience earned much more, between $50,000 and $65,000 a year. Benefits may include paid vacation days, insurance, retirement plans, profit sharing, and tuition-reimbursement plans.

OUTLOOK

Job opportunities for mechanical engineering technicians are expected to grow as fast as the average through 2010, according to the U.S. Department of Labor. Manufacturing companies will be looking for more ways to apply the advances in mechanical technology to their operations. Opportunities will be best for technicians who are skilled in new manufacturing concepts, materials, and designs.

However, the employment outlook for engineering technicians is influenced by the economy. Hiring will fluctuate with the ups and downs of the nation's overall economic situation.

FOR MORE INFORMATION

For information on accredited programs, contact:

Accreditation Board for Engineering and Technology
111 Market Place, Suite 1050
Baltimore, MD 21202-4012
Tel: 410-347-7700
Email: accreditation@abet.org
Web: http://www.abet.org

For information about the field of mechanical engineering, contact:

American Society of Mechanical Engineers
Three Park Avenue
New York, NY 10016-5990
Tel: 800-843-2763
Email: infocentral@asme.org
Web: http://www.asme.org

For information on high school programs that provide opportunities to learn about engineering technology, contact:

Junior Engineering Technical Society
1420 King Street, Suite 405
Alexandria, VA 22314
Tel: 703-548-5387
Email: jetsinfo@jets.org
Web: http://www.jets.org

For certification information, contact:

National Institute for Certification in Engineering Technologies
1420 King Street
Alexandria, VA 22314-2794
Tel: 888-476-4238
Web: http://www.nicet.org

MEDICAL ASSISTANTS

School Subjects **Biology** **Mathematics**	*Salary Range* **$17,000 to $23,000** **to $33,000+**
Personal Skills **Helping/teaching** **Technical/scientific**	*Certification or Licensing* **Voluntary** *Outlook*
Work Environment **Primarily indoors** **Primarily one location**	**Much faster than the average**

THE JOB

Medical assistants help physicians in offices, hospitals, and clinics by performing clerical or clinical duties, or both. The larger the office, the greater the chance that the assistant will specialize in one type of work. In their clinical duties, medical assistants help physicians by preparing patients for examination or treatment. They may check and record patients' blood pressure, pulse, temperature, height, and weight.

Medical assistants often ask patients questions about their medical histories and record the answers in the patients' file. In the examining room, medical assistants may be responsible for arranging medical instruments and handing them to the physician as requested during an examination. Medical assistants may prepare patients for X rays and laboratory examinations, as well as administer electrocardiograms. They may apply dressings, draw blood, and give injections. They also may give patients instructions about taking medications, managing their diet, or restricting their activities before laboratory tests or surgery. In addition, medical assistants may collect specimens such as throat cultures for laboratory tests and may be responsible for sterilizing examining room instruments and equipment.

PROFESSIONAL AND PERSONAL REQUIREMENTS

Voluntary certification is available from certain professional organizations. The Registered Medical Assistant (RMA) credential is awarded by American Medical Technologists, and the American Association of Medical Assistants awards a credential for Certified Medical Assistant (CMA). Medical assistants generally do not need to be licensed. Some states require medical assistants to pass a test or take a course before they can perform certain tasks such as taking X rays.

As a medical assistant, you must be able to interact with patients and other medical personnel. You must be dependable and compassionate and have the desire to help people. You also must be able to carry out detailed instructions accurately. You must also respect patients' privacy by keeping medical information confidential.

STARTING OUT

Students enrolled in college or other post-high school medical assistant programs may learn of available positions through their school placement offices. High school guidance counselors may have information about positions for students about to graduate. Newspaper want ads and state employment offices are other good places to look for leads. Graduates may also wish to call local physicians' offices to find out about unadvertised openings.

EARNINGS

The earnings of medical assistants vary widely, depending on experience, skill level, and location. According to the *Occupational Outlook Handbook,* median annual earnings of medical assistants were $23,000 in 2000. The lowest 10 percent earned less than $16,700, and the highest 10 percent earned more than $32,850 a year. Median annual earnings of medical assistants who worked in offices and clinics of medical doctors were $23,610, and in hospitals they were $22,950.

OUTLOOK

Employment for medical assistants will grow much faster than the average through 2010, according to the U.S. Department of Labor. Most openings will occur to replace workers who leave their jobs, but many will be the result of a predicted surge in the number of physicians' offices, clinics, and other outpatient care facilities. The growing number of elderly Americans who need medical treatment is also a factor for this increased demand for health services. In addition, new and more complex paperwork for medical insurance, malpractice insurance, government programs, and other purposes will create a growing need for assistants in medical offices.

Experienced and formally trained medical assistants are preferred by many physicians, so these workers have the best employment outlook. Word-processing skills, other computer skills, and formal certification are all definite assets.

FOR MORE INFORMATION

For information on a career as a medical assistant, contact the following organizations:

American Association of Medical Assistants
20 North Wacker Drive, Suite 1575
Chicago, IL 60606-2963
Tel: 312-899-1500
Web: http://www.aama-ntl.org

American Medical Technologists
710 Higgins Road
Park Ridge, IL 60068-5765
Tel: 847-823-5169
Email: mail@amt1.com
Web: http://www.amt1.com

MEDICAL LABORATORY TECHNICIANS

School Subjects **Biology** **Chemistry** *Personal Skills* **Following instructions** **Technical/scientific** *Work Environment* **Primarily indoors** **Primarily one location**	*Salary Range* **$19,000 to $28,000** **to $42,000+** *Certification or Licensing* **Required by certain states** *Outlook* **About as fast as the average**

THE JOB

Medical laboratory technicians perform routine tests in medical laboratories. These tests help physicians and other medical personnel diagnose and treat disease. Technicians prepare samples of body tissue; perform laboratory tests, such as urinalysis and blood counts; and make chemical and biological analyses of cells, tissue, blood, or other body specimens. They usually work under the supervision of a medical technologist or a laboratory director. Medical laboratory technicians may work in many fields or specialize in one specific medical area, such as cytology (the study of cells), hematology (blood), or histology (body tissue).

Medical laboratory technicians frequently handle test tubes and other glassware and use precision equipment, such as microscopes and automated blood analyzers. Technicians also are often responsible for making sure machines are functioning and supplies are adequately stocked.

PROFESSIONAL AND PERSONAL REQUIREMENTS

Students who have earned an associate's degree are eligible for certification from several different agencies. They may become a certified Medical Laboratory Technician (MLT) by the Board of

Registry of the American Society of Clinical Pathologists or the American Medical Technologists. In addition, the National Credentialing Agency for Laboratory Personnel offers certification for Clinical Laboratory Technicians (CLTs).

In some states, certification is all that is required for employment. In other states, state licensure is also required. School officials are the best source of information regarding state requirements.

Besides fulfilling the academic requirements, you must have good manual dexterity, normal color vision, the ability to follow orders, and a tolerance for working under pressure.

STARTING OUT

Graduates of medical laboratory technology schools usually receive assistance from faculty and school placement services to find their first jobs. Hospitals, laboratories, and other facilities employing medical laboratory technicians may notify local schools of job openings. Often the hospital or laboratory at which they received their practical training will offer full-time employment after graduation. Positions may also be secured using the various registries of certified medical laboratory workers. Newspaper job advertisements and commercial placement agencies are other sources of help in locating employment.

EARNINGS

Salaries of medical laboratory technicians vary according to employer and geographical area. The U.S. Department of Labor reports that median annual earnings of medical and clinical laboratory technicians were $27,540 in 2000. The lowest 10 percent earned less than $18,550, and the highest 10 percent earned more than $42,370.

Most medical laboratory technicians receive paid vacations and holidays, sick leave, hospitalization and accident insurance, and retirement benefits.

OUTLOOK

Because the number of new graduates entering this field has declined, employment shortages are occurring. This is good news for prospective laboratory technicians. The U.S. Department of Labor predicts that employment of medical laboratory workers will grow about as fast as the average for all other occupations through 2010.

The overall national effort to control health care costs and increased automation are two factors that may slow the growth of employment in this field. Despite these factors, the overall amount of medical laboratory testing will probably increase, as much of medical practice today relies on high-quality laboratory testing. Medical laboratory testing is an absolutely essential element in today's medicine. Well-trained technicians, who are flexible in accepting responsibilities and willing to continue their education throughout their careers, will enjoy good employment opportunities.

FOR MORE INFORMATION

For information on careers, certification, and continuing education, contact the following organizations:

American Medical Technologists
710 Higgins Road
Park Ridge, IL 60068-5765
Tel: 847-823-5169
Email: mail@amt1.com
Web: http://www.amt1.com

American Society for Clinical Laboratory Science
7910 Woodmont Avenue, Suite 530
Bethesda, MD 20814
Tel: 301-657-2768
Web: http://www.ascls.org

National Credentialing Agency for Laboratory Personnel
PO Box 15945-289
Lenexa, KS 66285
Tel: 913-438-5110, ext. 647
Email: nca-info@goamp.com
Web: http://www.nca-info.org

MEDICAL RECORD TECHNICIANS

School Subjects **Biology** **English**	*Salary Range* **$16,000 to $23,000** **to $35,000+**
Personal Skills **Following instructions** **Technical/scientific**	*Certification or Licensing* **Recommended**
Work Environment **Primarily indoors** **Primarily one location**	*Outlook* **Much faster than the average**

THE JOB

Medical record technicians compile, code, and maintain patient records. They also tabulate and analyze data from groups of records in order to assemble reports. They review records for completeness and accuracy; assign codes to diseases, operations, diagnoses, and treatments according to detailed standardized classification systems; and post the codes on the medical record, thus making the information on the record easier to retrieve and analyze. Medical record technicians transcribe medical reports; maintain indices of patients, diseases, operations, and other categories of information; compile patient census data; and file records or supervise others who do so. In addition, they may direct the day-to-day operations of the medical records department. They maintain the flow of records and reports to and from other departments, and they sometimes assist medical staff in special studies or research that draws on information in the records.

PROFESSIONAL AND PERSONAL REQUIREMENTS

Medical record technicians who have completed an accredited training program are eligible to take a national qualifying examination to earn the credential of Registered Health Information Technician (RHIT). Most health care institutions prefer to hire individuals with an RHIT credential, as it signifies that they have met the standards established by the American Health

Information Management Association (AHIMA) as the mark of a qualified health professional.

As a medical record technician, you must have the capacity to do consistently reliable and accurate routine work. Computer skills also are essential, and some experience in transcribing dictated reports may be useful. You must also be discreet, as you will deal with records that are private and sometimes sensitive.

STARTING OUT

Most successful medical record technicians are graduates of two-year accredited programs. These programs offer placement services and can help graduates find job leads. For those who have taken the accrediting exam and become RHITs, The AHIMA offers a resume referral service.

You may also apply directly to the personnel departments of hospitals, nursing homes, outpatient clinics, and surgery centers. Many job openings are also listed in the classified advertising sections of local newspapers and with private and public employment agencies.

EARNINGS

According to the *Occupational Outlook Handbook,* median annual earnings of medical records and health information technicians were $22,750 in 2000. Salaries ranged from less than $15,710 to more than $35,170. Technicians who are not RHITs typically earn somewhat less.

OUTLOOK

Employment prospects through 2010 are excellent. According to the U.S. Department of Labor, employment in this field will grow by 54.1 percent between 2000 and 2010. The demand for well-trained medical record technicians will grow rapidly and will continue to exceed the supply. This expectation is related to the health care needs of a population that is both growing and aging and the trend toward more technologically sophisticated medicine and greater use of diagnostic procedures. It is also related to the increased requirements of regulatory bodies that scrutinize both costs and quality of care of health care providers. Because of the fear of medical malpractice lawsuits, doctors and other health care providers are documenting their diagnoses and treatments in greater detail. Also, because of the high cost of health care, insurance companies, government agencies, and courts are examining medical records with a more critical eye. These factors combine to ensure a healthy job outlook for medical record technicians.

FOR MORE INFORMATION

For information on earnings, careers in health information management, and accreditation, contact:

American Health Information Management Association
233 N. Michigan Avenue, Suite 2150
Chicago, IL 60601-5800
Tel: 312-233-1100
Email: info@ahima.org
Web: http://www.ahima.org

For a list of schools offering accredited programs in health information management, contact:

Commission on Accreditation of Allied Health Education Programs
35 East Wacker Drive, Suite 1970
Chicago, IL 60601-2208
Tel: 312-553-9355
Email: caahep@caahep.org
Web: http://www.caahep.org

MEDICAL SECRETARIES

School Subjects **English** **Health**	*Salary Range* **$17,000 to $30,000** **to $37,000**
Personal Skills **Communication/ideas** **Following instructions**	*Certification or Licensing* **Voluntary**
Work Environment **Primarily indoors** **Primarily one location**	*Outlook* **About as fast as the average**

THE JOB

Medical secretaries are responsible for the administrative and clerical work in medical offices, hospitals, or private physicians' offices. They keep records, answer phone calls, order supplies, handle correspondence, bill patients, complete insurance forms, and transcribe dictation. Medical secretaries might also keep financial records and handle other bookkeeping. They greet patients, schedule appointments, obtain medical histories, arrange hospital admissions, and schedule surgeries.

Doctors rely on medical secretaries to keep administrative operations under control. They are often the information clearinghouses for the office. They schedule appointments, provide information to callers, organize and maintain paper and electronic files, and type letters. Medical secretaries must be familiar with office equipment such as facsimile machines, photocopiers, and telephone systems. They also use computers to run spreadsheet, word-processing, database-management, or desktop publishing programs.

PROFESSIONAL AND PERSONAL REQUIREMENTS

Certification is not required for a job as a medical secretary, but obtaining it may bring you increased opportunities, earnings, and responsibility. The International Association of Administrative Professionals offers the Certified Professional Secretary (CPS) designation. To achieve CPS certification, candidates must meet certain experience requirements and pass a rigorous exam covering a number of general secretarial topics. There is no licensing requirement for this job.

As a medical secretary, you must use good judgment and discretion in dealing with confidential medical records. The work requires confidence in dealing with the public, both in person and on the telephone. You should have a pleasant personality and a desire to help others in a dependable and conscientious manner.

STARTING OUT

When looking for a job, try applying directly to hospitals, clinics, and physicians' offices. Potential positions might be listed with school or college placement centers or in newspaper want ads. Networking with medical secretaries is another inside track to job leads because employers tend to trust employee recommendations.

EARNINGS

According to 2000 Wageweb data, the mean salary for medical secretaries was approximately $29,598 a year. Beginning workers earned an average of $22,266; more-experienced secretaries earned an average of $36,999.

The U.S. Department of Labor reports that medical secretaries earned a median annual salary of $23,430 in 2000. Salaries ranged from less than $16,510 to more than $34,510.

Most employers offer vacation, sick leave, and medical benefits. Many also include life, dental, and vision care insurance, retirement benefits, and profit sharing.

OUTLOOK

While the demand for secretaries in the general sector is expected to show little change or grow more slowly than the average for all occupations, the U.S. Department of Labor projects a higher demand for medical secretaries, expecting the occupation to grow as fast as the average through 2010.

Health services are demanding more from their support personnel and are increasing salary levels accordingly. Technological advances are making secretaries more productive and able to handle the duties once done by managers or other staff. The distribution of work has shifted; secretaries receive fewer requests for typing and filing jobs. Instead, they do more technical work requiring computer skills beyond keyboarding. As a result, job opportunities will be best for those who are up to date on the latest programs and technological advances.

FOR MORE INFORMATION

For information on training to become a medical secretary, contact:

Arlington Career Institute
901 Avenue K
Grand Prairie, TX 75050
Tel: 800-394-5445
Email: ACRI1@swbell.net
Web: http://www.themetro.com/aci

For information on professional certification, contact:

International Association of Administrative Professionals
PO Box 20404
10502 NW Ambassador Drive
Kansas City, MO 64195-0404
Tel: 816-891-6600
Email: service@iaap-hq.org
Web: http://www.iaap-hq.org

The Mayo Clinic is a major employer of medical secretaries. Visit its Web site for more information.

Mayo Clinic
Web: http://www.mayo.edu

MEDICAL TRANSCRIPTIONISTS

School Subjects **Biology** **English** *Personal Skills* **Communication/ideas** **Technical/scientific** *Work Environment* **Primarily indoors** **Primarily one location**	*Salary Range* **$18,000 to $25,000** **to $35,000** *Certification or Licensing* **Recommended** *Outlook* **Faster than the average**

THE JOB

Medical transcriptionists transcribe, or type, an oral report recorded by a doctor or another health care professional. They work for primary care physicians as well as health care professionals in various medical specialties, including cardiology, immunology, oncology, podiatry, radiology, and urology. The medical transcriptionist usually types up the report while listening to the recording through a headset, using a foot pedal to stop or rewind the report as necessary. Some doctors dictate over the telephone, and others use the Internet.

The report consists of information gathered during a patient's office appointment or hospital visit and covers the patient's medical history and treatment. Often doctors will use abbreviations while dictating. The medical transcriptionist must be familiar with and type out the full words of those abbreviations.

Some transcriptionists have additional responsibilities. They may deal with patients, answer the phone, handle the mail, and perform other clerical tasks. Transcriptionists may be asked to file or deliver their reports to other doctors, lawyers, or other people who request them.

PROFESSIONAL AND PERSONAL REQUIREMENTS

The American Association for Medical Transcription administers a two-part certification examination. Those who pass the exam become Certified Medical Transcriptionists (CMTs).

Certification is good for three years, at which point recertification is necessary to keep the CMT designation. While medical transcriptionists do not need to be certified to find a job, it is highly recommended as a sign of achievement and professionalism. CMTs will probably more readily find employment and earn higher salaries.

You need to love language and grammar and be accurate and precise in your work as a medical transcriptionist. You should be able to concentrate and be prepared to sit in one place for long periods at a time, either typing or reading. An ability to work independently will help you whether you are self-employed or have an office position, since you do most of your work sitting at a computer.

STARTING OUT

It can be difficult to get started in this field, especially if you do not have any work experience. Some medical transcriptionists start out working as administrative assistants or receptionists in doctors' offices. They become acquainted with medical terminology and office procedures, and they make important contacts in the medical profession. A smaller doctor's office may be more apt to hire an inexperienced medical transcriptionist than a hospital or transcription service would be.

An apprenticeship position or internship will give you needed on-the-job experience. Once you have some experience, you can look for another position through classified ads, job search agencies, or Internet resources. You can also find job leads through word of mouth and professional contacts.

EARNINGS

According to the *Occupational Outlook Handbook,* medical transcriptionists had median hourly earnings of $12.15 in 2000, or about $25,000 for full-time work. The lowest 10 percent made less than $8.66 per hour (or an annual salary of about $18,000), and the highest 10 percent made more than $16.70 per hour (about $35,000 annually). Medical transcriptionists who worked for mailing, reproduction, and stenographic services earned a median hourly wage of $11.47. Those employed in hospitals earned $12.14 an hour, and those who worked in offices and clinics of medical doctors earned $12.25 an hour.

Medical transcriptionists working in a hospital or company setting can expect to have the usual benefits, including paid vacation, sick days, and health insurance. Self-employed medical transcriptionists have to make arrangements for their own health and retirement plans and other benefits.

OUTLOOK

As Internet security issues are resolved, its use for receiving dictation and returning transcriptions will likely become more popular. The Internet offers a quick way to communicate and transfer documents, which is useful for medical transcriptionists who work far away from their employers or clients. As voice recognition technology improves and better recognizes complex medical terminology, it, too, will be used more, and medical transcriptionists will do less typing.

Even with these technological advances, there will continue to be a need for medical transcriptionists. They will still have to review electronically created documents. And given that people are living longer, they will require more medical tests and procedures, which will all need to be documented and transcribed. The U.S. Department of Labor reports that employment of medical transcriptionists is expected to grow faster than the average through 2010.

FOR MORE INFORMATION

For information on career and tips for students, contact:

American Association for Medical Transcription
100 Sycamore Avenue
Modesto, CA 95354-0550
Tel: 800-982-2182
Email: aamt@aamt.org
Web: http://www.aamt.org

This publication contains an assortment of articles of interest to health information management professionals, including medical transcriptionists.

Advance for Health Information Professionals
Web: http://www.advanceforhim.com

MICROELECTRONICS TECHNICIANS

School Subjects	Salary Range
Mathematics	**$25,000 to $40,000**
Physics	**to $58,000+**
Personal Skills	*Certification or Licensing*
Mechanical/manipulative	**Voluntary**
Technical/scientific	*Outlook*
Work Environment	**About as fast as the average**
Primarily indoors	
Primarily one location	

THE JOB

Microelectronics technicians work in research laboratories, assisting engineering staff in developing and constructing prototype and custom-designed microchips. Microchips, often called simply "chips," are tiny but extremely complex electronic devices that control the operations of many kinds of communications equipment, consumer products, industrial controls, aerospace guidance systems, and medical electronics. The process of manufacturing chips is called fabrication.

Microelectronics technicians work closely with electronics engineers, who design components, build and test the parts, and prepare for large-scale manufacturing. Components usually require the integrated operation of several or many different types of chips.

Microelectronics technicians generally work from a diagram produced by the design engineer. The technician constructs the component and then uses a variety of sophisticated, highly sensitive equipment to test its performance. Test results are reported to the engineering staff. The technician may be required to help in evaluating the results, preparing reports based on these evaluations, and completing the technical writing of the component's specifications.

PROFESSIONAL AND PERSONAL REQUIREMENTS

The International Society of Certified Electronics Technicians offers voluntary designation to technicians with four years of experience or formal education. There is no licensing requirement for the job.

As a microelectronics technician, you must be able to follow the design engineer's specifications and instructions exactly. Similar diligence and attention to detail are necessary when following the different procedures for testing the new components. You will also need an understanding of the underlying technology.

STARTING OUT

Most schools provide job placement services to students completing their degree program. Many offer on-the-job training as a part of the training program. An internship or other real-life experience is desirable but not necessary. Many companies will provide new employees with on-site training programs.

Newspapers and trade journals are full of openings in electronics, and some companies recruit new hires directly on campus. Government employment offices are also good sources when looking for job leads.

EARNINGS

According to the U.S. Department of Labor, median annual earnings of electrical and electronics engineering technicians were $40,020 in 2000. Salaries ranged from less than $25,210 to more than $58,320. Median annual earnings of technicians who worked in the electronic components and accessories industry were $35,500. Those in managerial or supervisory positions earn higher salaries, ranging between $33,000 and $50,000 per year. Wage rates vary greatly, according to skill level, type of employer, and location. Most employers offer some fringe benefits, including paid holidays and vacations, sick leave, and life and health insurance.

OUTLOOK

Jobs in the electronics industry are expected to grow as fast as the average through 2010, according to the U.S. Department of Labor. This is because of increasing competition within the industry and the rapid technological advances that characterize the electronics industry. Electronics is a rapidly growing industry, and the use of electronic technology will become more and more important in every aspect of people's lives. This in turn will create a demand for workers with the skills and training to sustain the industry's growth. In addition, as more and more manufacturers adapt electronic technology to their products and manufacturing processes, the need for skilled personnel will also increase.

The increasing reliability and durability of electronic technology, however, will have some effect on the need for technicians. Similarly, increasing imports of microelectronics products, components, and technology may represent a decrease in production in this country, which will in turn decrease the numbers of microelectronics technicians needed here. Nevertheless, the government will continue to account for a large part of the demand for microelectronics components, technology, and personnel.

FOR MORE INFORMATION

For information on certification, contact:

International Society of Certified Electronics Technicians
3608 Pershing Avenue
Fort Worth, TX 76107-4527
Tel: 817-921-9101
Email: info@iscet.org
Web: http://www.iscet.org

MUSICIANS

School Subjects **English** **Music** *Personal Skills* **Artistic** **Communication/ideas** *Work Environment* **Indoors and outdoors** **Primarily multiple locations**	*Salary Range* **$0 to $37,000 to $100,000+** *Certification or Licensing* **Required for certain** **positions** *Outlook* **About as fast as the average**

THE JOB

Musicians perform, compose, conduct, arrange, and teach music. They may play before live audiences in clubs or auditoriums, or they may perform on television or radio, in motion pictures, or in a recording studio. Musicians play in symphony orchestras, various styles of bands, or they work as solo performers. Some classical musicians accompany singers and choirs and may perform in churches and temples. Many performing musicians supplement their incomes through teaching part-time. Others teach music full-time, perhaps playing for audiences only on occasion.

PROFESSIONAL AND PERSONAL REQUIREMENTS

Musicians who want to teach in state elementary and high schools must be state certified. To obtain a state certificate, musicians must satisfactorily complete a degree-granting course in music education at an institution of higher learning. About 600 institutions in the United States offer programs in music education that qualify students for state certificates. Musicians who do not meet public school music education requirements can teach in private schools and recreation associations or give private sessions. Music teachers may also obtain certification from the Music Teachers National Association.

Beyond training, education, and study, you will need a strong love of music to endure the arduous training and working life of a musician. An uncommon degree of dedication, self-discipline, and drive is necessary to become an accomplished musician and to be recognized in the field.

STARTING OUT

As a young musician, you need to gain experience performing in front of audiences, whether through your school or through community musical groups. You should audition as often as possible, because experience at auditioning is very important. Whenever possible, take part in seminars and internships offered by orchestras, colleges, and associations.

Popular musicians often begin playing at low-paying social functions and at small clubs or restaurants. If people like their performances, these musicians usually move on to bookings at larger rooms in better clubs. Continued success leads to a national reputation and possible recording contracts.

If you are interested in teaching, apply directly to schools. College and university placement offices often have listings of positions. Professional associations frequently list teaching openings in their newsletters and journals, as do newspapers.

EARNINGS

The *Occupational Outlook Handbook* reports that median annual earnings of musicians, singers, and related workers were $36,740 in 2000. According to the American Federation of Musicians, musicians in the major U.S. symphony orchestras earned salaries of between $24,720 and $100,196 during the 2001 performance season. Featured musicians and soloists can earn much more, especially those with an international reputation.

Popular musicians are usually paid per concert or gig. On average, pay per musician ranges from $30 to $300 or more per night. The most successful popular musicians, of course, can earn millions of dollars each year. By the end of the 1990s, some artists, in fact, had signed recording contracts worth $20 million or more.

The salaries received by music teachers in public elementary and secondary schools are the same as for other teachers. According to the U.S. Department of Labor, public elementary school and high school teachers had median yearly earnings of $41,820 in 1999-2000.

Unlike other workers, most musicians also do not enjoy such benefits as sick leave or paid vacations. Some musicians, on the other hand, who work under contractual agreements, do receive benefits, which usually have been negotiated by artists' unions.

OUTLOOK

The U.S. Department of Labor predicts that employment of musicians will grow about as fast as the average through 2010. The demand for musicians will be greatest in theaters, bands, and restaurants as the public continues to spend more money on recreational activities.

The opportunities for careers in teaching music are expected to grow at an average rate in elementary schools and in colleges and universities but at a slower rate in secondary schools. Some public schools facing severe budget problems have eliminated music programs altogether, making competition for jobs at that level even keener.

It is difficult to make a living solely as a musician. Most must hold down other jobs while pursuing their music careers. They are advised to be as versatile as possible, playing various kinds of music and more than one instrument. More importantly, musicians must be committed to pursuing their craft.

FOR MORE INFORMATION

The AGMA is a union for professional musicians. The Web site has information on upcoming auditions, news announcements for the field, and membership information.

American Guild of Musical Artists (AGMA)
1430 Broadway, 14th Floor
New York, NY 10018
Tel: 212-265-3687
Web: http://www.musicalartists.org

This organization provides information on competitions for students.

Music Teachers National Association
441 Vine Street, Suite 505
Cincinnati, OH 45202-2811
Tel: 888-512-5278
Email: mtnanet@mtna.org
Web: http://www.mtna.org

NUCLEAR MEDICINE TECHNOLOGISTS

School Subjects **Computer science** **Mathematics** *Personal Skills* **Helping/teaching** **Technical/scientific** *Work Environment* **Primarily indoors** **Primarily one location**	*Salary Range* **$32,000 to $44,000** **to $59,000+** *Certification or Licensing* **Required by certain states** *Outlook* **Faster than the average**

THE JOB

Nuclear medicine technologists work directly with patients, preparing and administering radioactive drugs. All work is supervised by a physician. Because of the nature of radioactive material, the drug preparation requires adherence to strict safety precautions. All safety procedures are overseen by the Nuclear Regulatory Commission.

After administering the drug to the patient, the technologist operates a gamma scintillation camera that takes pictures of the radioactive drug as it passes through or accumulates in parts of the patient's body. These images are then displayed on a computer screen, where the technologist and physician can examine them. The images can be used to diagnose diseases or disorders in such organs as the heart, brain, lungs, liver, kidneys, and bones. Nuclear medicine is also used for therapeutic purposes, such as to destroy abnormal thyroid tissue or ease the pain of a terminally ill patient.

Nuclear medicine technologists also have administrative duties. They must keep thorough records of the procedures performed, check all diagnostic equipment and record its use and maintenance, and keep track of radioactive drugs administered. Technologists may also perform laboratory testing of a patient's body specimens, such as blood or urine. They are also responsible for maintaining medical records for review by the attending physician.

PROFESSIONAL AND PERSONAL REQUIREMENTS

Nuclear medicine technologists must know the minimum federal standards for use and administration of nuclear drugs and equipment. Twenty-one states now require technologists to be licensed. Certification or registration are also available through the Nuclear Medicine Technology Certification Board (NMTCB) and the American Registry of Radiologic Technologists (ARRT). Many nuclear medicine technologist positions, especially those in hospitals, are open only to certified or registered technologists. Information on becoming registered or certified is available from the ARRT and the NMTCB. (See the end of this article for contact information.) There is no licensing requirement for the job.

If you are interested in a nuclear medicine technology career, you should have a strong sense of teamwork, compassion for others, and self-motivation.

STARTING OUT

Graduates of specialized training programs and two- and four-year programs usually receive placement assistance from their educational institutions, which have a vested interest in placing as many graduates as possible. You can also check help wanted ads in local papers and professional journals for job leads or get involved in a professional organization, such as the Society of Nuclear Medicine, that gives members opportunities to network.

EARNINGS

Naturally, individual earnings vary based on factors such as a person's level of education and experience. Also, those who work overtime and on-call can add to their yearly income. The U.S. Department of Labor reports that the median annual salary for all nuclear medicine technologists was $44,130 in 2000. The lowest-paid 10 percent of technologists earned less than $31,910 annually, and the highest-paid 10 percent made more than $58,500 per year. The department also notes that the middle 50 percent of nuclear medicine technologists earned between $38,150 and $52,190 annually.

Typical benefits for hospital workers include health insurance, paid vacations and sick leave, and pension plans.

OUTLOOK

According to the U.S. Department of Labor, employment of nuclear medicine technologists should grow faster than the average through 2010. The Society of Nuclear Medicine estimates that 10 to 12 million nuclear imaging and therapeutic procedures are performed in the United States each year. Advances in medical diagnostic procedures could lead to increased use of nuclear medicine technology in the diagnosis and treatment of more diseases, including cancer treatment and cardiology. Most new job opportunities are expected to be in areas with large hospitals.

FOR MORE INFORMATION

For information about career opportunities as a nuclear medicine technologist, contact:

American Society of Radiologic Technologists
15000 Central Avenue, SE
Albuquerque, NM 87123-3917
Tel: 800-444-2778
Email: asrtbod@asrt.org
Web: http://www.asrt.org

For information on certification and state licensing, contact the following organizations:

American Registry of Radiologic Technologists
1255 Northland Drive
St. Paul, MN 55120-1155
Tel: 651-687-0048
Web: http://www.arrt.org

Joint Review Committee on Educational Programs in Nuclear Medicine Technology
1 Second Avenue East, Suite C
Polson, MT 59860-2320
Tel: 406-883-0003
Web: http://www.jrcnmt.org

Nuclear Medicine Technology Certification Board
2970 Clairmont Road, Suite 935
Atlanta, GA 30329
Tel: 404-315-1739
Email: board@nmtcb.org
Web: http://www.nmtcb.org

OCCUPATIONAL THERAPY ASSISTANTS AND AIDES

School Subjects **Health** **Psychology**	*Salary Range* **$14,000 to $34,000** **to $45,000+**
Personal Skills **Helping/teaching** **Mechanical/manipulative**	*Certification or Licensing* **Required (assistants)** **Voluntary (aides)**
Work Environment **Primarily indoors** **Primarily one location**	*Outlook* **Much faster than the average**

THE JOB

The goal of occupational therapy is to improve a patient's quality of life by compensating for limitations caused by age, illness, or injury. It differs from physical therapy because it focuses not only on physical rehabilitation, but also on psychological well-being. Occupational therapy emphasizes improvement of the activities of daily living, including such functions as personal hygiene, dressing, eating, and cooking.

Occupational therapy assistants (OTAs) help people with mental, physical, developmental, or emotional limitations using a variety of activities to improve basic motor functions and reasoning abilities. They work under the direct supervision of an occupational therapist, helping to plan, implement, and evaluate rehabilitation programs designed to regain patients' self-sufficiency and restore their physical and mental functions.

OTAs help patients improve mobility and productivity using a variety of activities and exercises. They may use adaptive techniques and equipment to help patients perform tasks many take for granted. For example, they may have their patients use a reacher, a long-handled device that pinches and grabs small items, such as keys or books, from the floor or a shelf.

Occupational therapy aides help OTAs and occupational therapists by doing such things as clerical work, preparing therapy equipment for a client's use, and keeping track of supplies. Aides are responsible for materials and equipment used during therapy. They assemble and clean equipment and make certain the therapists and assistants have what they need for a patient's therapy session. They answer telephones, schedule appointments, order supplies and equipment, and complete insurance forms and other paperwork.

PROFESSIONAL AND PERSONAL REQUIREMENTS

Certification or licensing is not required for occupational therapy aides. Occupational therapy assistants must pass the certifying test of the National Board for Certification in Occupational Therapy. After passing this test, assistants receive the designation Certified Occupational Therapy Assistant (COTA). Licensure requirements for assistants vary by state, so you will need to check with the licensing board of the state in which you want to work for specific information.

To work in this field, you must be able to take directions. OTAs and aides should have a pleasant disposition, strong people skills, and a desire to help those in need. Aides, in particular, need to be detail oriented in order to keep track of paperwork and equipment. It is important for assistants and aides to work well as a team.

STARTING OUT

The placement center of your community college or technical school can provide a listing of jobs available in the occupational therapy field. Job openings are also usually posted in hospital human resource departments. You should also contact professional organizations, such as the American Occupational Therapy Association, for more information.

EARNINGS

According to the U.S. Department of Labor, the median yearly income of occupational therapy assistants was $34,340 in 2000. The lowest-paid 10 percent earned approximately $23,970 or less annually, while the highest-paid 10 percent made approximately $45,370 or more. According to a 2000 salary survey by the American Occupational Therapy Association, occupational therapy assistants had an average yearly salary of $30,130.

Naturally, experience, location, and type of employer all factor into the salaries paid.

Median annual earnings of occupational therapist aides were $20,710 in 2000, according to the U.S. Department of Labor. The lowest 10 percent earned less than $14,370; the highest 10 percent earned more than $35,900.

Benefits for full-time workers depend on the employer. They generally include health and life insurance, paid sick and vacation time, holiday pay, and a retirement fund.

OUTLOOK

According to the *Occupational Outlook Handbook,* careers in occupational therapy are fast growing, with an employment increase of about 40 percent through 2010. However, only a small number of new jobs will actually be available due to the small size of these occupations. Occupational growth will stem from an increased number of elderly people. Although more people are living well into their 70s, 80s, and in some cases, 90s, they often need the kinds of services occupational therapy provides. Medical technology has greatly improved, saving many lives that in the past would be lost through accidents, stroke, or other illnesses. Such people need rehabilitation therapy as they recuperate. Hospitals and employers are hiring more therapy assistants to help with the workload and to reduce costs.

FOR MORE INFORMATION

For additional information on careers and education, contact:

American Occupational Therapy Association
4720 Montgomery Lane
PO Box 31220
Bethesda, MD 20824-1220
Tel: 301-652-2682
Web: http://www.aota.org

For information on certification, contact:

National Board for Certification in Occupational Therapy
800 South Frederick Avenue, Suite 200
Gaithersburg, MD 20877-4150
Tel: 301-990-7979
Web: http://www.nbcot.org

OFFICE ADMINISTRATORS

School Subjects **Business** **Speech**	*Salary Range* **$22,000 to $36,000** **to $60,000+**
Personal Skills **Communication/ideas** **Leadership/management**	*Certification or Licensing* **None available**
Work Environment **Primarily indoors** **Primarily one location**	*Outlook* **Little change or more slowly** **than the average**

THE JOB

Office administrators, also called *office managers,* direct and coordinate the work activities of workers within an office. They are usually responsible for interviewing prospective employees and making recommendations on hiring. They train new workers, explain office policies and performance criteria, and delegate work responsibilities. They supervise office clerks and other workers in their tasks and confer with other supervisory personnel in planning department activities. They evaluate the progress of their staff and work with upper management to ensure that productivity and quality goals are met. Office administrators may recommend increases in salaries, promote workers when approved, or fire them, if necessary. Administrators often meet with other office personnel to discuss job-related issues or problems, and they are responsible for maintaining a positive office environment.

PROFESSIONAL AND PERSONAL REQUIREMENTS

There is no certification or licensing available in this field.

Offices can be hectic places. Deadlines on major projects can create tension, especially if some workers are sick or overburdened. As an office administrator, you will have to constantly juggle the demands of your superiors with the capabilities of your subordinates. You need an even temperament and an ability to work well with others to keep the office running smoothly.

Additional important attributes are organizational ability, judgment, attention to detail, dependability, and trustworthiness.

STARTING OUT

Often, a firm will recruit office administrators from its clerical staff. A clerk with potential supervisory abilities may be given periodic supervisory responsibilities. Later, when an opening occurs for an administrator, that person may be promoted to a full-time position.

If you have previous office work experience, contact personnel departments of individual firms directly. It will help if your work experience is similar in nature to the office in which you are applying. Your school's placement office and help wanted advertisements are also good sources for assistance.

You may also want to consider working as a *temporary worker*, often referred to as *temps*. Working as a temp provides the advantage of getting a firsthand look at a variety of office settings and making many contacts.

EARNINGS

According to the *Occupational Outlook Handbook*, office administrators earned an average of about $36,420 a year in 2000. Fifty percent earned between $28,090 and $47,350 a year. The lowest-paid 10 percent earned less than $22,070, and the top 10 percent earned over $60,600.

The size and geographic location of the company and the individual's skills can be key determinants of earnings. Higher wages will be paid to those who work for larger private companies located in and around major metropolitan areas. Full-time workers also receive paid vacations and health and life insurance. Some companies offer year-end bonuses and stock options.

OUTLOOK

According to the U.S. Department of Labor, the employment rate of office administrators is projected to change little or grow at a rate more slowly than the average for all occupations through 2010. The increased use of data-processing and other automated equipment as well as corporate downsizing may reduce the number of administrators in the next decade.

However, this profession will still offer good employment prospects because of its sheer size. A large number of job openings will occur as administrators transfer to other industries or leave the workforce for other reasons. Since some clerical occupations will be affected by increased automation, some office administrators may have smaller staffs and be asked to perform more professional tasks. Employment opportunities will be especially good for those trained to operate computers and other types of modern office machinery.

FOR MORE INFORMATION

For information on seminars, conferences, and news on the industry, contact:

American Management Association International
1601 Broadway
New York, NY 10019-7420
Tel: 212-586-8100
Email: customerservice@amanet.org
Web: http://www.amanet.org

National Association of Executive Secretaries and Administrative Assistants
900 South Washington Street, Suite G-13
Falls Church, VA 22046
Tel: 703-237-8616
Web: http://www.naesaa.com

For a career brochure, contact:

National Management Association
2210 Arbor Boulevard
Dayton, OH 45439-1580
Tel: 937-294-0421
Email: nma@nma1.org
Web: http://www.nma1.org

For information on careers and related education, contact:

Canadian Management Centre of the American Management Association
150 York Street, 5th Floor
Toronto, ON M5H 3S5 Canada
Email: cmcinfo@amanet.org
Web: http://www.cmcamai.org

ORTHOTIC AND PROSTHETIC TECHNICIANS

School Subjects **Biology** **Technical/shop** *Personal Skills* **Helping/teaching** **Mechanical/manipulative** *Work Environment* **Primarily indoors** **Primarily one location**	*Salary Range* **$18,000 to $30,000** **to $41,000** *Certification or Licensing* **Voluntary** *Outlook* **Faster than the average**

THE JOB

Orthotic technicians and *prosthetic technicians* make, fit, repair, and maintain orthotic and prosthetic devices according to specifications and under the guidance of orthotists and prosthetists. Orthotic devices, sometimes also referred to as orthopedic appliances, are braces used to support weak or ineffective joints or muscles. Orthotic devices are also used to correct physical defects, such as spinal deformities.

Prosthetic devices are artificial limbs and plastic cosmetic devices. These devices are designed and fitted to the patient by prosthetists or orthotists. Technicians then make the device according to the specifications prepared by orthotists and prosthetists. Part of their work involves making models of patients' torsos, limbs, or amputated areas. Most of the technicians' efforts, however, go into the actual building of the devices. Some technicians specialize in either orthotic devices or prosthetic devices, while others are trained and able to work with both types.

PROFESSIONAL AND PERSONAL REQUIREMENTS

There are presently no licensing requirements for orthotic and prosthetic technicians. There is, however, a program for voluntary certification conducted by the American Board for

Certification in Orthotics and Prosthetics (commonly called ABC). Depending on their area of concentration, technicians who pass the examination are designated as Registered Technician, Orthotic (RTO), Registered Technician, Prosthetic (RTP), or Registered Technician, Prosthetic-Orthotic (RTPO). To maintain registration, a technician must complete a certain number of ABC-approved professional continuing education credits every five years.

To be a successful orthotic or prosthetic technician, you will need to enjoy working with your hands and have excellent eye-hand coordination. You must also be patient and detail oriented, since this work will involve using precise measurements and working on a piece until it is an exact fit. Technicians should be committed to lifelong learning, as new technologies, materials, and processes are continuously being developed. A good sense of color will also be helpful because your responsibilities may include matching the color of a device to a patient's skin tone.

STARTING OUT

Graduates of one- or two-year programs of formal instruction usually have the easiest time finding a first job. Your teachers and placement offices will have valuable advice and information about local employers. Also, check into some of the trade publications for the orthotics and prosthetics industry. For example, the *O&P Almanac*, distributed by the American Orthotic and Prosthetic Association, often carries classified advertising with listings of job openings.

EARNINGS

Technicians who have received their certification earn an average of approximately $3.50 more per hour than those who are noncertified, which translates into a difference of more than $7,000 yearly. Other factors influencing salary differences include the technician's work experience and the location, size, and type of employer. According to the *2000 O&P Business and Salary Survey Report*, certified technicians who had up to two years of work experience earned an average of $14.50 per hour. This hourly wage would translate into a yearly salary of approximately $30,160 for full-time work. Certified technicians with two to five years' experience earned an average of $17.61 per hour (approximately $36,630 annually). Those with more than five years of experience made an average of $19.78 an hour (approximately $41,140 per year). By comparison, the report also noted the lowest hourly pay for noncertified technicians with less than two years' experience averaged $8.69 per hour (approximately $18,075 annually).

OUTLOOK

Employment for orthotic and prosthetic technicians is expected to grow at a rate faster than the average. The need for technicians is driven by such circumstances as the rapid growth of the health care industry, improving technologies, and our country's aging population. According to a study prepared for the National Commission on Prosthetic Education, by the year 2015, the aging baby boomer population will largely increase the demand for both orthotists and prosthetists. By 2020, the number of people who have an amputation and are in need of prostheses will increase by 47 percent.

In addition, continuing developments in this field will mean that more people with different kinds of disabilities will be candidates for new or improved orthotic and prosthetic devices. As the need for orthotic and prosthetic devices and the variety of the devices themselves grow, so will the demand for skilled technicians.

FOR MORE INFORMATION

For information on certification, contact:

American Board for Certification in Orthotics and Prosthetics
330 John Carlyle Street, Suite 210
Alexandria, VA 22314
Tel: 703-836-7114
Web: http://www.abcop.org

For the O&P Almanac *and news relating to the field, contact:*

American Orthotic and Prosthetic Association
330 John Carlyle Street, Suite 200
Alexandria, VA 22314
Tel: 571-431-0876
Web: http://www.aopanet.org

PACKAGING MACHINERY TECHNICIANS

School Subjects	Salary Range
Mathematics	**$13,000 to $47,000**
Technical/shop	**to $70,000**
Personal Skills	*Certification or Licensing*
Mechanical/manipulative	**Voluntary**
Technical/scientific	
	Outlook
Work Environment	**Faster than the average**
Primarily indoors	
Primarily multiple locations	

THE JOB

Packaging machinery technicians work with automated machinery that packages products into bottles, cans, bags, boxes, cartons, and other containers. Their jobs entail building machines, installing and setting up equipment, training operators to use the equipment, maintaining equipment, troubleshooting, and repairing machines.

There are several subspecialties within this field. *Machinery builders,* also called *assemblers,* assist engineers in the development and modification of new and existing machinery designs. *Field service technicians,* also called *field service representatives,* install new machinery at customers' plants and train in-plant machine operators and maintenance personnel on its operation and maintenance. *Automated packaging machine mechanics,* also called *maintenance technicians*, perform scheduled preventive maintenance as well as make repairs.

PROFESSIONAL AND PERSONAL REQUIREMENTS

A voluntary certification program is available for engineering technicians through the National Institute for Certification in Engineering Technologies. Certification is available at various levels and in different specialty fields. The Institute of Packaging

Professionals also offers the following voluntary certifications: Certified Professional in Training (CPT) for those with less than six years of experience in packaging, and Certified Packaging Professional (CPP) for those with at least six years of experience.

If you are interested in this field, you should have mechanical and electrical aptitude, manual dexterity, and the ability to work under time pressure. You should have analytical and problem-solving skills as well as good communication skills.

STARTING OUT

If you are enrolled in a technical program, you may find job leads through your school's job placement service. Many jobs in packaging are unadvertised; you can find out about them through contacts with professionals in the industry. You can also learn about openings from teachers, school administrators, and industry contacts acquired during training.

You can apply directly to machinery manufacturing companies or companies with manufacturing departments. Local employment offices may list job openings. Sometimes companies hire part-time or summer help in other departments, such as the warehouse or shipping. These jobs may provide an opportunity to move into other areas of the company.

EARNINGS

In general, technicians earn approximately $20,000 a year to start and with experience can increase their salaries to about $33,000. Seasoned workers with two-year degrees who work for large companies may earn between $50,000 and $70,000 a year, particularly those in field service jobs or in supervisory positions.

According to Abbott-Langer Associates, packaging equipment operators in the food industry earned an average of $28,288 a year in 2000. Machine repairers earned an average of $30,472. The U.S. Bureau of Labor Statistics reports that median annual earnings for all workers in packaging machinery were $46,976 in 2000. Packaging machine operators and tenders earned an annual median of $19,660, with salaries ranging from $13,250 to $33,810.

Benefits vary and depend upon company policy but generally include paid holidays, vacations, sick days, and medical and dental insurance. Some companies also offer tuition assistance programs, pension plans, profit sharing, and 401-K plans.

OUTLOOK

Packaging machinery technicians are in high demand both by companies that manufacture packaging machinery and by companies that use packaging machinery. With the growth of the packaging industry, which grosses more than $100 billion a year, a nationwide shortage of trained packaging technicians has developed over the last 20 years. There are far more openings than there are qualified applicants.

The introduction of computers, robotics, fiber optics, and vision systems into the industry has added new skill requirements and job opportunities for packaging machinery technicians. There is already widespread application of computer-aided design and computer-aided manufacturing. The use of computers in packaging machinery will continue to increase, with computers communicating with other computers on the status of operations and providing diagnostic maintenance information and production statistics. The role of robotics, fiber optics, and electronics will also continue to expand. To be prepared for the jobs of the future, packaging machinery students should seek training in the newest technologies.

FOR MORE INFORMATION

For information on educational programs, certification, and the packaging industry, contact the following organizations:

Institute of Packaging Professionals
1601 North Bond Street, Suite 101
Naperville, IL 60563
Tel: 630-544-5050
Email: info@iopp.org
Web: http://www.iopp.org

National Institute for Certification in Engineering Technologies
1420 King Street
Alexandria, VA 22314-2794
Tel: 888-476-4238
Web: http://www.nicet.org

PAINTERS AND SCULPTORS

School Subjects	Salary Range
Art	**$10,000 (or less) to $31,000**
History	**to $71,000+**
Personal Skills	*Certification or Licensing*
Artistic	**None available**
Communication/ideas	*Outlook*
Work Environment	**About as fast as the average**
Indoors and outdoors	
One location with travel	

THE JOB

Painters use watercolors, oils, acrylics, and other substances to paint pictures or designs onto flat surfaces. *Sculptors* design and construct three-dimensional artwork from various materials, such as stone, concrete, plaster, and wood. Painters and sculptors use their creative abilities to produce original works of art. They are generally classified as fine artists rather than commercial artists because they are responsible for selecting the theme, subject matter, and medium of their artwork.

PROFESSIONAL AND PERSONAL REQUIREMENTS

There is no certification or licensing available in this field.

An important requirement for your career as a painter or sculptor is artistic ability. Of course, this is entirely subjective, and it is perhaps more important that you believe in your own ability and potential. Apart from being creative and imaginative, you should exhibit such traits as patience, determination, independence, and sensitivity.

You will also need good business and marketing skills if you intend to support yourself through art. As a small-business owner, you must be able to market and sell your products to wholesalers, retailers, and the general public.

STARTING OUT

If you are interested in exhibiting or selling your products, you should investigate your potential markets. Reference books, such as *Artist's Market,* may be helpful, as well as library books that offer information on business laws, taxes, and related issues. Local fairs and art shows often provide opportunities for new artists to display their work. Art councils are a good source of information on upcoming fairs in the area.

You can also sell your work on consignment. When a painter or sculptor sells work this way, a store or gallery displays an item; when the item is sold, the artist gets the price of that item minus a commission that goes to the store or gallery. Artists who sell on consignment should read contracts very carefully.

EARNINGS

More than 50 percent of artists are self-employed—a figure over five times greater than in other occupations. As freelancers, artists can set their hours and prices. Those employed by businesses usually work for the motion picture and television industries, wholesale or retail trades, or public relations firms. According to the *Occupational Outlook Handbook,* salaried, full-time artists in 2000 earned an average of $31,190 annually. Fifty percent earned between $20,460 and $42,720; the top 10 percent earned over $70,560. Some internationally known artists may command millions of dollars for their work.

Artists often work long hours and earn little, especially when they are first starting out. The price they charge is up to them, but much depends on the value the public places on their work. A particular item may sell for a few dollars or tens of thousands of dollars, or any price in between.

OUTLOOK

Employment for visual artists is expected to grow as fast as the average. However, because they are usually self-employed, much of their success depends on the amount and type of work created, the drive and determination in selling the artwork, and the interest or readiness of the public to appreciate and purchase the work. Continued population growth, higher incomes, and increased appreciation for fine art will create a demand for visual artists.

It often takes several years for an artist's work and reputation to be established. Many artists have to support themselves through other employment. There are numerous employment opportunities for commercial artists in such fields as publishing, advertising, fashion and design, and teaching. Painters and sculptors should consider employment in these and other fields. They should be prepared, however, to face strong competition from others who are attracted to these fields.

FOR MORE INFORMATION

The following organization helps artists market and sell their art. It offers marketing tools, a newsletter, a directory of artists, and reference resources.

ArtNetwork
PO Box 1360
Nevada City, CA 95959
Tel: 800-383-0677
Email: info@artmarketing.com
Web: http://www.artmarketing.com

For general information on ceramic arts study, contact:

National Art Education Association
1916 Association Drive
Reston, VA 20191-1590
Tel: 703-860-8000
Email: naea@dgs.dgsys.com
Web: http://www.naea-reston.org

The following organization provides an information exchange and sharing of professional opportunities.

Sculptors Guild
The Soho Building
110 Greene Street, Suite 601
New York, NY 10012
Tel: 212-431-5669

PARALEGALS

School Subjects **English** **Government**	*Salary Range* **$23,000 to $35,000** **to $56,000+**
Personal Skills **Communication/ideas** **Following instructions**	*Certification or Licensing* **Voluntary**
Work Environment **Primarily indoors** **Primarily multiple locations**	*Outlook* **Faster than the average**

THE JOB

Paralegals support lawyers in a variety of ways, including assisting in trial preparations, investigating facts, and preparing documents such as affidavits and pleadings. Although the lawyer assumes responsibility for the paralegal's work, the paralegal may take on all the duties of the lawyer except for setting fees, appearing in court, accepting cases, and giving legal advice.

Paralegals spend much of their time in law libraries, researching laws and previous cases, and compiling facts to help lawyers prepare for trial. As part of their research, paralegals often interview witnesses as well. After analyzing the laws and facts that have been compiled for a particular client, the paralegal often writes a report that the lawyer may use to determine how to proceed with the case. If a case is brought to trial, the paralegal helps prepare legal arguments and draft pleadings to be filed in court. Paralegals also organize and store files and correspondence related to cases.

PROFESSIONAL AND PERSONAL REQUIREMENTS

Paralegals are not required to be licensed or certified. Instead, when lawyers employ paralegals, they often follow guidelines designed to protect the public from the practice of law by unqualified persons.

Paralegals may choose to become certified by the National Association of Legal Assistants Certifying Board. Paralegals who pass the test may use the title Certified Legal Assistant

(CLA) after their names. The National Federation of Paralegal Associations also offers a designation for paralegals. Those who pass this exam and maintain the continuing education requirement may use the designation Registered Paralegal (RP).¯

Communication skills, both verbal and written, are vital to working as a paralegal. You must be able to think logically and learn new laws and regulations quickly. Research skills, computer skills, and people skills are also necessary for success.

STARTING OUT

Although some law firms promote legal secretaries to paralegal status, most employers prefer to hire individuals who have completed paralegal programs. To have the best opportunity at getting a quality job in the paralegal field, you should attend a paralegal school. In addition to providing a solid background in paralegal studies, most schools help graduates find jobs.

The National Federation of Paralegal Associations recommends using job banks that are sponsored by paralegal associations across the country. For paralegal associations that may be able to help, see the addresses listed at the end of this article.

EARNINGS

The size and location of the firm and the education and experience of the employee are some factors that determine the annual earnings of paralegals. Starting salaries for those with one year or less paralegal experience were $38,100 in 1999, according to the National Federation of Paralegal Associations.

The U.S. Department of Labor reports that paralegals earned median annual earnings of $35,360 in 2000. The highest 10 percent earned more than $56,060, while the lowest 10 percent earned less than $23,350. Paralegals employed by the federal government averaged $48,560 annually in 2000.

OUTLOOK

The employment outlook for paralegals through 2010 is very good; growth of 33 percent is expected during this time span. In the private sector, paralegals can work in banks, insurance companies, real estate firms, and corporate legal departments. In the public sector, there is a growing need for paralegals in the courts and community legal service programs, government agencies, and consumer organizations.

The growth of this occupation, to some extent, is dependent on the economy. Businesses are less likely to pursue litigation cases when profit margins are down, thus curbing the need for new hires.

FOR MORE INFORMATION

For information regarding accredited educational facilities, contact:

American Association for Paralegal Education
407 Wekiva Springs Road, Suite 241
Longwood, FL 32779
Tel: 407-834-6688
Email: info@aafpe.org
Web: http://www.aafpe.org

For general information about careers in the law field, contact:

American Bar Association
Service Center
541 North Fairbanks Court
Chicago, IL 60611
Tel: 312-988-5522
Email: service@abanet.org
Web: http://www.abanet.org

For information about educational and licensing programs, certification, and paralegal careers, contact:

National Association of Legal Assistants
1516 South Boston Avenue, Suite 200
Tulsa, OK 74119
Tel: 918-587-6828
Email: nalanet@nala.org
Web: http://www.nala.org

For career brochures, contact:

National Federation of Paralegal Associations
PO Box 33108
Kansas City, MO 64114-0108
Tel: 816-941-4000
Email: info@paralegals.org
Web: http://www.paralegals.org

PEDORTHISTS

School Subjects **Biology** **Technical/shop**	*Salary Range* **$20,000 to $35,000** **to $65,000**
Personal Skills **Helping/teaching** **Mechanical/manipulative**	*Certification or Licensing* **Recommended (certification)** **Required by certain states** **(licensing)**
Work Environment **Primarily indoors** **Primarily one location**	*Outlook* **Faster than the average**

THE JOB

Pedorthists treat patients' foot problems by designing and fitting therapeutic footwear based on doctors' prescriptions. They examine and make impressions of patients' feet to get the exact measurements and contours. If the foot problem can be corrected by using footwear that has already been created, pedorthists will make minor adjustments to this ready-made device to fit the patient's needs. Sometimes, pedorthists must design new footwear that meets the specific needs of the patient.

Once pedorthists have designed the device, they try it on the patient to make sure the fit is correct. Often, pedorthists schedule many trial fittings, making numerous adjustments, to be sure the footwear is absolutely correct. They also must keep precise, detailed records that are used to create reports for patients' doctors.

Pedorthists specialize in a variety of areas, including adult foot deformities, amputations, arthritis, congenital deformities, diabetes, geriatrics, overuse injuries, pediatrics, sports-related injuries, and trauma.

PROFESSIONAL AND PERSONAL REQUIREMENTS

Voluntary certification is offered by the Board for Certification in Pedorthics. Every three years, pedorthists must renew their credential by attending continuing education classes.

A number of states require pedorthists to be licensed. You should contact your state's department of labor to learn more about licensing requirements.

Pedorthists work closely with patients, physicians, and other health care workers. Because of this, you will need strong written and oral communication skills if you choose this line of work. You must also be in good physical condition, since you will be repeatedly kneeling, sitting, or standing as you work with patients.

STARTING OUT

The most direct way to enter this field is to earn your degree with summer internships built in. Most likely, the internships will turn into jobs or into leads to other possible job opportunities. Although certification is important, it's not necessary to break into the field.

The Pedorthic Footwear Association sponsors several national and regional seminars each year. These seminars focus on specialty areas within pedorthics, such as diabetes, sports-related injuries, and geriatrics. These events provide many educational opportunities for the beginning pedorthist and allow the beginner to meet and talk with experienced pedorthists.

EARNINGS

Pedorthists just entering the field will usually start out making $20,000 to $28,000 a year. With certification and hands-on experience, pedorthists can make $30,000 to $35,000 annually. Those at the top of their field may earn up to $65,000. Earnings depend on the type of facility and the location of the pedorthists' employer.

Pedorthists working in shoe stores and clinics usually receive paid sick days, holidays, vacation days, and some level of insurance. Retirement savings plans are usually offered as well. Most hospitals provide insurance and other benefits but usually don't offer as many days off. However, some hospitals offer discounted or free medical services to their employees.

OUTLOOK

Jobs are abundant for pedorthists for many reasons. The sports and fitness boom shows no signs of declining. Many people involved in different sports activities will need special braces, inserts, and devices to maintain a high level of activity. Also, sports-related injuries are increasingly common, so skilled pedorthists who are able to treat such injuries will be in high demand.

Advancing age brings many chronic conditions such as arthritis and bone disease that require the help of a pedorthist. Many people with these problems will require special equipment and advice from the pedorthist. The growing elderly population has created a great need for pedorthists. As a result of these factors, the future of pedorthics is stable and ever growing.

FOR MORE INFORMATION

For certification information, contact:

Board for Certification in Pedorthics
2517 Eastlake Avenue E, Suite 200
Seattle, WA 98102
Tel: 800-560-2025
Email: info@cpeds.org
Web: http://www.cpeds.org

For information about the pedorthist profession and free brochures, contact:

Pedorthic Footwear Association
7150 Columbia Gateway Drive, Suite G
Columbia, MD 21046
Tel: 410-381-7278
Email: info@pedorthics.org
Web: http://www.pedorthics.org

PHARMACY TECHNICIANS

School Subjects **Biology** **Chemistry**	*Salary Range* **$18,000 to $24,000** **to $26,000+**
Personal Skills **Following instructions** **Technical/scientific**	*Certification or Licensing* **Required by certain states** *Outlook*
Work Environment **Primarily indoors** **Primarily one location**	**Much faster than the average**

THE JOB

Pharmacy technicians give technical assistance to registered pharmacists. Technicians usually work in chain or independent drug stores, hospitals, community ambulatory care centers, home health care agencies, nursing homes, and the pharmaceutical industry. They maintain patient records; count, package, and label medication doses; prepare and distribute sterile products; and fill orders for stock supplies such as over-the-counter products.

As their roles increase, trained pharmacy technicians become more specialized. They can work in narcotics control, nuclear pharmacy, and home health care and assist with pharmaceuticals in operation rooms and emergency rooms. Specially trained pharmacy technicians are also employed as data entry technicians, lead technicians, supervisors, and technician managers.

PROFESSIONAL AND PERSONAL REQUIREMENTS

At least three states license pharmacy technicians, and all 50 states have adopted a written, standardized test for voluntary certification of technicians. Some states, including Texas and Louisiana, require certification of pharmacy technicians. Even if the state in which you hope to work does not require certification, you should consider getting it. Certification will enhance your credentials, demonstrate to employers your commitment to the profession, and possibly qualify you for higher pay.

To work as a pharmacy technician, you must be precision minded, honest, and mature because you are depended on for accuracy, especially in hospitals. You must be able to precisely follow written or oral instructions, as a wide variety of people, including physicians, nurses, pharmacists, and patients, rely on your actions. You will also need computer aptitude in order to effectively record pharmaceutical data.

STARTING OUT

Pharmacy technicians often are hired by the hospital or agency where they interned. Other sources of job openings are employment agencies and newspaper ads.

In some cases you may be able to pursue education and certification while employed as a pharmacy technician. Some chain drugstores pay certification fees for their techs and reward them with higher hourly pay.

EARNINGS

A fall 2000 salary survey conducted by Pharmacy OneSource and *Pharmacy Week* found that technicians working in hospitals, for example, generally earned more per hour than those working in retail. In addition, technicians with certification earned more per hour than those without. According to the survey, certified technicians had median hourly wages of $11.31 (approximately $23,525 a year), while non-certified technicians had median hourly wages of $9.65 ($20,072 a year).

A technician's experience is another factor that influences earnings. According to Salary.com, beginning technicians in 2001 may expect yearly earnings as low as approximately $18,350, while those with at least four years of experience may make approximately $26,150 or more per year.

Benefits that technicians receive depend on their employers but generally include medical and dental insurance, retirement savings plans, and paid sick, personal, and vacation days.

OUTLOOK

The U.S. Department of Labor projects much faster than average employment growth for pharmacy technicians through 2010. As the role of the pharmacist shifts to consultation, more technicians will be needed to assemble and dispense medications. A strong demand is emerging for technicians with specialized training to work in specific areas, such as emergency room and nuclear pharmacy. An increasing number of pharmacy technicians will be needed as the number of older Americans (who, on average, require more prescription medications) continues to rise.

Aspiring pharmacy technicians should be aware that they might need more education in the future to gain certification as a result of the growing number of complex medications and new drug therapies on the market.

FOR MORE INFORMATION

Contact the AAPT for more information on membership and continuing education. The association's Web site also has helpful links for those interested in this field.

American Association of Pharmacy Technicians (AAPT)
PO Box 1447
Greensboro, NC 27402
Tel: 877-368-4771
Email: aapt@bellsouth.net
Web: http://www.pharmacytechnician.com

For more information on accredited pharmacy technician training programs, contact:

American Society of Health-System Pharmacists
7272 Wisconsin Avenue
Bethesda, MD 20814
Tel: 301-657-3000
Web: http://www.ashp.org

To learn more about certification and training, contact:

Pharmacy Technician Certification Board
2215 Constitution Avenue, NW
Washington, DC 20037-2985
Tel: 202-429-7576
Web: http://www.ptcb.org

Pharmacy Week *is a newsletter for professionals and pharmacy students. Check out the Web site for articles, industry news, job listings, and continuing education information.*

Pharmacy Week
Web: http://www.pharmacyweek.com

PHLEBOTOMY TECHNICIANS

School Subjects **Biology** **Chemistry** *Personal Skills* **Helping/teaching** **Technical/scientific** *Work Environment* **Primarily indoors** **Primarily one location**	*Salary Range* **$17,000 to $21,000** **to $40,000+** *Certification or Licensing* **Required by certain states** *Outlook* **About as fast as the average**

THE JOB

Phlebotomy technicians draw blood from patients or donors in hospitals, blood banks, clinics, physicians' offices, or other facilities. They assemble equipment, verify patient identification numbers, and withdraw blood using a finger prick or a syringe. They label, transport, and store blood for analysis or for other medical purposes.

Before taking blood, the phlebotomy technician takes the patient's medical history, temperature, and pulse and checks to see how much blood has been ordered by the patient's physician to be drawn. Next, the site of the withdrawal is located, and the blood sample is carefully and systematically taken.

After collection, the phlebotomy technician labels the blood, coordinates its number with the physician's order, and transports the blood to a storage facility or to another laboratory worker. The technician also checks to make sure that the patient is not lightheaded or nauseous, notes any adverse reactions, and administers first aid or other medical assistance if necessary.

PROFESSIONAL AND PERSONAL REQUIREMENTS

Certification and licensing for phlebotomy technicians vary by state and employer. Several agencies grant certification, including American Medical Technologists, the American Society of Phlebotomy Technicians, and the Board of Registry of the

American Society of Clinical Pathologists. Contact these organizations for more information.

You should enjoy working with people and be an effective communicator and good listener to succeed in this line of work. You need to be attentive to detail and able to work under pressure. In addition, you should have patience and good manual dexterity to draw blood from patients with the least amount of discomfort.

STARTING OUT

Newspapers and publications serving health care professionals list job advertisements. If you are attending an accredited training program, you may also be recruited by an employer directly. Some programs offer job placement assistance as well.

EARNINGS

Experience, level of education, employer, and work performed determine the salary ranges for phlebotomy technicians. According to a survey by the American Society of Clinical Pathologists' Board of Registry, the median beginning hourly salary for phlebotomy technicians was $8.10 in 2000 (or approximately $16,800 a year). The median hourly salary for more experienced workers was $9.90 ($20,590 a year). The highest-paid phlebotomy technicians earned $11.80 or more per hour ($24,544 a year). A specialist in blood bank technology with a bachelor's degree and advanced training can usually expect a starting salary of approximately $40,000 a year.

Benefits such as vacation time, sick leave, insurance, and other fringe benefits vary by employer but are usually consistent with other full-time health care workers.

OUTLOOK

The demand for phlebotomy technicians in the United States is highest in small hospitals. As the percentage of our population aged 65 or older continues to rise, the demand for all kinds of health care professionals will increase as well. There is a demand for workers who are qualified to draw blood at the bedside of patients. The growing number of patients with certain diseases, such as HIV and AIDS, also increases the need for phlebotomy technicians.

FOR MORE INFORMATION

The following organizations provide information on phlebotomy technician careers, certification, and employment opportunities.

American Association of Blood Banks
8101 Glenbrook Road
Bethesda, MD 20814-2749
Tel: 301-907-6977
Email: aabb@aabb.org
Web: http://www.aabb.org

American Medical Technologists
710 Higgins Road
Park Ridge, IL 60068-5765
Tel: 847-823-5169
Email: mail@amt1.com
Web: http://www.amt1.com

American Society of Phlebotomy Technicians
PO Box 1831
Hickory, NC 28603
Tel: 828-294-0078
Web: http://www.aspt.org

For information on accredited training programs, contact:

National Accrediting Agency for Clinical Laboratory Sciences
8410 West Bryn Mawr, Suite 670
Chicago, IL 60631
Tel: 773-714-8880
Email: info@naacls.org
Web: http://www.naacls.org

PHOTOGRAPHERS

School Subjects **Art** **Chemistry**	*Salary Range* **$14,000 to $22,000** **to $47,000+**
Personal Skills **Artistic** **Communication/ideas**	*Certification or Licensing* **None available**
Work Environment **Indoors and outdoors** **Primarily multiple locations**	*Outlook* **About as fast as the average**

THE JOB

Photographers take, develop, and print pictures of people, places, objects, and events, using a variety of cameras and photographic equipment. They work in publishing, advertising, public relations, science, and business as well as in personal photographic services. They may also work as fine artists.

Photography is both an artistic and technical occupation. Photographers must know how to use cameras and adjust focus, shutter speeds, apertures, lenses, and filters. They must understand the types and speeds of films and the use of light and shadow.

Some photographers send their film to laboratories to be developed and printed, but others do it themselves. These processes require knowledge about chemicals such as developers and fixers and how to use enlarging equipment.

Digital photography is a relatively new development. Film is replaced by microchips that record pictures in digital format. They can then be downloaded onto a computer's hard drive, and the photographer uses special software to manipulate the images on screen. Digital photography is used primarily for electronic publishing and advertising.

Photographers usually specialize in one of several areas: portraiture, commercial and advertising photography, photojournalism, fine art, educational photography, or scientific photography.

PROFESSIONAL AND PERSONAL REQUIREMENTS

There are no certification or licensing requirements for this field.

If you hope to become a photographer, you should possess manual dexterity, good eyesight and color vision, and artistic ability. You need an eye for form and line, an appreciation of light and shadow, and the ability to use imaginative and creative approaches to photographs or film, especially in commercial work. In addition, you should be patient and accurate and enjoy working with detail.

Self-employed, or freelance, photographers need good business skills. They must be able to manage their own studios, including hiring and managing photographic assistants and other employees, keeping records, and maintaining photographic and business files. Marketing and sales skills are also important to a successful freelance photography business.

STARTING OUT

Some photographers enter the field as apprentices, trainees, or assistants. As a trainee, you can work in a darkroom, camera shop, or developing laboratory. You might be asked to move lights and arrange backgrounds for a commercial or portrait photographer or motion picture photographer. You will need to spend many months learning this kind of work before you move into a job behind a camera.

In many large cities, there are schools of photography, which may be a good way to start in the field. Jobs as a press photographer are available at many newspapers and magazines published in the United States and abroad. Some photographers go into business for themselves as soon as they have finished their formal education. Setting up a studio may not require a large capital outlay, but beginners may find that success does not come easily.

EARNINGS

The U.S. Department of Labor reports that salaried photographers earned median annual salaries of $22,300 in 2000. Salaries ranged from less than $13,760 to more than $46,890. Self-employed photographers often earn more than salaried photographers, but their earnings depend on general business conditions.

Photographers who combine scientific training and photographic expertise can work as scientific photographers and often earn a higher salary than other photographers. They also usually receive consistently larger advances in salary than do others, so that their income, both as beginners and as experienced photographers, places them well above the average in their field.

Photographers in salaried jobs usually receive benefits such as paid holidays, vacations, and sick leave and medical insurance.

OUTLOOK

Employment of photographers will increase about as fast as the average for all occupations through 2010, according to the *Occupational Outlook Handbook*. The demand for visual images should remain strong in education, communication, entertainment, marketing, and research. As the Internet grows and more newspapers and magazines turn to electronic publishing, demand will increase for photographers to produce digital images. Additionally, as the population grows, demand should increase for photographers who specialize in portraiture.

Photography is a highly competitive field. There are far more photographers than positions available. Only those who are extremely talented and highly skilled can support themselves as self-employed photographers. Many photographers work another job in addition to taking pictures.

FOR MORE INFORMATION

To access job leads and News Photographer *magazine, contact:*

National Press Photographers Association
3200 Croasdaile Drive, Suite 306
Durham, NC 27705
Tel: 919-383-7246
Web: http://www.nppa.org

This organization provides training, publishes its own magazine, and offers various services for its members.

Professional Photographers of America
229 Peachtree Street, NE, Suite 2200
Atlanta, GA 30303
Tel: 404-522-8600
Web: http://www.ppa.com

PHYSICAL THERAPY ASSISTANTS

School Subjects **Biology** **Health** *Personal Skills* **Helping/teaching** **Mechanical/manipulative** *Work Environment* **Primarily indoors** **Primarily one location**	*Salary Range* **$23,000 to $34,000** **to $46,000+** *Certification or Licensing* **Required by certain states** *Outlook* **Much faster than the average**

THE JOB

Physical therapy assistants help to restore physical function in people with injury, birth defects, or disease. They assist with a variety of techniques, such as exercise, massage, heat, and water therapy. Working directly under the supervision of physical therapists, assistants teach and help patients improve functional activities required in their daily lives, such as walking, climbing, and moving from one place to another. Assistants observe patients during treatments, record the patients' responses and progress, and report these to the physical therapist, either orally or in writing. They fit and instruct patients on how to use braces, artificial limbs, crutches, canes, walkers, wheelchairs, and other devices. They may make physical measurements to assess the effects of treatments or to evaluate patients' range of motion, length and girth of body parts, and vital signs. Physical therapy assistants act as members of a team and regularly confer with other members of the physical therapy staff.

PROFESSIONAL AND PERSONAL REQUIREMENTS

More than 40 states require regulation of physical therapy assistants in the form of registration, certification, or licensure. Typically, graduation from an accredited program and passing a written exam are needed for licensing. Because requirements vary by state, you will need to check with your state's licensure board for specific information.

You will need stamina, patience, and determination, and you should genuinely like and understand people to do this work. You should be reasonably strong and enjoy physical activity to help patients with their therapy exercises. Manual dexterity and good coordination are needed to adjust equipment and assist patients. You should be able to lift, climb, stoop, and kneel.

STARTING OUT

The best place to find a job may be your school's placement center. You can apply to the physical therapy departments of local hospitals, rehabilitation centers, extended-care facilities, and other potential employers. Other places to look for openings are the classified ads of newspapers, professional journals, and with private and public employment agencies. In locales where training programs have produced many physical therapy assistants, competition for jobs may be keen. In this case, you may want to widen your job search to other locations where there is less competition, especially suburban and rural areas.

EARNINGS

Salaries for physical therapy assistants vary considerably depending on geographic location, employer, and level of experience. Physical therapy assistants earned median annual salaries of $33,870 in 2000, according to the U.S. Department of Labor. The lowest 10 percent earned less than $23,150; the highest 10 percent earned more than $45,610. According to a 2000 member survey by the American Physical Therapy Association, a majority of physical therapy assistants (26.3 percent) reported earning between $30,001 and $35,000 annually. The two largest groups after that were those making less than $25,000 annually (24 percent) and those earning between $25,001 and $30,000 per year (23.9 percent). A reported 14.9 percent earned between $35,001 and $40,000 annually.

Fringe benefits vary, although they usually include paid holidays and vacations, health insurance, and pension plans.

OUTLOOK

Employment prospects are very good for physical therapy assistants. The U.S. Department of Labor predicts that employment will grow by almost 45 percent through 2010. Demand for rehabilitation services is expected to continue to grow much more rapidly than the average for all occupations, and the rate of turnover among workers is relatively high. Many new positions for physical therapy assistants are expected to open up as hospital programs that aid the disabled expand and as long-term facilities seek to offer residents more adequate services.

The baby boom generation is getting older, thus creating a need for more physical rehabilitation. In addition, as more adults engage in strenuous physical exercise, more musculoskeletal injuries will result, thus increasing demand for physical therapy services.

FOR MORE INFORMATION

For additional education and career information, contact:

American Physical Therapy Association
1111 North Fairfax Street
Alexandria, VA 22314-1488
Tel: 800-999-2782
Web: http://www.apta.org

PLASTICS TECHNICIANS

School Subjects **Chemistry** **Mathematics** *Personal Skills* **Mechanical/manipulative** **Technical/scientific** *Work Environment* **Primarily indoors** **Primarily one location**	*Salary Range* **$14,000 to $30,000** **to $61,000** *Certification or Licensing* **Voluntary** *Outlook* **Decline**

THE JOB

Plastics technicians help engineers, scientists, research groups, and manufacturers design, develop, manufacture, and market plastics products. The duties of plastics technicians can be grouped into five general categories: research and development, mold and tool making, manufacturing, sales and service, and related technical tasks.

In research and development, technicians work in laboratories to create new materials or to improve existing ones.

Plastics technicians with drafting skills are employed as mold and tool designers or as drawing detailers.

Technicians in plastics manufacturing work in molding, laminating, or fabricating. They help to make aircraft, aerospace and mass-transit vehicles, boats, satellites, surfboards, recreational vehicles, and furniture.

Plastics technicians are also needed in the sales departments of suppliers, manufacturers, molding companies, laminators, and fabricators. Sales representatives provide a liaison between the customer and the company, assist in product and mold design, and solve problems that may arise in manufacturing.

Plastics technicians are also important in certain related fields. Companies that make computers, appliances, electronic devices, aircraft, and other products rely heavily on plastics technicians to design, purchase, and integrate plastics into the company's manufacturing process.

PROFESSIONAL AND PERSONAL REQUIREMENTS

Certification isn't required of plastics technicians, but is available through the Society of the Plastics Industry in four areas: blow molding, extrusion, injection molding, or thermoforming.

As a plastics technician, you should have good hand-eye coordination and manual dexterity to perform a variety of tasks, especially building laminated structures. You should also have good communication skills, since you must interact with a variety of co-workers including various engineers, chemists, supervisors, designers, estimators, and other technicians. You must be able to follow both oral and written instructions in order to be able to create a product according to precise specifications and demands.

STARTING OUT

Your school's placement center is a good source for job leads. Ask if any recruiting agents will be visiting your school and, if so, schedule a time to interview or attend an informational session. Another good way to start off your career is by joining a student chapter of the Society of Plastics Engineers. Student members receive newsletters and technical journals and can attend professional seminars. These contacts are invaluable when seeking employment.

EARNINGS

According to the 2000 U.S. Bureau of Labor Statistics data, median annual salaries for plastics workers ranged from $14,000 for those who operate molding, coremaking, and other machines to $61,000 for model makers and pattern makers.

Benefits often include paid vacations, health and dental insurance, pension plans, credit union services, production bonuses, stock options, and industry-sponsored education. These benefits will vary with the size and nature of the company.

OUTLOOK

The plastics industry is currently suffering from the effects of a slowing economy and higher production costs. The U.S. Department of Labor projects that employment in the plastics industry will decline through 2010, with a loss of approximately 24,000 jobs. Production jobs are particularly at risk, but the outlook is somewhat better for certain professional occupations, such as computer specialists. Workers with technical and advanced degrees will have the best opportunities. Marketing and sales occupations are expected to decline as a result of company restructuring and mergers.

FOR MORE INFORMATION

The APC is a trade industry that offers a great deal of information about the plastics industry and maintains an informative Web site:

American Plastics Council (APC)
1300 Wilson Boulevard, Suite 800
Arlington, VA 22209
Tel: 800-243-5790
Web: http://www.americanplasticscouncil.org

For information about scholarships, seminars, and training, contact:

Plastics Institute of America
University of Massachusetts-Lowell
333 Aiken Street
Lowell, MA 01854
Tel: 978-934-3130
Web: http://pia.caeds.eng.uml.edu

For information on student membership, contact:

Society of Plastics Engineers
14 Fairfield Drive
PO Box 403
Brookfield, CT 06804-0403
Tel: 203-775-0471
Email: info@4spe.org
Web: http://www.4spe.org

PLUMBERS AND PIPEFITTERS

School Subjects **Chemistry** **Physics**	*Salary Range* **$22,000 to $38,000** **to $63,000+**
Personal Skills **Following instructions** **Mechanical/manipulative**	*Certification or Licensing* **Required by certain states**
Work Environment **Primarily indoors** **Primarily multiple locations**	*Outlook* **About as fast as the average**

THE JOB

Plumbers and *pipefitters* install and repair pipes and pipe systems that carry water, steam, air, or other liquids and gases for sanitation and industrial purposes. Plumbers also install plumbing fixtures, appliances, and heating and refrigerating units.

Because little difference exists between the work of the plumber and the pipefitter in most cases, the two are often considered to be one trade. However, some crafts workers specialize in one field or the other, especially in large cities.

The work of pipefitters differs from that of plumbers mainly in its location and the variety and size of pipes used. Plumbers work primarily in residential and commercial buildings, whereas pipefitters are generally employed by large industrial locations (such as oil refineries, refrigeration plants, and defense establishments), where more complex systems of piping are used.

Plumbers and pipefitters work with heating, water, and drainage systems, especially those that must be connected to public utilities systems. Some of their jobs include replacing burst pipes and installing and repairing sinks, bathtubs, water heaters, hot water tanks, garbage disposal units, dishwashers, and water softeners. Plumbers and pipefitters also may work on septic tanks and sewers. During the final construction stages of both commercial and residential buildings, they install heating and air-conditioning units and connect radiators, water heaters, and plumbing fixtures.

PROFESSIONAL AND PERSONAL REQUIREMENTS

Plumbers may need a license in many areas. To obtain this license, plumbers must pass a special examination to demonstrate their knowledge of local building codes as well as their all-around knowledge of the trade. To become a plumbing contractor in most places, a master plumber's license must be obtained.

To be a successful plumber, you should like to solve a variety of problems and not object to being called on during evenings, weekends, or holidays to perform emergency repairs. As in most service occupations, you should be able to get along well with all kinds of people. Though you may often work alone, you might also eventually direct the work of helpers and should enjoy the company of those in the other construction trades.

STARTING OUT

To become an apprentice, contact local plumbing, heating, and air-conditioning contractors who employ plumbers, the state employment service bureau, or the local union branch of the United Association of Journeymen and Apprentices of the Plumbing, Pipefitting, Sprinkler Fitting Industry. Individual contractors or contractor associations often sponsor local apprenticeship programs. Generally, graduates of apprenticeship programs are able to secure a permanent position in the firm with which they trained.

EARNINGS

The *Occupational Outlook Handbook* reports the median hourly salary for salaried plumbers and pipefitters was $18.19 in 2000 (or approximately $37,800 a year). Wages ranged from $10.71 to $30.06 an hour (or $22,000 to $63,000 annually). Hourly pay rates for apprentices usually start at 50 percent of the experienced worker's rate and increase by 5 percent every six months until a rate of 95 percent is reached. Benefits for union workers usually include health insurance, sick time, and vacation pay, as well as pension plans.

OUTLOOK

Employment opportunities for plumbers and pipefitters are expected to grow about as fast as the average for all jobs through

2010, according to the U.S. Department of Labor. Construction projects are usually only short-term in nature, and more plumbers will find steady work in renovation, repair, and maintenance. Since pipework is becoming more important in large industries, more workers will be needed for installation and maintenance work, especially where refrigeration and air-conditioning equipment are used. Employment opportunities fluctuate with local economic conditions, although the plumbing industry is less affected by economic trends than other construction trades.

FOR MORE INFORMATION

For more information about becoming a plumber or pipefitter, contact the following organizations:

Plumbing-Heating-Cooling Contractors Association
180 South Washington Street
PO Box 6808
Falls Church, VA 22040
Tel: 800-533-7694
Email: naphcc@naphcc.org
Web: http://www.naphcc.org

United Association of Journeymen and Apprentices of the Plumbing, Pipefitting, Sprinkler Fitting Industry of the United States and Canada
901 Massachusetts Avenue, NW
Washington, DC 20001
Tel: 202-628-5823
Web: http://www.ua.org

POLICE OFFICERS

School Subjects **Physical education** **Psychology**	*Salary Range* **$24,000 to $40,000** **to $86,000+**
Personal Skills **Following instructions** **Leadership/management**	*Certification or Licensing* **None available**
Work Environment **Indoors and outdoors** **Primarily multiple locations**	*Outlook* **Faster than the average**

THE JOB

Police officers perform many duties relating to public safety. Their chief duties include preserving the peace, preventing criminal acts, enforcing the law, investigating crimes, and arresting those who violate the law. They are also responsible for directing traffic, community relations, and controlling crowds at public events. If police officers patrol a beat or work in small communities, their duties may be many and varied. In large city departments, their work may be highly specialized. Police officers are employed at the federal, state, county, and city level. They are under oath to uphold the law 24 hours a day.

There are many specific positions within police work. *Internal affairs investigators* are employed to police the police. *Specialized officers* supervise in special situations, such as missing persons or fraud. *Police clerks* perform clerical and community-oriented tasks. *State police officers* (sometimes known as *state troopers* or *highway patrol officers*) patrol the highways and enforce the laws and regulations of those traveling on them.

PROFESSIONAL AND PERSONAL REQUIREMENTS

There is no certification or licensing available in this field. To become an officer, you will be required to pass written tests designed to measure your intelligence and general aptitude for police work. You also need to pass a physical examination, usually including tests of physical agility, dexterity, and strength. Your personal history, background, and character undergo careful scrutiny because honesty and law-abiding characteristics are essential traits for law-enforcement officers. An important requirement is that you have no arrest record.

As a police officer, you should enjoy working with people and be able to cooperate with others. You must have a strong degree of emotional control and the ability to think clearly and logically during emergency situations.

STARTING OUT

If you are interested in police work, apply directly to local civil service offices or examining boards. In some locations, written examinations may be given to groups at specified times. In smaller communities, you may have to apply directly to the police department or city government offices in the community where you reside. If you are interested in becoming a state police officer, apply directly to your state civil service commission or state police headquarters, which are generally located in your state's capital.

EARNINGS

According to the U.S. Department of Labor, police officers in 2000 earned an annual average salary of $39,790; the lowest 10 percent earned less than $23,790 a year, while the highest 10 percent earned over $58,900 annually. Police officers in supervisory positions earned median salaries of $57,210 a year in 2000, with a low of $34,660 and a high of more than $86,060. Salaries for police officers range widely based on geographic location. Police departments in the North and West generally pay more than those in the South.

Most police officers receive periodic and annual salary increases up to a limit set for their rank and length of service. Overtime pay may be given for certain work shifts or emergency duty. In these instances, officers are usually paid straight or time-and-a-half pay, while extra time off is sometimes given as compensation.

Because most police officers are civil service employees, they receive generous benefits, including health insurance and paid vacation and sick leave, and they enjoy increased job security.

OUTLOOK

Employment of police officers is expected to increase faster than the average for all occupations through 2010, according to the U.S. Department of Labor. In response to increasing crime rates, some police departments across the country are expanding the number of patrol officers. However, budget problems faced by many municipalities may limit growth.

Job opportunities will be affected by technological, scientific, and other changes occurring today in police work. Automation in traffic control is limiting the number of officers needed in this area, while the increasing reliance on computers is creating demands for new kinds of police work. New approaches in social science and psychological research are also changing the methodology used in working with public offenders. These trends indicate a future demand for more educated, specialized personnel.

This occupation has a very low turnover rate. However, new positions will open as current officers retire, leave the force, or move into higher positions. Retirement ages are relatively low in police work compared to other occupations; many police officers retire while in their forties to pursue a second career.

FOR MORE INFORMATION

For information on summer camps, scholarships, and other resources for young people interested in police work, contact:

American Police Hall of Fame and Museum
3801 Biscayne Boulevard
Miami, FL 33137
Tel: 305-573-0070
Web: http://www.aphf.org

The National Association of Police Organizations is a coalition of police unions and associations that work to advance the interests of law enforcement officers through legislation, political action, and education.

National Association of Police Organizations
750 First Street, NE, Suite 920
Washington, DC 20002
Tel: 202-842-4420
Web: http://www.napo.org

PRESCHOOL TEACHERS

School Subjects	Salary Range
Art	**$12,000 to $18,000**
English	**to $65,000**
Personal Skills	*Certification or Licensing*
Communication/ideas	**Recommended**
Helping/teaching	*Outlook*
Work Environment	**About as fast as the average**
Primarily indoors	
Primarily one location	

THE JOB

Preschool teachers promote general education of children under the age of five. They help students develop physically, socially, and emotionally, work with them on language and communication skills, and help cultivate their cognitive abilities. Teachers plan and lead activities developed in accordance with the specific ages and needs of the children. They may work with their youngest students on learning the days of the week and to recognize colors, seasons, and animal names and characteristics. They help older students with number and letter recognition and even simple writing skills.

Preschool teachers adopt many parental responsibilities for the children. They greet the children in the morning and supervise them throughout the day. Often these responsibilities can be quite demanding and complicated. For most children, preschool is their first time away from home and family for an extended period of time. A major portion of a preschool teacher's day is spent helping children adjust to being away from home and encouraging them to play together. This is especially true at the beginning of the school year. Teachers may need to gently reassure children who become frightened or homesick.

Some schools and districts consider *kindergarten teachers,* who teach students approximately five years of age, to be preschool teachers. For the purposes of this article, kindergarten teachers will be included in this category.

PROFESSIONAL AND PERSONAL REQUIREMENTS

In some states, licensure may be required. Many states accept the Child Development Associate (CDA) credential or an associate or bachelor's degree as sufficient requirements for work in a preschool facility. Individual state boards of education can provide specific licensure information. Kindergarten teachers working in public elementary schools almost always need teaching certification similar to that required by other elementary school teachers in the school. Other types of licensure or certification may be required, depending on the school or district. These may include first-aid or cardiopulmonary resuscitation training.

Because young children look up to adults and learn through example, it is especially important that preschool teachers be good role models. If you are interested in becoming a teacher, you should remember that everything you say and do in the classroom will affect the children you teach. Patience, a sense of humor, and respect for children are essential qualities of a preschool teacher.

STARTING OUT

Contact child care centers, nursery schools, Head Start programs, and other preschool facilities to identify job opportunities. Often jobs for preschool teachers are listed in the classified section of newspapers. In addition, many school districts and state boards of education maintain job listings of available teaching positions. If no permanent positions are available at preschools, you may be able to find opportunities to work as a substitute teacher. Most preschools and kindergartens maintain a substitute list and refer to it frequently.

EARNINGS

Although there have been some attempts to correct the discrepancies in salaries between preschool teachers and other teachers, salaries in this profession tend to be lower than for teaching positions in public elementary and high schools. Because some preschool programs are only in the morning or afternoon, many teachers work part-time. As part-time workers, they often do not receive medical insurance or other benefits and may get paid minimum wage to start.

According to the U.S. Department of Labor, preschool teachers earned a median salary of about $17,810 a year in 2000. The department reports that kindergarten teachers, which the department classifies separately from preschool teachers, earned median salaries that ranged from $37,610 to $42,080 in 2000. The lowest 10 percent earned less than $23,020, while the highest 10 percent earned $64,920.

OUTLOOK

Employment opportunities for preschool teachers are expected to increase faster than the average for all occupations through 2010, according to the U.S. Department of Labor. Specific job opportunities vary from state to state and depend on demographic characteristics and level of government funding. Jobs should be available at private child care centers, nursery schools, Head Start facilities, public and private kindergartens, and laboratory schools connected with universities and colleges.

Employment for all teachers, including preschool teachers, will vary by region and state. The U.S. Department of Labor predicts that Southern and Western states, particularly Georgia, California, Texas, and Arizona, will have strong increases in enrollments, while schools located in the Northeast and Midwest may experience declines in enrollment.

FOR MORE INFORMATION

For information about certification, contact:

Council for Professional Recognition
2460 16th Street, NW
Washington, DC 20009-3575
Tel: 800-424-4310
Web: http://www.cdacouncil.org

For information about student memberships and training opportunities, contact:

National Association of Child Care Professionals
PO Box 90723
Austin, TX 78709-0723
Tel: 800-537-1118
Email: admin@naccp.org
Web: http://www.naccp.org

QUALITY CONTROL TECHNICIANS

School Subjects **Mathematics** **Physics**	*Salary Range* **$17,000 to $33,000** **to $40,000+**
Personal Skills **Mechanical/manipulative** **Technical/scientific**	*Certification or Licensing* **Voluntary**
Work Environment **Primarily indoors** **Primarily one location**	*Outlook* **About as fast as the average**

THE JOB

Quality control technicians work with engineers to test and inspect materials and products during all phases of production. Their main responsibility is to ensure that specified levels of quality are met. Technicians may test random samples of products or monitor automated equipment and production workers that inspect products during manufacturing. Using engineering blueprints, drawings, and specifications, technicians measure and inspect parts for dimensions, performance, and mechanical, electrical, and chemical properties. They set tolerances, or acceptable deviations from engineering specifications, and they identify rejects and items that need to be reworked.

Quality control technicians also record and evaluate test data. Using statistical quality control procedures, technicians prepare charts and write summaries about how well a product conforms to existing standards. Most importantly, they offer suggestions to quality control engineers on how to modify existing quality standards and manufacturing procedures. Their work helps to achieve the optimum product quality from existing or proposed new equipment.

PROFESSIONAL AND PERSONAL REQUIREMENTS

Many quality control technicians pursue voluntary certification from professional organizations to indicate that they have achieved a certain level of expertise. The American Society for

Quality offers certification at a number of levels, including Quality Engineer Certification (QEC) and Quality Technician Certification (QTC). Requirements include having a certain amount of work experience, having proof of professionalism, and passing a written examination. Many employers value this certification and take it into consideration when making new hires or giving promotions.

To succeed as a quality control technician, you need scientific and mathematical aptitude. You should have good eyesight and good manual skills, including the ability to use hand tools. You should also be able to follow technical instructions and to make sound judgments about technical matters.

STARTING OUT

Students enrolled in two-year technical schools may learn of openings through their schools' job placement services. In many cases, employers prefer to hire technicians with some work experience in their particular industry. If you have had summer or part-time employment or participated in a work-study or internship program, you will have greater job opportunities.

You may also learn about openings through help-wanted ads or by using the services of state and private employment services. Apply directly to companies that employ quality control technicians. You can identify and research such companies by using job resource guides and other reference materials available at most public libraries.

EARNINGS

Earnings vary according to the type of work, the industry, and the geographic location. Most beginning quality control technicians who are graduates of two-year technical programs earn salaries ranging from $17,000 to $21,000 a year. Experienced technicians with two-year degrees earn salaries that range from $21,000 to $40,000 a year; some senior technicians with special skills or experience may earn much more.

Technicians who are certified typically earn higher salaries than those who are not. According to the American Society for Quality, a 2000 salary survey reveals that certified quality technicians earned approximately $38,360, while those without certification made approximately $32,860 annually.

Most companies offer benefits that include paid vacations and holidays, health insurance, pension plans, profit sharing, 401-K plans, and tuition assistance programs.

OUTLOOK

The employment outlook for quality control technicians depends, to some degree, on general economic conditions. Although many economists forecast low to moderate growth in manufacturing operations through 2010, employment opportunities for quality control personnel should remain steady or increase slightly as many companies place increased emphasis on quality control activities.

Opportunities for quality control technicians should be good in the food and beverage industries, pharmaceutical firms, electronics companies, and chemical companies. Technicians also may find employment in industries using robotics equipment or in the aerospace, biomedical, bioengineering, environmental controls, and transportation industries. Lowered rates of manufacturing in the automotive and defense industries will decrease the number of quality control personnel needed for these areas. Declines in employment in some industries may occur because of the increased use of automated equipment that tests and inspects parts during production operations.

FOR MORE INFORMATION

For information on certification and student chapters, contact:

American Society for Quality
600 North Plankinton Avenue
Milwaukee, WI 53203
Tel: 800-248-1946
Web: http://www.asq.org

Visit the ASTM's Web site to read articles from its magazine Standardization News.

American Society for Testing and Materials (ASTM)
100 Barr Harbor Drive
PO Box C700
West Conshohocken, PA 19428-2959
Tel: 610-832-9585
Web: http://www.astm.org

RADIOLOGIC TECHNOLOGISTS

School Subjects	Salary Range
Biology	**$25,000 to $36,000**
Mathematics	**to $52,000+**
Personal Skills	*Certification or Licensing*
Helping/teaching	**Voluntary (certification)**
Technical/scientific	**Required by certain states (licensing)**
Work Environment	*Outlook*
Primarily indoors	**Faster than the average**
Primarily one location	

THE JOB

Radiologic technologists operate equipment that creates images of the body's tissues, organs, and bones for medical diagnoses and therapy. Before an X-ray examination, radiologic technologists may administer drugs or chemical mixtures to the patient to better highlight internal organs. They place the patient in the correct position between the X-ray source and film and protect body areas that are not to be exposed to radiation. After determining the proper duration and intensity of the exposure, they operate the controls to beam X rays through the patient, expose the photographic film, and create the image.

In addition to administering X rays, technologists may also use radiation to treat diseased or affected areas of a patient's body. They expose the patient to specified concentrations of radiation for prescribed times to help kill diseased cells and keep them from multiplying.

PROFESSIONAL AND PERSONAL REQUIREMENTS

Radiologic technologists can become certified through the American Registry of Radiologic Technologists (ARRT) after graduating from an accredited program in radiography, radiation therapy, or nuclear medicine. After becoming certified, many technologists choose to register with the ARRT. Registration is an annual procedure required to maintain the certification. Although registration and certification are voluntary, many jobs are open only to technologists who have acquired these credentials.

An increasing number of states have licensing requirements. According to the American Society of Radiologic Technologists, licenses are required in 35 states and Puerto Rico to work in radiologic technology. Check with the state in which you hope to work about its licensing requirements.

You need to be a responsible individual with a mature and caring nature in order to work as a radiologic technologist. You should be personable and compassionate and enjoy interacting with all types of people, including those who are very ill. A compassionate attitude is essential to deal with patients who may be frightened or in pain.

STARTING OUT

If you receive your training from a school that lacks accreditation or if you learn on the job, you may have difficulty in qualifying for many positions, especially those with a wide range of assignments. If you are enrolled in a hospital educational program, you may be able to get a job with the hospital upon completion of the program. If you are in a degree program, you can get help finding a job through your school's placement office.

EARNINGS

According to the U.S. Department of Labor, median annual earnings of radiologic technologists and technicians were $36,000 in 2000. The lowest-paid 10 percent, which typically includes those just starting out in the field, earned less than $25,310. The highest-paid 10 percent, which typically includes those with considerable experience, earned more than $52,050.

Median earnings of radiologic technologists and technicians who worked in medical and dental laboratories were $39,400 in 2000. Those who worked in hospitals earned a median of $36,280, and those who worked in offices and clinics of medical doctors earned $34,870.

The same vacation and sick leave provisions as other employees cover most technologists. In addition, most employers offer benefits such as health insurance and pensions.

OUTLOOK

Overall, employment for radiologic technologists is expected to grow faster than the average through 2010, according to the U.S. Department of Labor. The demand for qualified technologists in some areas of the country far exceeds the supply. This shortage is particularly acute in rural areas and small towns. Those who are willing to relocate to these areas will have increased job prospects. Another way to broaden job opportunities is by training to do more than one type of imaging procedure.

In the years to come, increasing numbers of radiologic technologists will be employed in non-hospital settings, such as physicians' offices, clinics, health maintenance organizations, government agencies, and diagnostic imaging centers. This pattern will be part of the overall trend toward holding down health care costs by delivering more care outside of hospitals. Nevertheless, hospitals will remain the major employers of radiologic technologists for the near future.

FOR MORE INFORMATION

For information on certification and educational programs, contact:

American Registry of Radiologic Technologists
1255 Northland Drive
St. Paul, MN 55120-1155
Tel: 651-687-0048
Web: http://www.arrt.org

For information about the field and to access a job bank, contact:

American Society of Radiologic Technologists
15000 Central Avenue, SE
Albuquerque, NM 87123-3917
Tel: 800-444-2778
Web: http://www.asrt.org

For an educational resource guide, contact:

Society of Diagnostic Medical Sonography
2745 Dallas Parkway, Suite 350
Plano, TX 75093-4706
Tel: 800-229-9506
Web: http://www.sdms.org

REAL ESTATE AGENTS AND BROKERS

School Subjects **Business** **Mathematics**	*Salary Range* **$14,000 to $28,000** **to $144,000+**
Personal Skills **Communication/ideas** **Helping/teaching**	*Certification or Licensing* **Required**
Work Environment **Primarily indoors** **Primarily multiple locations**	*Outlook* **Little change or more slowly** **than the average**

THE JOB

Real estate agents and *brokers* help clients buy, sell, rent, or lease a piece of real estate. Brokers are businesspeople who sell, rent, or manage property. Real estate agents are salespeople who are either self-employed or hired by brokers. Sometimes the term agent is applied to both real estate brokers and agents.

Brokers' main responsibility is to actively solicit property listings for their agency. Once the listing is obtained, brokers must analyze the property to best present it to prospective buyers. Frequently, the broker counsels the owner about the asking price for the property.

When the property is ready to be shown, it is the job of real estate agents to find prospective buyers. When a buyer is found, the agent must bring the buyer and seller together at price terms agreeable to both. Once both parties have signed the contract, the real estate broker and agent must see to it that all special terms of the contract are carried out before the closing date.

PROFESSIONAL AND PERSONAL REQUIREMENTS

Every state and the District of Columbia requires that real estate agents and brokers be licensed. For the general license, most states require agents to be at least 18 years old, have between 30 and 60 hours of classroom training, and pass a written examination on real estate fundamentals and state laws. Brokers must pass a more extensive examination and complete between 60 and 90 hours of classroom training. Additionally, many states require brokers to have prior experience selling property or a formal degree in real estate.

You need to possess a pleasant personality and a neat appearance in order to work as a real estate agent or broker. You also need to be knowledgeable, organized, and detail oriented and have a good memory for names, faces, and business details, such as taxes, zoning regulations, and local land-use laws.

STARTING OUT

You can apply directly to local real estate firms or be referred through public and private employment services. Brokers looking to hire agents may run newspaper advertisements. Contact firms in your own community, where your knowledge of the neighborhood can work to your advantage.

There are advantages to joining either a small or a large organization. In a small office, you will train informally under an experienced agent. Your duties will be broad and varied but possibly menial. However, this is a good chance to learn all the basics of the business. In larger firms, you may proceed through a more standardized training process and specialize in one phase of the real estate field, such as commercial real estate, mortgage financing, or property management.

EARNINGS

Compensation in the real estate field is based largely upon commission. Agents usually split commissions with the brokers who employ them, in return for providing the office space, advertising support, sales supervision, and the use of the broker's name. When two or more agents are involved in a transaction (for example, one agent listing the property for sale and another selling it), the commission is usually divided between the two on the basis of an established formula. Agents can earn more if they both list and sell the property.

According to the U.S. Department of Labor, median annual earnings of salaried real estate agents, including commission, were $27,640 in 2000. Salaries ranged from less than $14,460 to more than $78,540. Median annual earnings of salaried real estate brokers, including commission, were $47,690 in 2000, and salaries ranged from less than $18,080 to more than $143,560 a year.

Agents and brokers may supplement their income by appraising property, placing mortgages with private lenders, or selling insurance. Since earnings are irregular and economic conditions unpredictable, agents and brokers should maintain sufficient cash reserves for slack periods.

OUTLOOK

According to the *Occupational Outlook Handbook,* employment of real estate agents and brokers is expected to grow more slowly than the average for all occupations through 2010. Despite slow growth, turnover within the field is high. New job opportunities surface as agents retire or transfer to other types of work.

The country's expanding population creates additional demand for real estate services. A trend toward mobility, usually among Americans in their prime working years, indicates a continued need for real estate professionals. In addition, a higher percentage of affluence among this working group indicates that more Americans will be able to own their own homes.

The field of real estate is easily affected by changes in the economy. Periods of prosperity bring a lot of business. Conversely, a downturn leads to a lower number of real estate transactions, resulting in fewer sales and commissions for agents and brokers.

FOR MORE INFORMATION

For information on licensing, contact:

Association of Real Estate License Law Officials
PO Box 230159
Montgomery, AL 36123-0159
Tel: 334-260-2902
Email: mailbox@arello.org
Web: http://www.arello.org

For information on commercial real estate, contact:

Society of Industrial and Office Realtors
700 11th Street, NW, Suite 510
Washington, DC 20001
Tel: 202-737-1150
Email: admin@sior.com
Web: http://www.sior.com

RECREATION WORKERS

School Subjects	Salary Range
Physical education **Theater/dance**	**$15,000 to $17,000** **to $31,000**
Personal Skills **Following instructions** **Helping/teaching**	*Certification or Licensing* **Required for certain** **positions**
Work Environment **Indoors and outdoors** **Primarily one location**	*Outlook* **Faster than the average**

THE JOB

Recreation workers help groups and individuals enjoy and use their leisure time constructively. They organize and administer physical, social, and cultural programs.

With the help of volunteers, recreation workers employed by local governments and voluntary agencies coordinate various programs at locations such as community centers, neighborhood playgrounds, recreational and rehabilitation centers, prisons, hospitals, and homes for children and the elderly. Programs may include arts and crafts, dramatics, music, dancing, swimming, games, camping, nature study, and other pastimes. Workers may also help organize special events such as festivals, contests, pet and hobby shows, and various outings. *Recreation supervisors* have overall responsibility for coordinating the work of the workers who carry out the programs and may supervise several recreation centers or an entire region.

Other positions in the field include recreation center directors, recreation leaders, recreation aides, camp counselors, camp directors, and social directors.

PROFESSIONAL AND PERSONAL REQUIREMENTS

Many recreation professionals apply for certification as evidence of their professional competence. The National Recreation and Park Association (NRPA), the American Camping Association, and the National Employee Services and

Recreation Association award certificates to individuals who meet their standards. More than 40 states have adopted NRPA standards for park/recreation professionals. The federal government employs many recreation leaders in national parks, the armed forces, the Department of Veterans Affairs, and correctional institutions. It may be necessary to pass a civil service examination to qualify for these positions.

Personal qualifications for recreation work include a desire to work with people, an outgoing personality, an even temperament, and an ability to lead and influence others. You should have good health and stamina and be able to stay calm and think clearly and quickly in emergencies.

STARTING OUT

Your school's placement office is a good place to stop when looking for your first job. Many graduates begin as either recreation leaders or specialists and, after several years of experience, can become recreation directors. You can also enter a trainee program that leads directly to recreation administration within a year or so.

EARNINGS

Full-time recreation workers can earn from $7 an hour to $15 an hour (approximately $14,500 to $31,000 a year) depending on job responsibilities and experience. Some top-level managers earn considerably more.

Salaries in industrial recreation are higher. Newly hired recreation workers in industry have starting salaries of about $18,000 to $24,000 a year. Camp directors average about $1,600 per month in municipally operated camps; in private camps, earnings are higher. Camp counselors employed seasonally are paid anywhere from $200 to $800 a month. Recreation workers in local government earn about $16,600 a year, while those employed by civic and social associations earn about $14,100 annually.

OUTLOOK

The U.S. Department of Labor predicts that employment opportunities for recreation workers will increase faster than the average through 2010. The expected expansion in the recreation field will result from increased leisure time and income for the population as a whole. A continuing interest in fitness and health and a growing elderly population in nursing homes, senior centers, and retirement communities will also increase the demand for recreation programs.

Recreation programs that depend on government funding are most likely to be affected in times of economic downturns when budgets are reduced. During such times, competition will increase significantly for jobs in the private sector. Due to such predicted budget reductions, employment for recreation workers in local government is predicted to grow more slowly than the average for all other occupations.

In any case, competition is expected to be keen because the field is open to college graduates regardless of major; as a result, there are more applicants than there are job openings. Opportunities will be best for individuals who have formal training in recreation and for those with previous experience.

FOR MORE INFORMATION

For information on industry trends and accredited schools, contact:

American Association for Leisure and Recreation
1900 Association Drive
Reston, VA 20191
Tel: 703-476-9527
Email: aalr@aahperd.org
Web: http://www.aahperd.org/aalr

For information on certification, contact:

American Camping Association
5000 State Road 67 North
Martinsville, IN 46151-7902
Tel: 765-342-8456
Web: http://www.acacamps.org

For information on career opportunities and certification, contact:

National Recreation and Park Association
22377 Belmont Ridge Road
Ashburn, VA 20148-4501
Tel: 703-858-0784
Email: info@nrpa.org
Web: http://www.nrpa.org

REGISTERED NURSES

School Subjects	Salary Range
Biology	**$32,000 to $45,000**
Chemistry	**to $92,000+**
Personal Skills	*Certification or Licensing*
Helping/teaching	**Required**
Technical/scientific	*Outlook*
Work Environment	**Faster than the average**
Primarily indoors	
Primarily multiple locations	

THE JOB

Registered nurses (RNs) help individuals, families, and groups to achieve health and prevent disease. They care for the sick and injured in hospitals and other health care facilities, physicians' offices, private homes, public health agencies, schools, camps, and industry. Some registered nurses are employed in private practice.

Registered nurses work under the direct supervision of nursing departments and in collaboration with physicians. Two-thirds of all nurses work in hospitals. There are many different kinds of RNs, such as general duty nurses, surgical nurses, maternity nurses, head nurses and supervisors, private duty nurses, office nurses, occupational health (or industrial) nurses, school nurses, community health (or public health) nurses, and advanced practice nurses.

PROFESSIONAL AND PERSONAL REQUIREMENTS

All states and the District of Columbia require a license to practice nursing. To obtain a license, graduates of approved nursing schools must pass a national examination. Nurses may be licensed by more than one state. In some states, continuing education is a condition for license renewal. Different titles require different education and training levels.

Stamina, both physical and mental, is a must for this occupation. You will be spending much of the day on your feet, either walking or standing. Handling patients who are ill or infirm can also be very exhausting. Sick people are often very demanding, or they may be depressed or irritable. Despite this, you must retain your composure and should be cheerful to help patients achieve emotional balance. You must also be patient and have a caring, nurturing attitude. As part of a health care team, you must be able to follow orders and work under close supervision.

STARTING OUT

The only way to become a registered nurse is through completion of one of three kinds of educational programs, plus passing the licensing examination. After these requirements have been met, you can apply for employment directly to hospitals, nursing homes, home care agencies, temporary nursing agencies, companies, and government agencies that hire nurses. Jobs can also be obtained through school placement offices, by signing up with employment agencies specializing in placement of nursing personnel, or through your state's employment office. Other sources of jobs include nurses' associations, professional journals, and newspaper want ads.

EARNINGS

According to the *Occupational Outlook Handbook,* registered nurses had median annual earnings of $44,840 in 2000. Salaries ranged from less than $31,890 to more than $64,360. Earnings of RNs vary according to employer. Those who worked for personnel supply services earned $46,860; at hospitals, $45,780; and at nursing and personal care facilities, $41,330.

According to WageWeb.com, nurse managers earn from $49,478 to $64,999, with an average of $57,193. Nurse directors earn from $73,688 to $91,745, with an average of $82,690.

Salary is determined by several factors: setting, education, and work experience. Most full-time nurses are given flexible work schedules as well as health and life insurance; some are offered education reimbursement and year-end bonuses. A staff nurse's salary is limited only by the amount of work he or she is willing to take on. Many nurses take advantage of overtime work and shift differentials. About 10 percent of all nurses hold more than one job.

OUTLOOK

The U.S. Department of Labor projects registered nurses to be one of the top 25 occupations with fastest growth, high pay, and low unemployment. Two-thirds of all nursing jobs are found in hospitals. However, because of administrative cost cutting, increased nurses' workloads, and rapid growth of outpatient services, hospital nursing jobs will experience slower than average growth. Employment in home care and nursing homes is expected to grow rapidly. Many nurses will also be needed to help staff the growing number of outpatient facilities, such as health maintenance organizations (HMOs), group medical practices, and ambulatory surgery centers.

FOR MORE INFORMATION

Visit the AACN Web site for information on schools and careers.

American Association of Colleges of Nursing (AACN)
One Dupont Circle, Suite 530
Washington, DC 20036
Tel: 202-463-6930
Web: http://www.aacn.nche.edu

For information about state-approved programs and information on nursing, contact the following organizations:

National League for Nursing
61 Broadway
New York, NY 10006
Tel: 800-669-1656
Web: http://www.nln.org

National Organization for Associate Degree Nursing
11250 Roger Bacon Drive, Suite 8
Reston, VA 20190-5202
Tel: 703-437-4377
Web: http://www.noadn.org

This Web site provides information on nursing careers, nursing schools, and scholarships.

Discover Nursing
Web: http://www.discovernursing.com

RESPIRATORY THERAPISTS

School Subjects	Salary Range
Health	**$23,000 to $38,000**
Mathematics	**to $55,000**
Personal Skills	*Certification or Licensing*
Helping/teaching	**Recommended**
Technical/scientific	*Outlook*
Work Environment	**Faster than the average**
Primarily indoors	
Primarily one location	

THE JOB

Respiratory therapists evaluate, treat, and care for patients with deficiencies or abnormalities of their cardiopulmonary (heart/lung) system, either providing temporary relief from chronic ailments or administering emergency care where life is threatened.

Working under a physician's direction, these workers set up and operate respirators, mechanical ventilators, and other devices. They monitor the functioning of the equipment and the patients' response to the therapy. Therapists also maintain patients' charts, assist with breathing exercises, and inspect, test, and order repairs for respiratory therapy equipment.

PROFESSIONAL AND PERSONAL REQUIREMENTS

More than 40 states regulate respiratory care personnel through licensing or certification. Requirements vary, so you will need to check with your state's regulatory board for specific information.

The National Board for Respiratory Care offers voluntary certification to graduates of accredited programs. The certifications are Certified Respiratory Therapist (CRT) and Registered Respiratory Therapist (RRT). As of January 1, 2002, you must have at least an associate degree to be eligible to take the CRT exam. Anyone desiring certification must take the CRT exam first. After successfully completing this exam, those who are eligible can take the RRT exam. CRTs who meet further education and experience requirements can qualify for the RRT credential. Certification is highly recommended because many employers require this credential.

As a respiratory therapist, you must enjoy working with people. You need to be sensitive to patients' physical and psychological needs. You also must pay strict attention to detail, remain calm in emergencies, and be able to follow instructions and work as part of a team. Mechanical ability and manual dexterity are necessary to operate much of the respiratory equipment.

STARTING OUT

After high school, you can apply directly to local hospitals for jobs as respiratory therapy assistants. If your goal is to become a therapist or technician, however, you will need to enroll in a formal respiratory therapy educational program. After completing such a program, you can use your school's placement office to help find a job. Otherwise, you can apply directly to individual local health care facilities.

EARNINGS

Respiratory therapists earned median salaries of $37,680 in 2000, according to the *Occupational Outlook Handbook*. The lowest 10 percent earned less than $28,620, and the highest 10 percent earned more than $50,660. Median annual earnings of respiratory therapy technicians were $32,860 in 2000. Salaries ranged from less than $22,830 to more than $46,800.

According to 2000 data from the American Association for Respiratory Care, those in staff positions reported a mean wage of $16.66 per hour, or $34,650 annually, for full-time work. Those holding positions as supervisors reported a mean hourly wage of $20.99, or approximately $43,660 per year. Those in director positions had a mean hourly wage of $26.45, or approximately $55,015 annually.

Hospital workers receive benefits that include health insurance, paid vacations and sick leave, and pension plans.

OUTLOOK

Employment growth for respiratory therapists is expected to be more rapid than the average for all occupations through 2010. The fields of neonatal care and gerontology are growing. Also, there is a greater incidence of cardiopulmonary and AIDS-related diseases, coupled with more advanced methods of diagnosing and treating them.

Employment opportunities for respiratory therapists should be very favorable in the rapidly growing field of home health care, although this area accounts for only a small number of respiratory therapy jobs. There should also be numerous openings for respiratory therapists in equipment rental companies and in firms that provide respiratory care on a contract basis.

FOR MORE INFORMATION

For information on scholarships, continuing education, job listings, and careers in respiratory therapy, contact:

American Association for Respiratory Care
11030 Ables Lane
Dallas, TX 75229
Tel: 972-243-2272
Web: http://www.aarc.org

For more information on allied health care careers as well as a listing of accredited programs, contact:

Commission on Accreditation of Allied Health Education Programs
35 East Wacker Drive, Suite 1970
Chicago, IL 60601-2208
Tel: 312-553-9355
Web: http://www.caahep.org

For a list of CoARC-accredited training programs, contact:

Committee on Accreditation for Respiratory Care (CoARC)
1248 Harwood Road
Bedford, TX 76021-4244
Tel: 800-874-5615
Web: http://www.coarc.com

For information on licensing and certification, contact:

National Board for Respiratory Care
8310 Nieman Road
Lenexa, KS 66214-1579
Tel: 913-599-4200
Web: http://www.nbrc.org

RESTAURANT AND FOOD SERVICE MANAGERS

School Subjects **Business** **Health** *Personal Skills* **Communication/ideas** **Leadership/management** *Work Environment* **Primarily indoors** **Primarily one location**	*Salary Range* **$19,000 to $32,000** **to $60,000+** *Certification or Licensing* **None available** *Outlook* **About as fast as the average**

THE JOB

Restaurant and food service managers work in restaurants ranging from fast-food establishments to elegant hotel dining rooms. They work in settings varying from school cafeterias to hospital food services. Whatever the environment, managers coordinate and direct the work of the employees who prepare and serve food and perform other related functions.

Restaurant managers set work schedules for wait staff and host staff. Food service managers are responsible for buying the food and equipment necessary for the operation of the restaurant or facility, and they may help with menu planning. They inspect the premises periodically to ensure compliance with health and sanitation regulations.

Restaurant and food service managers perform many clerical and financial duties, such as keeping records, directing payroll operations, handling large sums of money, and taking inventories. They generally supervise any advertising or sales promotions for their operations and establish and maintain contacts with customers and vendors.

PROFESSIONAL AND PERSONAL REQUIREMENTS

There is no certification or licensing available in this field. The National Restaurant Association Educational Foundation offers a voluntary Foodservice Management Professional (FMP) certification to qualified restaurant and food service managers. See the end of this article for contact information.

Experience in all areas of restaurant and food service work is an important requirement to succeed as a manager. Business and industry-related knowledge is also necessary for this line of work, as is stamina to endure long and often irregular hours. Desirable personality characteristics include poise, self-confidence, and an ability to get along with people.

STARTING OUT

Many restaurants and food service facilities provide self-sponsored, on-the-job training for prospective managers. As a result, you can start out as a food service worker and eventually move up the ladder within your organization's workforce, finally arriving at the managerial position. However, you will do better to have specialized training. With advanced education, you have a better chance to move directly into a manager-trainee position and then on to a managerial position.

EARNINGS

The earnings of salaried restaurant and food service managers vary a great deal, depending on the type and size of the establishment. According to the *Occupational Outlook Handbook,* median annual earnings of food service managers were $31,720 in 2000. The lowest 10 percent earned less than $19,200, and the highest 10 percent earned more than $53,090. Those in charge of the largest restaurants and institutional food service facilities often earn more than $60,000. Managers of fast-food restaurants average about $25,000 per year. In addition to a base salary, most managers receive bonuses based on profits, which can range from $2,000 to $7,500 a year.

OUTLOOK

Employment for well-qualified restaurant and food service managers will grow as fast as the average through 2010, especially for those with associate or bachelor's degrees. New restaurants are always opening to meet increasing demand. It has been estimated that at least 44 percent of all of the food consumed in the United States is eaten in restaurants and hotels.

Many job openings will arise from the need to replace managers retiring from the workforce. Also, population growth will result in an increased demand for eating establishments and, in turn, a need for managers to oversee them. As the elderly population increases, managers will be needed to staff dining rooms located in hospitals and nursing homes.

Economic downswings have a great effect on eating and drinking establishments. During a recession, people have less money to spend on luxuries such as dining out, thus hurting the restaurant business. However, greater numbers of working parents and their families are finding it convenient to eat out or purchase carryout food from a restaurant.

FOR MORE INFORMATION

For information on restaurant management careers, education, and certification, contact the following organizations:

International Council on Hotel, Restaurant, and Institutional Education
2613 North Parham Road, 2nd Floor
Richmond, VA 23294
Tel: 804-346-4800
Email: info@chrie.org
Web: http://chrie.org

National Restaurant Association Educational Foundation
175 West Jackson Boulevard, Suite 1500
Chicago, IL 60604-2702
Tel: 800-765-2122
Email: info@foodtrain.org
Web: http://www.nraef.org

RETAIL MANAGERS

School Subjects	*Salary Range*
Business	**$17,000 to $28,000**
Mathematics	**to $100,000+**
Personal Skills	*Certification or Licensing*
Helping/teaching	**None available**
Leadership/management	*Outlook*
Work Environment	**Little change or more slowly**
Primarily indoors	**than the average**
Primarily one location	

THE JOB

Retail managers are responsible for the profitable operation of retail trade establishments. They oversee the selling of food, clothing, furniture, sporting goods, novelties, and many other items. Their primary duties include hiring, training, and supervising other employees; maintaining the physical facilities; managing inventory; monitoring expenditures and receipts; and maintaining good public relations. Other duties vary according to the type of merchandise sold, size of store, and number of employees. In small, owner-operated stores, managers often are involved in accounting, data processing, marketing, research, sales, and shipping. In large retail corporations, however, managers may be involved in only one or two activities.

PROFESSIONAL AND PERSONAL REQUIREMENTS

There is no certification or licensing available for this field.

As a retail manager, you may be required to work long, irregular hours. You should have good communication skills and enjoy working with and supervising people. Diplomacy often is necessary when creating schedules for workers and in disciplinary matters. There is a great deal of responsibility in retail management, and such positions often are stressful. A calm disposition and ability to handle stress will serve you well when balancing the needs of workers, customers, and supervisors.

STARTING OUT

Many new college graduates are able to find managerial positions through their schools' placement service. Some of the large retail chains engage in campus recruitment.

Not all store managers, however, are college graduates. Many store managers are promoted to their positions from jobs of less responsibility within the organization. Some may be in the retail industry for more than a dozen years before being promoted. Those with more education often receive promotions faster.

Regardless of your educational background, if you are interested in the retail industry, you should consider working in a retail store at least part-time or during the summer to get experience and measure your interest in working in retail. Although there may not be an opening when you first submit an application, high turnover of employees in retail can result in a vacancy in time.

EARNINGS

Salaries depend on the size of the store, the responsibilities of the job, and the number of customers served. According to the *Occupational Outlook Handbook,* median annual earnings of supervisors of retail sales workers, including commission, were $27,510 in 2000. Salaries ranged from less than $16,910 to more than $52,590 a year. Median annual earnings of grocery store managers were $27,380, and managers of drugstores and proprietary stores earned $27,250. Those who managed miscellaneous shopping goods stores had median annual earnings of $25,750, and department store managers earned $23,530. Managers who oversee an entire region for a retail chain can earn more than $100,000.

In addition to a salary, some stores offer their managers special bonuses, or commissions, which are typically connected to the store's performance. Many stores also offer employee discounts on store merchandise.

OUTLOOK

Employment of retail managers is expected to grow more slowly than the average for all occupations through 2010. Although retailers have reduced their management staff to cut costs and make operations more efficient, there still are good opportunities in retailing. However, competition for jobs probably will continue to increase, and computerized systems for inventory control may reduce the need for some managers. Applicants with the best educational backgrounds and work experience will have the best chances of finding jobs.

FOR MORE INFORMATION

For information on jobs in retail, contact:

International Mass Retail Association
1700 North Moore Street, Suite 2250
Arlington, VA 22209
Tel: 703-841-2300
Web: http://www.imra.org

For materials on educational programs in the retail industry, contact:

National Retail Federation
325 7th Street, NW, Suite 1000
Washington, DC 20004
Tel: 800-673-4692
Web: http://www.nrf.com

ROBOTICS TECHNICIANS

School Subjects **Computer science** **Mathematics**	*Salary Range* **$25,000 to $35,000** **to $50,000+**
Personal Skills **Mechanical/manipulative** **Technical/scientific**	*Certification or Licensing* **None available**
Work Environment **Primarily indoors** **Primarily one location**	*Outlook* **About as fast as the average**

THE JOB

Robotics technicians assist robotics engineers with the design, development, production, testing, operation, repair, and maintenance of robots and robotic devices. The majority of robotics technicians work within the field of computer-integrated manufacturing or programmable automation.

In order to install and repair robots and robotic equipment, technicians need knowledge of electronics, electrical circuitry, mechanics, pneumatics, hydraulics, and computer programming.

Companies that have only a few robots don't always hire their own robotics technicians. Instead they use *robot field technicians* who work for a robotic manufacturer. These technicians travel to manufacturing sites and other locations where robots are used to repair and service robots and robotic equipment.

Technicians involved with the design and development of new robotic devices are sometimes referred to as *robotics design technicians*. As part of a design team, they work closely with robotics engineers. The robotics design job starts as the engineers analyze the tasks and settings to be assigned and decide what kind of robotics system will best serve the necessary functions.

Other kinds of robotics technicians include *robot operators*, who operate robots in specialized settings, and *robotics trainers*, who train other employees in the installation, use, and maintenance of robots.

PROFESSIONAL AND PERSONAL REQUIREMENTS

There is no certification or licensing available in this field.

If you are interested in working as a robotics technician, you need manual dexterity, good hand-eye coordination, and mechanical and electrical aptitudes. You should also be willing to continue your education and training to remain competitive in this constantly changing field.

STARTING OUT

In the past, most people entered robotics technician positions from positions as automotive workers, machinists, millwrights, computer repair technicians, and computer operators. Companies retrained them to troubleshoot and repair robots rather than hire new workers. Although this still occurs today, there are many more opportunities for formal education and training specifically in robotics engineering, and robotics manufacturers are more likely to hire graduates of robotics programs, both at the technician and engineer levels.

Places to search for employment include your school's job placement services, advertisements in professional magazines and newspapers, or job fairs.

EARNINGS

According to the U.S. Department of Labor, robotics technicians who are graduates of a two-year robotics program earn between $25,000 and $35,000 a year. With increased training and experience, technicians can earn $50,000 or more.

Employers offer a variety of benefits that can include the following: paid holidays, vacations, personal days, and sick leave; medical, dental, disability, and life insurance; pension and retirement plans; profit sharing; and educational assistance programs.

OUTLOOK

Employment opportunities for robotics technicians are closely tied to economic conditions in the United States and in the global marketplace. The Robotics Industry Association (RIA) reports that the robotics market fell 30 percent in 2001, primarily due to economic recession and the continued slowdown in equipment expenditures. The RIA estimates that some 118,000 robots are now working in U.S. factories, making the United States the world's second-largest robotics user, after Japan.

The use of industrial robots is expected to grow as robots become more programmable and flexible and as manufacturing processes become more automated. Growth is also expected in nontraditional applications, such as education, health care, security, and nonindustrial purposes. Employment in robotics will depend on future demand for new applications as well as available capital to spend on research and development. Competition for engineering and technician jobs with be stiff.

FOR MORE INFORMATION

For information on competitions and student membership, contact:

Association for Unmanned Vehicle Systems
3401 Columbia Pike, Suite 400
Arlington, VA 22204
Tel: 703-920-2720
Web: http://www.auvsi.org

For career information, company profiles, training seminars, and educational resources, contact:

Robotic Industries Association
900 Victors Way
PO Box 3724
Ann Arbor, MI 48106
Tel: 734-994-6088
Web: http://www.roboticsonline.com

For information on educational programs, competitions, and student membership in the SME, contact:

Society of Manufacturing Engineers (SME)
One SME Drive
Dearborn, MI 48121
Tel: 800-733-4763
Web: http://www.sme.org

SECURITY GUARDS

School Subjects **Business** **Psychology** Personal Skills **Communication/ideas** **Mechanical/manipulative** Work Environment **Indoors and outdoors** **One location with travel**	Salary Range **$13,000 to $18,000** **to $29,000+** Certification or Licensing **Recommended** Outlook **Faster than the average**

THE JOB

Security guards are responsible for protecting public and private property against theft, fire, vandalism, illegal entry, and acts of violence. They may work for a variety of clients, including large stores, art museums, factories, laboratories, data processing centers, and political candidates.

Some security guards work for government agencies or for private companies hired by government agencies. Their task is usually to guard secret or restricted installations domestically or in foreign countries. They spend much of their time patrolling areas, which they may do on foot, on horseback, or in automobiles or aircraft. They monitor activities in an area through the use of surveillance cameras and video screens. Their assignments usually include detecting and preventing unauthorized activities, searching for explosive devices, standing watch during secret and hazardous experiments, and performing other routine police duties within government installations.

Specific jobs within this field include security officers, bouncers, golf-course rangers, gate tenders, and bank guards.

PROFESSIONAL AND PERSONAL REQUIREMENTS

Certification, which is recommended though not required, is offered by the American Society for Industrial Security.

Virtually every state has licensing or registration requirements for security guards who work for contract security agencies. To be granted a license, individuals generally must be 18 years of age, have no convictions for perjury or acts of violence, pass a background investigation, and complete classroom training.

Good general health (especially vision and hearing), alertness, emotional stability, and the ability to follow directions are important characteristics for you to have as a security guard. Many jobs stipulate that guards meet certain criteria related to height, weight, and physical fitness.

Guards employed by the federal government must be U.S. armed forces veterans, have some previous experience as guards, and pass a written examination. Many positions require experience with firearms.

STARTING OUT

If you are interested in a career in security services, apply directly to security companies and government agencies. Some jobs may be available through state or private employment services.

Training requirements are generally increasing as modern, highly sophisticated security systems become more common. Many employers give newly hired security guards instruction before they start the job and also provide several weeks of on-the-job training. Guards receive training in protection, public relations, report writing, crisis deterrence, first aid, and drug control.

EARNINGS

Average starting salaries for security guards vary according to their level of training and experience and the location where they work. Median annual earnings for security guards were $17,570 in 2000, according to the U.S. Department of Labor. Experienced security guards earned more than $28,660 per year in 2000, while the least-experienced guards earned less than $12,860 annually.

Entry-level guards working for contract agencies may receive little more than the minimum wage, however. In-house guards generally earn higher wages and have greater job security and better advancement potential.

Security guards employed by federal government agencies earned starting salaries of $21,950 to $27,190 per year in 2001. Median earnings for guards were $28,960. The location of the work also affects earnings, with higher pay in locations with a higher cost of living.

Government employees typically enjoy good job security and generous benefits. Benefits for positions with private companies vary significantly.

OUTLOOK

Employment for guards and other security personnel is expected to increase faster than the average through 2010, as crime rates rise with the overall population growth. Public concern about crime, vandalism, and terrorism continues to increase. The U.S. Department of Labor estimates that the employment of security guards should grow by 35 percent through 2010. Many job openings will be created as a result of the high turnover of workers in this field.

A factor adding to this demand is the trend for private security firms to perform duties previously handled by police officers. Private security firms employ security guards to protect many government sites, such as nuclear testing facilities. Private companies also operate many training facilities for government security technicians and guards as well as provide police services for some communities.

FOR MORE INFORMATION

For information on educational programs and certification procedures, contact:

American Society for Industrial Security
1625 Prince Street
Alexandria, VA 22314-2818
Tel: 703-519-6200
Email: asis@asisonline.org
Web: http://www.asisonline.org

For information on union membership, contact:

Security, Police, and Fire Professionals of America
25510 Kelly Road
Roseville, MI 40866
Tel: 800-228-7492
Web: http://www.spfpa.org

SEMICONDUCTOR TECHNICIANS

School Subjects **Chemistry** **Mathematics** *Personal Skills* **Communication/ideas** **Technical/scientific** *Work Environment* **Primarily indoors** **Primarily one location**	*Salary Range* **$18,000 to $25,000** **to $40,000+** *Certification or Licensing* **Voluntary** *Outlook* **Faster than the average**

THE JOB

Semiconductor technicians test new kinds of semiconductor devices being designed for use in modern electronic equipment. Although the word semiconductor is often used to refer to microchips or integrated circuits, a semiconductor is actually the basic material of these devices. Semiconductor materials are treated to act with properties between that of an insulator, which does not conduct electrical current, and that of a true conductor of electrical current, such as metal. Silicon is the most common material used as a semiconductor.

Working under the direction of engineers in research laboratory settings, semiconductor technicians assist in the design and planning for later production or help to improve production yields. They are responsible for ensuring that specifications are met and for identifying flaws and problems in the semiconductor material and design. Technicians may also assist in designing and building new test equipment. Some technicians may be responsible for maintaining the equipment and for training operators on its use.

PROFESSIONAL AND PERSONAL REQUIREMENTS

The International Society of Certified Electronics Technicians offers voluntary certification for various jobs in electronics.

A thorough understanding of semiconductors, electronics, and the production process is necessary to work in this field.

You also need investigative and research skills and a basic knowledge of computers and computer programs. Other important qualities include patience, perseverance, and attention to detail.

STARTING OUT

Semiconductor technician positions can be located through the job placement office of your community college or vocational training school. Many schools provide students with job interviews and introductions to companies in the community that are looking for qualified workers.

Job listings in the newspaper or at local employment agencies are also good places for locating job opportunities. You can also find lower-skilled positions in the semiconductor industry and work toward a promotion to a technician position.

EARNINGS

Because of the stringent requirements, qualified semiconductor technicians command salaries that tend to be higher than many other professions. Semiconductor technicians earned a median hourly salary of $12.23 in 2000, or roughly $25,500 per year, according to the U.S. Department of Labor. Ten percent of all workers earned less than $8.85 an hour ($18,400 a year), while the top 10 percent earned $19.10 or more an hour ($39,700 a year). Technicians earning the higher salaries have more education and have worked in the industry for many years.

OUTLOOK

The semiconductor industry is expected to remain a strong source of employment through 2010, according to the U.S. Department of Labor. The increasing demand for semiconductors and related devices in most areas of industry, manufacturing, and consumer services requires a steady supply of personnel trained in their development and processing. New applications for semiconductor technology are continually being created, and these, too, will spur the demand for trained technical staff. Advancements in technology will require increased and continuing educational requirements for those seeking and holding positions in this industry.

FOR MORE INFORMATION

For certification information, contact:

International Society of Certified Electronics Technicians
3608 Pershing Avenue
Fort Worth, TX 76107-4527
Tel: 817-921-9101
Email: info@iscet.org
Web: http://www.iscet.org

For industry information and educational programs, contact:

Semiconductor Equipment and Materials International
1401 K Street, NW, Suite 601
Washington, DC 20005
Tel: 202-289-0440
Email: semidc@semi.org
Web: http://www.semi.org

For industry information, contact:

Semiconductor Industry Association
181 Metro Drive, Suite 450
San Jose, CA 95110
Tel: 408-436-6600
Email: mailbox@sia-online.org
Web: http://www.semichips.org

SURGICAL TECHNOLOGISTS

School Subjects **Biology** **Health** *Personal Skills* **Helping/teaching** **Technical/scientific** *Work Environment* **Primarily indoors** **Primarily one location**	*Salary Range* **$20,000 to $29,000 to** **$40,000+** *Certification or Licensing* **Recommended** *Outlook* **Faster than the average**

THE JOB

Surgical technologists, also called *surgical technicians* or *operating room technicians,* are members of the surgical team who work in the operating room with surgeons, nurses, anesthesiologists, and other personnel before, during, and after surgery. They perform functions that ensure a safe and sterile environment.

To prepare a patient for surgery, they may wash, shave, and disinfect the area where the incision will be made. They arrange the equipment, instruments, and supplies in the operating room according to the preference of the surgeons and nurses. During the operation, they adjust lights and other equipment as needed. They count sponges, needles, and instruments used during the operation, hand instruments and supplies to the surgeon, and hold retractors and cut sutures as directed. Technologists maintain specified supplies of fluids such as saline, plasma, blood, and glucose and may assist in administering these fluids. Following the operation, they may clean and restock the operating room and wash and sterilize the used equipment using germicides, autoclaves, and sterilizers.

PROFESSIONAL AND PERSONAL REQUIREMENTS

Voluntary professional certification is available from the Liaison Council on Certification for the Surgical Technologist. Individuals can earn the Certified Surgical Technologist (CST) designation by graduating from an accredited educational program and passing a nationally administered certifying examination. Increasing numbers of hospitals are requiring certification as a condition of employment.

You must possess an educational background in the medical sciences, a strong sense of responsibility, a concern for order, and an ability to integrate a number of tasks at the same time to work as a surgical technologist. You need good manual dexterity to handle awkward surgical instruments with speed and agility. In addition, you will need physical stamina to stand through long surgical procedures.

STARTING OUT

Graduates of programs are often offered jobs in the same hospital in which they received their clinical training. Programs usually cooperate closely with hospitals in the area, which are usually eager to employ technologists educated in local programs. Available positions are also advertised in newspaper want ads.

EARNINGS

Salaries vary greatly in different institutions and localities. According to the *Occupational Outlook Handbook,* the average salary for surgical technologists was $29,020 in 2000, but salaries ranged from $20,490 to $40,310 a year (excluding overtime). Some technologists with experience earn much more. Most surgical technologists are required to be periodically on call—available to work on short notice in cases of emergency—and can earn overtime from such work.

Graduates of educational programs usually receive salaries higher than technologists without formal education. In general, technologists working on the East Coast and West Coast earn more than surgical technologists in other parts of the country. Surgical first assistants and private scrubs employed directly by surgeons tend to earn more than surgical technologists employed by hospitals.

OUTLOOK

According to the U.S. Department of Labor, the field of surgical technology is projected to experience rapid growth through 2010. Population growth, longevity, and improvement in medical and surgical procedures have all contributed to a growing demand for surgical services and hence for surgical technologists. As long as the rate at which people undergo surgery continues to increase, there will continue to be a need for this profession. Also, as surgical methods become increasingly complex, more surgical technologists will likely be needed.

An increasing number of surgical procedures are being performed in the offices of physicians and ambulatory surgical centers. As a result, employment for technologists in these non-hospital settings should grow much faster than the average.

FOR MORE INFORMATION

For information on education programs and certification, contact the following organizations:

Association of Surgical Technologists
7108-C South Alton Way
Centennial, CO 80112
Tel: 303-694-9130
Web: http://www.ast.org

Liaison Council on Certification for the Surgical Technologist
128 South Tejon Street, Suite 301
Colorado Springs, CO 80903
Tel: 800-707-0057
Email: mail@lcc-st.org
Web: http://www.lcc-st.org

SURVEYING AND MAPPING TECHNICIANS

School Subjects **Geography** **Mathematics**	*Salary Range* **$18,000 to $28,000** **to $47,000+**
Personal Skills **Following instructions** **Technical/scientific**	*Certification or Licensing* **Voluntary** *Outlook* **Faster than the average**
Work Environment **Primarily outdoors** **Primarily multiple locations**	

THE JOB

As essential assistants to civil engineers, surveyors, and map-makers, *surveying and mapping technicians* are usually the first to be involved in any job that requires precise plotting. This includes highways, airports, housing developments, mines, dams, bridges, and buildings of all kinds. Their main responsibility is to accurately record all readings and keep orderly field notes to check for accuracy.

Technicians may specialize if they join a firm that focuses on one or more particular types of surveying. For example, technicians involved in land surveying are skilled in technical measuring and tasks related to establishing township, property, and other tract-of-land boundary lines. Technicians who work for highway, pipeline, railway, or power line surveying firms help to establish grades, lines, and other points of reference for construction projects. Technicians who work for geodetic surveyors help take measurements of large masses of land, sea, or space.

Technological advances such as the Global Positioning System (GPS) and Geographic Information Systems (GIS) have revolutionized surveying and mapping work. Using these systems, surveying teams can track points on the Earth with radio signals transmitted from satellites and store this information in computer databases.

PROFESSIONAL AND PERSONAL REQUIREMENTS

Unlike professional land surveyors, there are no certification or licensing requirements to becoming a surveying and mapping technician. However, technicians who seek government employment must pass a civil service examination.

Many employers prefer certified technicians for promotions into higher positions with more responsibility. The American Congress on Surveying and Mapping offers four levels of voluntary certification. With each level, the technician must have more experience and pass progressively challenging examinations. If the technician hopes to one day work as a surveyor, he or she must be specially certified to work in a specific state.

You should be patient, orderly, systematic, accurate, and objective in your work. You must be willing to work cooperatively and have the ability to think and plan ahead. Because of the increasing technical nature of the work, you will need computer skills to be able to use highly complex equipment such as GPS and GIS technology.

STARTING OUT

If you plan on attending a technical institute or four-year college, check out your school's placement service for help in arranging examinations or interviews. Employers of surveying technicians often send recruiters to schools before graduation. Some community or technical colleges have work-study programs that provide cooperative part-time or summer work for pay. Employers involved with these programs often hire students full-time after graduation.

EARNINGS

According to the U.S. Department of Labor, the 2000 median hourly salary for all surveying and mapping technicians, regardless of the industry, was $13.48, or approximately $28,000 a year. The lowest 10 percent earned less than $8.45 an hour ($17,600 a year), and the highest 10 percent earned over $22.40 an hour ($46,600). Technicians working for the public sector in federal, state, and local governments generally earned more per hour than those working in the private sector for engineering and architectural services.

OUTLOOK

According to the *Occupational Outlook Handbook,* employment growth is expected to be faster than the average for all occupations through 2010. This better outlook may be attributed to the lower entry requirements and lower wages than those of other technician jobs.

One of the factors that is expected to increase the demand for surveying services is growth in urban and suburban areas. New streets, homes, shopping centers, schools, and gas and water lines will require property and boundary line surveys. Other factors are the continuing state and federal highway improvement programs and the increasing number of urban redevelopment programs.

The need to replace workers who have either retired or transferred to other occupations will also provide opportunities. In general, technicians with more education and skill training will have more job options. New technologies used in surveying and mapping such as GPS and GIS will provide openings to skilled technicians familiar with such advancements.

FOR MORE INFORMATION

For information on accredited surveying programs, certification, industry news, and other issues, contact the following organizations:

Accreditation Board for Engineering and Technology, Inc.
111 Market Place, Suite 1050
Baltimore, MD 21202
Tel: 410-347-7700
Email: accreditation@abet.org
Web: http://www.abet.org

American Congress on Surveying and Mapping
6 Montgomery Village Avenue, Suite 403
Gaithersburg, MD 20879
Tel: 240-632-9716
Web: http://www.acsm.net

For more information on Geographic Information Systems (GIS), visit this site:

GIS.com
Web: http://www.gis.com

SYSTEMS SET UP SPECIALISTS

School Subjects	*Salary Range*
Business	**$29,000 to $35,000**
Computer science	**to $45,000+**
Personal Skills	*Certification or Licensing*
Mechanical/manipulative	**Voluntary**
Technical/scientific	*Outlook*
Work Environment	**Faster than the average**
Primarily indoors	
Primarily multiple locations	

THE JOB

Systems set up specialists are responsible for installing new computer systems and upgrading existing systems to meet the specifications of the client. These specialists install hardware, such as memory, sound cards, fax/modems, fans, microprocessors, and systems boards. They also load software and configure the hard drive appropriately. Some systems set up specialists install computer systems at the client's location. Installation might include normal hard drive or network server configurations as well as connecting peripherals such as printers, phones, fax machines, modems, and multiple terminals. They also provide technical support, giving initial training to users.

Systems set up specialists are employed by computer manufacturing companies or computer service companies nationwide, or they are employed as part of the technical support departments of many businesses. These specialists are sometimes called technical support technicians, desktop analyst/specialists, and PC set up specialists.

PROFESSIONAL AND PERSONAL REQUIREMENTS

There is no certification or licensing available in this field. A number of companies, such as Microsoft and Cisco, offer training programs in the use of their products that result in certification. There are also independent companies, such as STI Knowledge 2000, that provide training programs leading to certification. Generally these certifications are voluntary. Some employers may pay for part or all of the training cost.

You will need good manual dexterity and a curiosity about how things work to succeed as a systems specialist. Patience and problem-solving skills are important attributes.

STARTING OUT

Most positions in systems set up are considered entry level. If you plan to enter this field without a postsecondary education but with computer skills and experience, you will need to network with working computer professionals for potential employment opportunities. Jobs are advertised in the newspaper every week. In fact, many papers devote entire sections to computer-related positions. Also, don't forget the benefits of working with employment agencies. Another job-hunting technique is to conduct online searches on the World Wide Web. Many computer companies post employment opportunities and accept resumes and applications online.

If you plan to enter the field by completing an advanced degree (in computer technology, for example), work closely with your school's placement office. Many firms looking for computer professionals inform schools first, since they are assured of meeting candidates with a certain level of proficiency in the field.

EARNINGS

According to the *2000 Technical Support Salary Survey* conducted by the Association of Support Professionals and Softletter, systems set up specialists with entry-level customer service responsibilities earned a median income of $29,000 annually. Those working as support technicians had median annual earnings of $35,000. Senior support technicians, typically those with management responsibilities as well as experience and technical expertise, had a median annual salary of $45,000.

In some areas of the country, salaries for those in management positions may be higher. Computer professionals typically earn more in areas where there are clusters of computer companies, such as in California and parts of the East Coast. However, the high cost of living in these areas may offset the benefits of a higher salary.

Most full-time set up specialists work for companies that provide a full range of benefits, including health insurance, sick leave, and paid vacation. Specialists who operate their own businesses are responsible for providing their own benefits.

OUTLOOK

The U.S. Department of Labor predicts that demand for systems set up specialists will grow faster than the average for all other occupations through 2010. This outlook, however, may be somewhat tempered by the economic fluctuations in the technology industry as a whole.

As computers become more sophisticated, highly trained set up specialists will be needed to install them correctly. It is very important for set up specialists to stay up to date with technological advances through continuing education, seminars, or work training.

FOR MORE INFORMATION

For information regarding the industry, career opportunities, and student membership, contact:

Association for Computing Machinery
1515 Broadway
New York, NY 10036
Tel: 800-342-6626
Web: http://www.acm.org

For salary statistics and information on job opportunities, contact:

Association of Support Professionals
66 Mt. Auburn Street
Watertown, MA 02472
Tel: 617-924-3944
Web: http://www.asponline.com

To read articles from its magazine, Computer, *or for other information on scholarships, student chapters, and careers, contact:*

IEEE Computer Society
1730 Massachusetts Avenue, NW
Washington, DC 20036-1992
Tel: 202-371-0101
Web: http://www.computer.org

TEACHER AIDES

School Subjects **Art** **English** *Personal Skills* **Helping/teaching** **Leadership/management** *Work Environment* **Primarily indoors** **Primarily one location**	*Salary Range* **$12,000 to $17,000** **to $28,000+** *Certification or Licensing* **None available** *Outlook* **Faster than the average**

THE JOB

Teacher aides perform a wide variety of duties to help teachers run a classroom. Aides prepare instructional materials, help students with classroom work, and supervise students in the library, on the playground, and at lunch. They perform administrative duties such as photocopying, keeping attendance records, and grading papers.

Teacher aides work in public, private, and parochial preschools and elementary and secondary schools. Duties vary depending on the classroom teacher, school, and school district. Some teacher aides specialize in one subject, and some work in a specific type of school setting. These settings include bilingual classrooms, gifted and talented programs, classes for learning-disabled students and those with unique physical needs, and multi-age classrooms. These aides conduct many of the same duties but may provide more individual assistance to students.

PROFESSIONAL AND PERSONAL REQUIREMENTS

There is no certification or licensing available for aides. However, you should find out the specific job requirements from the school, school district, or state department of education in the area where you would like to work. Requirements vary from school to school and state to state. It is important to remember that an aide who is qualified to work in one state, or even one school, may not be qualified to work in another.

As a teacher aide, you must enjoy working with children and be able to handle their demands, problems, and questions with patience and fairness. You must be willing and able to follow instructions, but you should also be able to take the initiative in projects. Flexibility, creativity, and a cheerful outlook are definite assets for anyone working with children.

STARTING OUT

You can apply directly to schools and school districts for teacher aide positions. Many school districts and state departments of education maintain job listings, bulletin boards, and hotlines that list available job openings. Teacher aide jobs are often advertised in the classified section of the newspaper. Once hired, aides typically spend the first few months in special training and receive a beginning wage. After six months or so, they should have regular responsibilities and may receive a higher salary.

EARNINGS

Teacher aides are usually paid on an hourly basis and usually only during the nine or 10 months of the school calendar. Salaries vary depending on the school or district, the region of the country, and the duties the aides perform. Median annual earnings of teacher assistants in 2000 were $17,350, according to the U.S. Department of Labor. Salaries ranged from less than $12,260 to more than $27,550.

Benefits such as health insurance and vacation or sick leave may also depend on the school or district as well as the number of hours a teacher aide works. Many schools employ teacher aides only part-time and do not offer benefits. Other teacher aides may receive the same health and pension benefits as the teachers in their schools.

OUTLOOK

Growth in this field is expected to be faster than the average through 2010 because of an expected increase in the number of school-age children. The U.S. Department of Labor predicts that this field will grow by 22 percent between 2000 and 2010. As the number of students in schools increases, new schools and classrooms will be added, and more teachers and teacher aides will be hired. A shortage of teachers will cause administrators to hire more aides to help with larger classrooms.

The field of special education (working with students with specific learning, emotional, or physical concerns or disabilities) is expected to grow rapidly, and more aides will be needed in these areas. In addition, aides who want to work with young children in day care or extended day programs will have a relatively easy time finding work because more children are attending these programs while their parents are at work.

FOR MORE INFORMATION

To learn about current issues affecting paraprofessionals in education, visit the AFT Web site or contact:

American Federation of Teachers (AFT)
555 New Jersey Avenue, NW
Washington, DC 20001
Tel: 202-879-4400
Email: online@aft.org
Web: http://www.aft.org

To order publications or read current research and other information, contact:

Association for Childhood Education International
17904 Georgia Avenue, Suite 215
Olney, MD 20832
Tel: 800-423-3563
Email: aceihq@aol.com
Web: http://www.udel.edu/bateman/acei

For information about training programs and other resources, contact:

National Resource Center for Paraprofessionals
Utah State University
6526 Old Main Hill
Logan, UT 84322-6526
Tel: 435-797-7272
Email: info@nrcpara.org
Web: http://www.nrcpara.org

TECHNICAL SUPPORT SPECIALISTS

School Subjects **Computer science** **Mathematics** *Personal Skills* **Helping/teaching** **Technical/scientific** *Work Environment* **Primarily indoors** **Primarily one location**	*Salary Range* **$21,000 to $36,000** **to $63,000+** *Certification or Licensing* **Recommended** *Outlook* **Much faster than the average**

THE JOB

Technical support specialists investigate and resolve problems in computer functioning. They listen to customer complaints, walk customers through possible solutions, and write technical reports based on these problems. They have different duties depending on whom they assist and what they fix. Regardless of specialty, all technical support specialists must be very knowledgeable about the products with which they work and able to communicate effectively with users from different technical backgrounds. They must be patient with frustrated users and able to perform well under stress. Technical support is like solving mysteries, so support specialists should enjoy the challenge of problem solving and have strong analytical thinking skills.

PROFESSIONAL AND PERSONAL REQUIREMENTS

Though certification is not an industry requirement, it is highly recommended. According to the Help Desk Institute, most individuals wishing to qualify to work in a support/help desk environment will need to obtain certification within a month of being on the job. A number of organizations offer several different types of certification. For example, the Computing Technology Industry Association offers the "A+" certification for entry-level computer service technicians. The Help Desk Institute offers certification for those working in help desk positions.

As a support specialist, you should be patient, enjoy the challenges of problem solving, and be able to think logically. You should work well under stress and demonstrate effective communication skills. You should be naturally curious and enthusiastic about learning new technologies as they are developed.

STARTING OUT

Most technical support positions are considered entry level. They are found mainly in computer companies and large corporations and are plentiful in areas where clusters of computer companies are located, such as northern California and Seattle, Washington. If you are interested in obtaining a job in this field, you should scan the classified ads for openings in local businesses, and you may want to work with an employment agency for help in finding out about opportunities. Since many job openings are publicized by word of mouth, it is also very important to speak with as many working computer professionals as possible.

Students of computer technology should work closely with their schools' placement offices. Many employers inform placement offices at nearby schools of openings before ads are run in the newspaper. In addition, placement office staffs are generally very helpful with resume and interviewing techniques.

EARNINGS

Median annual earnings for technical support specialists were $36,460 in 2000, according to the U.S. Department of Labor. The highest 10 percent earned more than $63,480, while the lowest 10 percent earned less than $21,260. Those with more education, responsibility, and expertise have the potential to earn much more.

Technical support specialists earned the following median annual salaries by industry: professional and commercial equipment; $42,970; computer and data-processing services, $37,860; personnel supply services, $34,080; colleges and universities, $32,830; and miscellaneous business services, $21,070.

Most technical support specialists work for companies that offer a full range of benefits, including health insurance, paid vacation, and sick leave. Smaller service or start-up companies may hire support specialists on a contractual basis.

OUTLOOK

The U.S. Department of Labor predicts that the technical support specialist position will be one of the fastest growing of all occupations through 2010. Every time a new computer product is released on the market or another system is installed, there will be problems, whether from user error or technical difficulty. Therefore, there will always be a need for technical support specialists. Since technology changes so rapidly, it is very important for these professionals to keep up to date on advances. They should read trade magazines, surf the Internet, and talk with colleagues in order to know what is happening on the cutting edge.

FOR MORE INFORMATION

For information on internships, student membership, and the student magazine, Crossroads, *contact:*

Association for Computing Machinery
1515 Broadway
New York, NY 10036
Tel: 800-342-6626
Web: http://www.acm.org

For information on certification and training, contact the following:

Computing Technology Industry Association
1815 South Meyers Road, Suite 300
Oakbrook Terrace, IL 60181-5228
Tel: 630-678-8300
Web: http://www.comptia.org

Help Desk Institute
6385 Corporate Drive, Suite 301
Colorado Springs, CO 80919
Tel: 800-248-5667
Web: http://www.thinkhdi.com

For information on scholarships, student membership, and the student newsletter, looking.forward, *contact:*

IEEE Computer Society
1730 Massachusetts Avenue, NW
Washington, DC 20036-1992
Tel: 202-371-0101
Web: http://www.computer.org

VETERINARY TECHNICIANS

School Subjects **Biology** **Chemistry** *Personal Skills* **Helping/teaching** **Technical/scientific** *Work Environment* **Primarily indoors** **Primarily one location**	*Salary Range* **$15,000 to $20,000** **to $59,000** *Certification or Licensing* **Required by certain states** *Outlook* **Much faster than the average**

THE JOB

Veterinary technicians perform much of the laboratory testing procedures commonly associated with veterinary care. In fact, approximately 50 percent of a veterinary technician's duties involves laboratory testing. A veterinary technician may also assist the veterinarian with necropsies in an effort to determine the cause of an animal's death.

In a clinic or private practice, a veterinary technician assists the veterinarian with surgical procedures. This generally entails preparing the animal for surgery, administering and monitoring anesthesia, tracking surgical instruments, and monitoring vital signs. If an animal is very ill and has no chance for survival or if an overcrowded animal shelter is unable to find a home for a donated or stray animal, the veterinary technician may be required to assist in euthanizing (humanely killing) the animal.

During routine examinations and checkups, veterinary technicians help restrain the animals. They may perform ear cleaning and nail clipping procedures as part of regular animal care. Outside the examination and surgery rooms, veterinary technicians may record, replenish, and maintain pharmaceutical equipment and other supplies.

PROFESSIONAL AND PERSONAL REQUIREMENTS

Although the American Veterinary Medical Association (AVMA) determines the majority of the national codes for veterinary technicians, state codes and laws vary. Most states offer registration or certification, and graduation from an AVMA-accredited program is usually a prerequisite.

Most colleges and universities assist graduates with registration and certification arrangements. To keep abreast of new technology and applications in the field, practicing technicians may be required to complete a determined number of annual continuing education courses.

As a veterinary technician, you must be an effective communicator and proficient in basic computer applications. In clinical or private practice, it is usually the veterinary technician who conveys and explains treatment and subsequent animal care to the animal's owner. Technicians may have to help euthanize an animal that is very sick or severely injured and cannot get well. As a result, they must be emotionally stable and help pet owners deal with their grief and loss.

STARTING OUT

Veterinary technicians who complete an accredited program are often able to receive assistance in finding a job through their college's placement offices. Students who have completed internships may receive job offers from the place where they interned.

Graduates may also learn of clinic openings through classified ads in newspapers. Opportunities in zoos and research facilities are usually listed in specific industry periodicals such as *Veterinary Technician Magazine* and the Association of Zoo Veterinary Technicians' *AZVT News*.

EARNINGS

Earnings are generally low for veterinary technicians in private practices and clinics, but pay scales are steadily climbing due to their increasing demand. Better-paying jobs are in zoos and in research. However, those fields of practice are very competitive (especially zoos), and only a small percentage of highly qualified veterinary technicians are employed in these areas.

About 70 percent of veterinary technicians are employed in private or clinical practice and research. According to the AVMA, the average yearly salary of veterinary technicians is $20,161. Graduates of accredited programs who had work experience earned yearly salaries in the range of $15,000 to $59,000 in a high-end industry job. Earnings vary depending on practice setting, geographic location, level of education, and years of experience. Benefits vary and depend on each employer's policies.

OUTLOOK

Employment for veterinary technicians will grow much faster than the average for all other occupations through 2010, according to the U.S. Department of Labor. Veterinary medicine is a field that is not adversely affected by the economy, so it does offer stability. The public's love for pets coupled with higher disposable incomes will encourage continued demand for workers in this occupation.

FOR MORE INFORMATION

For more information on careers, schools, and resources, contact the following organizations:

American Veterinary Medical Association
1931 North Meacham Road, Suite 100
Schaumburg, IL 60173
Tel: 847-925-8070
Email: avmainfo@avma.org
Web: http://www.avma.org

Association of Zoo Veterinary Technicians
c/o White Oak Conservation Center/ASB
3823 Owens Road
Yulee, FL 32097
Web: http://www.azvt.org

National Association of Veterinary Technicians in America
PO Box 224
Battle Ground, IN 47920
Tel: 765-742-2216
Email: navta@navta.net
Web: http://www.navta.net

WASTEWATER TREATMENT PLANT TECHNICIANS

School Subjects **Chemistry** **Mathematics**	*Salary Range* **$19,000 to $31,000** **to $47,000+**
Personal Skills **Mechanical/manipulative** **Technical/scientific**	*Certification or Licensing* **Required by certain states**
Work Environment **Indoors and outdoors** **Primarily one location**	*Outlook* **About as fast as the average**

THE JOB

Wastewater treatment plant technicians work under the supervision of wastewater treatment plant operators. Technicians take samples and monitor treatment to ensure that water leaving the plant is safe for its intended use. Depending on the level of treatment, water is used for human consumption or for nonconsumptive purposes, such as field irrigation or discharge into natural water sources.

Wastewater treatment plant technicians' duties include regulating the flow of wastewater by adjusting pumps, valves, and other equipment; monitoring purification processes; collecting water samples and conducting laboratory tests; performing maintenance and minor repairs to equipment; and surveying streams and studying basin areas. They also prepare graphs, tables, and diagrams to illustrate survey data, answer public inquiries, and train new personnel.

PROFESSIONAL AND PERSONAL REQUIREMENTS

In most states, workers who control operations at wastewater treatment plants must be certified by the state. There is no nationwide standard, so different states administer different tests. Many states issue several classes of certification, depending on the size of the plant the worker is qualified to control.

Technicians must be familiar with the provisions of the Federal Clean Water Act and various state and local regulations that apply to their work. If you plan to work in a larger city or town, you may have to take a civil service exam or other tests that assess your aptitudes and abilities.

STARTING OUT

You can get help in locating job openings from the placement office of your school. Another source of information is the local office of your state's employment service. You may also directly contact state and local water pollution control agencies and the personnel offices of wastewater treatment facilities in areas where you would like to work.

The Internet is another useful resource for finding job leads. Professional associations, such as the Water Environment Foundation (http://www.wef.org), offer job listings in the wastewater field as part of their Web sites. Such sites are a good place for getting started in the field, as they also list internship or trainee positions available.

EARNINGS

Salaries of wastewater treatment plant technicians vary depending on factors such as the size of the plant, the workers' job responsibilities, and their level of certification. According to the *Occupational Outlook Handbook,* water and liquid waste treatment plant operators and technicians earned median annual salaries of $31,380 in 2000. The lowest 10 percent earned $19,120 or less, while the highest 10 percent earned $47,370 or more a year. In local government, plant operators earned a median salary of $31,120.

In addition to their pay, most technicians receive benefits such as life and health insurance, a pension plan, and reimbursement for education and training related to their job.

OUTLOOK

Through 2010, employment in this field is expected to grow as fast as the average for all occupations. The growth in demand for wastewater treatment will be related to the overall growth of the nation's population and economy. New treatment plants may be built, and existing ones will be upgraded, requiring additional trained personnel to manage their operations. Other openings will arise when experienced workers retire or transfer to new occupations. Technicians with formal training will have the best chances for new positions and promotions.

Workers in wastewater treatment plants are rarely laid off, even during a recession, because wastewater treatment is essential to public health and welfare. In the future, more wastewater professionals will probably be employed by private companies that contract to manage treatment plants for local governments.

FOR MORE INFORMATION

For information on the field of wastewater management, contact:

American Water Works Association
6666 West Quincy Avenue
Denver, CO 80235
Tel: 303-794-7711
Web: http://www.awwa.org

For information on education and training, contact the following organizations:

Environmental Careers Organization
179 South Street
Boston, MA 02111
Tel: 617-426-4375
Web: http://www.eco.org

National Environmental Training Association
5320 North 16th Street, Suite 114
Phoenix, AZ 85016
Tel: 602-956-6099
Email: neta@ehs-training.org
Web: http://www.ehs-training.org

For career information, contact or visit the following Web site:

Water Environment Federation
601 Wythe Street
Alexandria, VA 22314-1994
Tel: 800-666-0206
Web: http://www.wef.org

WEBMASTERS

School Subjects **Computer science** **Mathematics**	*Salary Range* **$20,000 to $50,000** **to $100,000+**
Personal Skills **Communication/ideas** **Technical/scientific**	*Certification or Licensing* **Voluntary** *Outlook*
Work Environment **Primarily indoors** **Primarily one location**	**Much faster than the average**

THE JOB

Webmasters design, implement, and maintain World Wide Web sites for corporations, educational institutions, not-for-profit organizations, government agencies, and other institutions. Webmasters should have working knowledge of network configurations, interface, graphic design, software development, business, writing, marketing, and project management. Because their job encompasses so many different responsibilities, in a large organization, the position is often held by a team of individuals rather than a single person. Duties may include securing space on the Web for new sites by contracting with an Internet service provider; developing the actual Web site; coding text in HyperText Markup Language (HTML); designing the graphic elements to the site; maintaining and updating pages and hyperlinks; and monitoring and reporting on Web site usage by measuring the amount of "hits" the site receives in a month.

PROFESSIONAL AND PERSONAL REQUIREMENTS

Certification is voluntary and is available at many colleges, universities, and technical schools throughout the United States, as well as through the International Webmasters Association.

Of course, a strong knowledge of computer technology is necessary, and employers usually require at least two years of experience with World Wide Web technologies. In addition to having computer skills, you need to be creative to work as a Webmaster. Good writing skills and an aptitude for marketing are also excellent qualities for Web site design.

STARTING OUT

Most people become Webmasters by moving into the position from another computer-related position within the same company. Since most large organizations already use computers for various functions, they may employ a person or several people to serve as computer "specialists." If these organizations decide to develop their own Web sites, they frequently assign the task to one of these employees who is already experienced with the computer system. Often, the person who ultimately becomes an organization's Webmaster at first just takes on the job in addition to his or her other, already established duties.

Another way that individuals find jobs in this field is through online postings of job openings. Many companies post Webmaster position openings online because the candidates they hope to attract are very likely to use the Internet for a job search. Therefore, you should use the World Wide Web to check job-related newsgroups. You should also use a Web search engine to locate openings.

EARNINGS

Interactive Week's 2001 salary survey reports that the median salary for Webmasters was between $30,000 and $40,000 a year, but pay ranged from less than $20,000 to $100,000 or more. In some cases, the demand for Webmasters is so great that some companies are offering stock options, sign-on bonuses, and other perks, in addition to high salaries. According to the National Association of Colleges and Employers, the starting salary for graduates with a bachelor's degree in computer sciences was approximately $52,723 in 2001; in computer programming, $48,602; and in information sciences and systems, $45,182.

Depending on the organization for which they work, Webmasters may receive a benefits package in addition to salary. A typical benefits package would include paid vacations and holidays, medical insurance, and perhaps a pension plan.

OUTLOOK

According to the U.S. Department of Labor, the field of computer and data processing services is projected to be the fastest-growing industry for the next decade. As a result, the employment rate of Webmasters and other computer specialists is expected to grow much faster than the average rate for all occupations through 2010.

As more and more businesses, not-for-profit organizations, educational institutions, and government agencies choose to "go online," the total number of Web sites will grow, as will the need for experts to design them. Companies are starting to view Web sites not as temporary experiments, but rather as important and necessary business and marketing tools.

One thing to keep in mind, however, is that when technology advances extremely rapidly, it tends to make old methods of doing things obsolete. Changes in technology could make the Web sites we are now familiar with a thing of the past. User-friendly software programs could make Web site design so easy and efficient that it no longer requires an "expert" to do it well. Webmasters who are concerned with job security should be willing to continue learning and using the very latest developments in technology, so that they are prepared to move into the future of online communication, whatever it may be.

FOR MORE INFORMATION

For information on membership and industry-related events, contact:

Association of Internet Professionals
4790 Irvine Boulevard, Suite 105-283
Irvine, CA 92620
Tel: 866-AIP-9700
Email: info@association.org
Web: http://www.association.org

For information on training and certification programs, contact the following organizations:

International Webmasters Association
119 East Union Street, Suite F
Pasadena, CA 91103
Tel: 626-449-3709
Web: http://www.iwanet.org

World Organization of Webmasters
9580 Oak Avenue Parkway, Suite 7-177
Folsom, CA 95630
Tel: 916-608-1597
Web: http://www.joinwow.org

WIRELESS SERVICE TECHNICIANS

School Subjects **Computer science** **Physics** *Personal Skills* **Mechanical/manipulative** **Technical/scientific** *Work Environment* **Primarily indoors** **Primarily multiple locations**	*Salary Range* **$35,000 to $45,000** **to $50,000+** *Certification or Licensing* **None available** *Outlook* **Much faster than the average**

THE JOB

Wireless service technicians are responsible for maintaining specified broadcast areas called cell sites. This includes the radio towers, cell site equipment, and often the building and grounds for the sites. Technicians routinely visit and monitor the functioning of the on-site equipment, performing preventive testing and maintenance. They are also responsible for troubleshooting and remedying problems that might arise. Most wireless service technicians spend their work time at various locations, visiting each of their cell sites as necessary.

In addition to routine maintenance and troubleshooting responsibilities, wireless service technicians have several other duties. They test the quality of the wireless reception by using a mobile phone in various locations within the coverage area. They also may work with technicians in the switching center to incorporate new cell sites into the network and make sure that the wireless calls are transmitted smoothly from one broadcast area to another.

PROFESSIONAL AND PERSONAL REQUIREMENTS

There is no certification or licensing available in this field.

The ability to work independently is one of the most important characteristics of a good wireless service technician. Most technicians work on their own, traveling from site to site and performing their duties with little or no supervision. As a result, you will need a high degree of self-discipline and responsibility. Because of the travel involved, you will also need a valid driver's license and good driving record.

STARTING OUT

One of the best ways to start looking for a job as a wireless service technician is to visit the Web sites of several wireless providers. Many wireless companies maintain job sections on their sites that list available positions. Another possibility is to browse through wireless industry publications, such as *Wireless Week* (http://www.wirelessweek.com), *Telephony* (http://www.internettelephony.com), and *Wireless Review* (http://www.wirelessreview.com).

You should attend technical job fairs, expos, or exchanges to meet and network with employers. Watch local newspapers for similar events in your community. Finally, an excellent source of job leads will be your college's placement office. Many wireless companies visit schools that offer the appropriate degree programs to recruit qualified students for employees. Some companies even offer a co-op program, in which students are hired on a part-time basis while they are still in school.

EARNINGS

Because there is such a demand for qualified and dependable employees in the wireless field, the qualified wireless technician can expect to receive a good salary. According to the U.S. Department of Labor, nonsupervisory workers in telephone communications earned a median salary of $743 a week, or approximately $38,600 annually, in 2000. Technicians earned a median rate of between $22 and $23 an hour, approximately $45,760 to $47,840 a year.

Most major wireless service providers offer a benefits package to their employees, which often includes health insurance, paid vacation, holiday, and sick days, and a pension or 401-K plan.

OUTLOOK

According to the U. S. Department of Labor, employment in the telecommunications industry is expected to grow at an average rate, increasing by approximately 12 percent in the next decade. However, job opportunities with wireless service providers, in particular, should be more plentiful. Providers will need technicians and other wireless workers to meet the growing demand for wireless service.

There are several reasons for the growing popularity of wireless service. Perhaps the most significant is the steady decrease in prices for cellular service. Since 1988, the average monthly bill for wireless service has gone from approximately $100 to approximately $41, according to the Cellular Telecommunications and Internet Association.

A second reason for the increase in usage is that coverage areas are increasingly broad and comprehensive. As more and more cell sites are added, more and more parts of the United States have cellular service.

A third factor in the growth is the continuous improvement in cellular phones and services due to technological advances. One of the most recent innovations is digital communication technology called personal communications services (PCS). PCS is expected to increase wireless phone use by offering better quality and range.

FOR MORE INFORMATION

For job postings, links to wireless industry recruiters, industry news, and training information, contact:

Cellular Telecommunications and Internet Association
1250 Connecticut Avenue, NW, Suite 800
Washington, DC 20036
Tel: 202-785-0081
Web: http://www.wow-com.com

For the latest on the wireless industry, job information, and information about Wireless Magazine, *contact:*

Wireless Industry Association
9746 Tappenbeck Drive
Houston, TX 77055
Tel: 800-624-6918
Email: mail@wirelessindustry.com
Web: http://wirelessdealers.com

Chapter Six
RELATED RESOURCES

The American Association of Community Colleges works with government and educational associations to promote the benefits of community colleges and higher education.

American Association of Community Colleges
One Dupont Circle, NW, Suite 410
Washington, DC 20036
Tel: 202-728-0200
Web: http://www.aacc.nche.edu

The DETC serves as a clearinghouse of information on distance learning. It also sponsors a nationally recognized accrediting agency and offers a free Directory of Accredited Institutions.

Distance Education and Training Council (DETC)
1601 18th Street, NW
Washington, DC 20009
Tel: 202-234-5100
Web: http://www.detc.org

The ERIC Clearinghouse provides educational literature, including information on community colleges and related topics.

ERIC Clearinghouse for Community Colleges
PO Box 951521
3051 Moore Hall
University of California-Los Angeles
Los Angeles, CA 90095-1521
Tel: 800-832-8256
Web: http://www.gseis.ucla.edu/ERIC

This association's Web site offers links to community and technical college information, including professional associations, instructional resources, distance education, education-related publications, and a variety of Web search tools.

League for Innovation in the Community College
4505 East Chandler Boulevard, Suite 250
Phoenix, AZ 85048
Tel: 480-705-8200
Web: http://www.league.org

Princeton Review offers students practical information and advice on topics such as financial aid, college majors, careers, and the everyday issues of college life. The site also lists information for thousands of two- and four-year colleges.

Princeton Review
2315 Broadway
New York, NY 10024
Tel: 212-874-8282
Web: http://www.princetonreview.com

This Web site has links to over 1,100 community colleges in the United States, Canada, and other selected foreign countries, and it offers other resources relating to community college education.

Maricopa Center for Learning and Instruction
Maricopa Community Colleges
2411 14th Street
Tempe, AZ 85250
Tel: 480-731-8300
Web: http://www.mcli.dist.maricopa.edu

This publication's Web site offers information on education trends, tips on saving for college, and news from community college campuses across the country.

Community College Week
Web: http://www.ccweek.com

This Web site aims to provide high school students with information about alternatives to four-year colleges, such as apprenticeships, internships, military opportunities, and enrollment at community, technical, and vocational colleges.

My Future
Web: http://www.myfuture.com

The following site is an excellent source for researching two-year programs and institutions.

U.S. Two-Year Colleges
Web: http://cset.sp.utoledo.edu/twoyrcol.html

INDEX

2+2 programs, 41

2+2+2 programs, 41–42

3+1 programs, 42

A

Abilities, 20

Accreditation, 35–39

    criteria for evaluating, 36–37

    defined, 36

    institutional, 36

    specialized program, 36

Accredited college, advantages of attending, 37

Accrediting Commission for Community and Junior Colleges/Western Association of Schools, 38

Accrediting Commission of the Distance Education and Training Council (DETC), 39

Adult day care coordinators, 47-49

Aeronautical and aerospace technicians, 50-52

Agribusiness technicians, 53-55

Agricultural business technicians, 53

Agricultural equipment technicians, 56-58

Aircraft mechanics, 59-61

Alcohol and drug abuse counselors, 62-64

American Association Community Colleges, viii

Animators, 83-85

Applications programmers, 98

Applied education programs, 4

Apprenticeships, 10

Aptitudes, 20

Assemblers, 251

Associate degrees, 7–12

    in applied arts and sciences, 8

in arts, 8

defined, 8–9

numbers of students earning, 5

reasons for seeking, 13–33

Automated packaging machine mechanics, 251

Automobile collision repairers, 65-57

Automobile service technicians, 68-70

B

Bay de Noc Community College, 8

Biomedical equipment technicians, 71-73, 128

Bodyworkers, 212

Bolles, Richard, 23

Broadcast engineers, 74-76

Broadcast operators, 74

Broadcast technicians, 74

Brooks, Gwendolyn, 12

Business and industry programs, 10–11

C

CAD designers, 104

CAD technicians, 104

Cardiovascular technologists, 77-79

Career Occupational Preference System, 33

Carpenters, 80-82

Cartoonists, 83-85

Caterers, 86-88

Certificates, 8, 10

Chefs, 107-109

Chemical technicians, 89-91

Chief business programmers, 98

Civil engineering technicians, 92-94

Class sizes, vii

Colorado Mountain College, 8–9

Commission on Colleges/Southern Association of Colleges and Schools, 38

Commission on Secondary Schools/Middle States Association of Colleges and Schools, 37–38

Community colleges, vii–viii, 7–8

    advantages of attending accredited, 37

    advantages offered by, vii

    apprenticeship programs at, 10

    associate degrees offered by, 8–9

    business and industry programs at, 10–11

    certificates granted by, 8, 10

    class sizes in, vii

    courses offered by, 7–8

    disadvantages of attending unaccredited

    hot programs in, 9

    licensure programs at, 11–12

    non-credit classes at, viii

    notable alumni, 12

    open door policy of, 8

    reasons for attending, 13–33

    student services at, vii–viii

Computer and office machine service technicians, 95-97

Computer networking, 9

Computer programmers, 98-100

Computer service technicians, 1

Computer support service owners, 101-103

Computer technicians/networking, 9

Computer-aided design drafters, 104-106

Computer-aided design technicians, 104-106

Construction electricians, 140

Continuing education classes, 7

Cooks, 107-109

Corrections officers, 110-112

Court reporters, 3, 113-115

Crystal, Billy, 12

D

Dental assistants, 116-118

Dental hygienists, 119-121

Desktop publishing specialists, 122-124

Diagnostic medical sonographers, 125-127

Dialysis patient-care technicians, 128

Dialysis technicians, 128-130

Dialyzer reprocessing technicians, 128

Dietetic technicians, 131-133

Disney, Walt, 12

Dispensing opticians, 134-136

Drafters, 137-139

E

EEG technologists, 143

Electrical repairers, 140

Electricians, 140-142

Electroneurodiagnostic technologists, 143-145

Electronics engineering technicians, 146-148

Embalmers, 170

Emergency medical technicians, 149-151

EMTs, 149

END technologists, 143

Engineering-electric/electronics, 9

Environmental technicians, 152-154

Executive housekeepers, 182

F

Fashion designers, 155-157

Fiber optics technicians, 158-160

Field service representatives, 251

Field service technicians, 251

Finish carpenters, 80

Fire safety technicians, 161-163

Firefighters, 164-166

Fluid power technicians, 167-169
Food service managers, 305-307
Forestry technicians, 1
Freeman, Morgan, 12
Funeral directors, 170
Funeral home workers, 170-172

G
General computer technologies, 9
General managers, 182
Generalists, 68
Graphic designers, 173-175
Grounds managers, 194-196

H
Hayes, Dennis, 12
Heating and cooling technicians, 2, 176-178
Higher Learning Commission of the North Central
    Association of Colleges and Schools, 36, 39
Highway patrol officers, 281
Home health LPNs, 206
Honolulu Community College, 9
Horticultural technicians, 179-181
Horticulturists, 179
Hotel managers, 182-184
Human services workers, 185-187

I
Industrial engineering technicians, 188-190
Institutional accreditation, 36
Interests, 28–30
Internal affairs investigators, 281

J
Junior colleges, vii, 7

K

Kindergarten teachers, 284

Kirkpatrick, Jeanne, 12

Kuder Career Planning System, 33

L

Laboratory testing technicians, 191-193

Landscapers, 194-196

Laser technicians, 197-199

Legal secretaries, 200-202

Lehrer, Jim, 12

Library technical assistants, 203

Library technicians, 203-205

Licensed practical nurses, 206-208

Licensed vocational nurses, 206

Licensure, 11–12

Life values, 23–25

Litigation secretaries, 200

LPNs, 206

M

Machinery builders, 251

Maintenance electricians, 140

Maintenance technicians, 251

Marine services technicians, 209-211

Massage therapists, 212-214

Masseurs, 212

Masseuses, 212

Massotherapists, 212

Mechanical engineering technicians, 215-217

Medical assistants, 218-220

Medical laboratory technicians, 221-223

Medical record technicians, 224-226

Medical secretaries, 227-229

Medical transcriptionists, 230-232

Mellencamp, John Cougar, 12

Merchant, Natalie, 12

Mfume, Kweisi, 12

Miami-Dade Community College, 8

Microelectronics technicians, 233-235

Morticians, 170

Mortuary science technician, 170

Motel managers, 182-184

Motion cartoonists, 83

Musicians, 236-238

N

Nephrology technicians, 128

New England Association of Schools and Colleges, 38

Non-credit classes, viii

Northern Maine Technical College, 9

Northwest Association of Schools and Colleges, 39

Nuclear medicine technologists, 239-241

O

Occupational therapy aides, 242-244

Occupational therapy assistants, 242-244

Office administrators, 245-247

Office managers, 245

Operating room technicians, 320

Orthotic technicians, 2, 248-250

OTAs, 242

P

Packaging machinery technicians, 251-253

Painters, 254-256

Paralegals, 257-259

Pedorthists, 260-262

Perot, H. Ross, 12

Personality attributes, 17–19

Pharmacy technicians, 263-265

Phlebotomy technicians, 266-268

Photographers, 269-271

Physical therapy assistants, 272-274

Pipefitters, 278-280

Plastics technicians, 275-277

Plumbers, 278-280

Police clerks, 281

Police officers, 281-283

Pollution control technicians, 152

Preschool teachers, 284-286

Professional students, 16

Prosthetic technicians, 2, 248-250

Q

Quality control technicians, 287-289

R

Radiologic technologists, 290-292

Real estate agents, 293-295

Real estate brokers, 293-295

Receiving institution, 41

Recreation supervisors, 296

Recreation workers, 296-298

Registered nurses, 299-301

Registered nursing, 9

Renal dialysis technicians, 128

Respiratory therapists, 302-304

Restaurant managers, 305-307

Retail managers, 308-310

RNs, 299

Robot field technicians, 311-313

Robot operators, 311

Robotics design technicians, 311

Robotics technicians, 311
Robotics trainers, 311
Rough carpenters, 80

S
School-To-Work programs, 4
Sculptors, 254-256
Security guards, 314-316
Self-assessment, 15–16
Self-Assessment Profile Sheet, 31–32
Self-Assessment Survey and Profile Sheet
    interests, 28–30
    life values, 23–25
    personality attributes, 17–19
    skills, 20–23
    temperaments, 19–20
    work values, 26–28
Self-Directed Search, 33
Semiconductor technicians, 317-319
Sending institution, 41
Significant influencing factors, 33
Skills, 20–23
Specialists, 68
Specialized officers, 281
Specialized program accreditation, 36
State police officers, 281
State troopers, 281
Students, transfer, 41–45
Student services, vii–viii
Surgical technicians, 320
Surgical technologists, 320-322
Surveying and mapping technicians, 323-325
Systems programmers, 98
Systems set up specialists, 326-328

T

Teacher aides, 329-331

Tech Prep programs, 4

Technical colleges, vii, 7

Technical institutes, 7

Technical support specialists, 332-334

Temperaments, 19–20

Temporary workers, 246

Temps, 246

Tracers, 138

Transfer student, 41

    checklist for, 45

    options for, 41–45

Trial secretaries, 200

U

Unaccredited college, disadvantages of attending, 37

Undertakers, 170

V

Values

    life, 23–25

    work, 26–28

Veterinary technicians, 2, 335-337

W

Wastewater treatment plant technicians, 338-340

Webmasters, 341-343

Western Michigan University Career Guidance Inventory, 33

What Color is Your Parachute Workbook (Bolles), 23

Wireless service technicians, 344-346

Work values, 26–28